Firewater

D1615980

Firewater

The Impact of the Whisky Trade
on the Blackfoot Nation

Hugh A. Dempsey

FIFTH
HOUSE

Copyright © 2002 Hugh A. Dempsey

All rights reserved. No part of this publication may be reproduced, stored in a retrieval system, or transmitted, in any form or by any means, electronic, mechanical, recording, or otherwise, without the prior written permission of the publisher, except in the case of a reviewer, who may quote brief passages in a review to print in a magazine or newspaper, or broadcast on radio or television. In the case of photocopying or other reprographic copying, users must obtain a licence from the Canadian Copyright Licencing Agency.

Front cover background courtesy Glenbow Archives, Calgary, Alberta
Front cover painting, "Joe Kipp's Trading Post," 1898, by Charles Marion Russell, courtesy Buffalo Bill Historical Center, Cody, WY; Gift of Charles Ulrick and Josephine Bay Foundation, Inc.; 1.85

Cover and interior design by Rachel Hershfield/Folio Publication Design

The publisher gratefully acknowledges the support of The Canada Council for the Arts and the Department of Canadian Heritage.

THE CANADA COUNCIL | LE CONSEIL DES ARTS
FOR THE ARTS | DU CANADA
SINCE 1957 | DEPUIS 1957

We acknowledge the financial support of the Government of Canada through the Book Publishing Industry Development Program for our publishing activities.

The author gratefully acknowledges the support of The Alberta Foundation of the Arts.

The Alberta Foundation for the Arts   Alberta COMMUNITY DEVELOPMENT
COMMITTED TO THE DEVELOPMENT OF CULTURE AND THE ARTS

Printed in Canada by Transcontinental Printing.

02 03 04 05 06 / 5 4 3 2 1

First published in the United States in 2002 by
Fitzhenry & Whiteside
121 Harvard Avenue, Suite 2
Allston, MA 02134

National Library of Canada Cataloguing in Publication Data

Dempsey, Hugh A., 1929-
Firewater

Includes bibliographical references and index.
ISBN 1-894004-96-5

1. Whiskey industry--Great Plains--History--19th century. 2. Siksika Indians--History. 3. Northwest, Canadian--History--1870-1905. I. Title.
E99.S54D45 2002   971.2'004973   C2002-910778-4

Fifth House Ltd.
A Fitzhenry & Whiteside Company
1511-1800 4 Street SW
Calgary, Alberta, Canada
T2S 2S5

1-800-387-9776
www.fitzhenry.ca

Contents

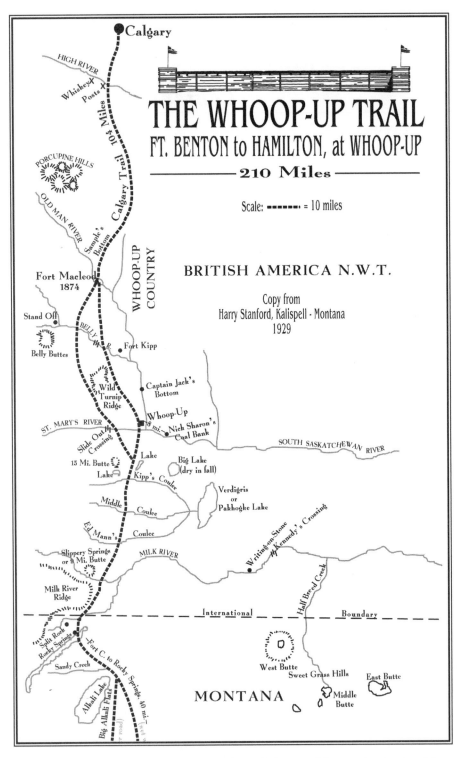

This map was originally drawn by ex-Mountie Harry Stanford in 1929. The map above is adapted from Gerald L. Berry's The Whoop-Up Trail *(Edmonton, AB: Applied Art Products, 1953), pp. 56–57.*

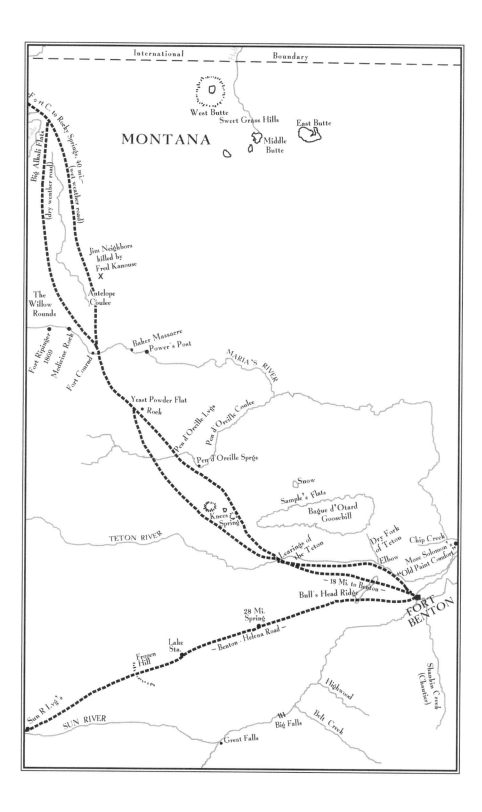

International Boundary

MONTANA

West Butte
Sweet Grass Hills
East Butte
Middle Butte

Fort C. to Rocky Springs 40 mi. — (wet weather road)

(dry weather road)

Big Alkali Flats

The Willow Rounds

Jim Neighbors killed by Fred Kanouse X

Antelope Coulee

Fort Ripinger 1860
Medicine Rock
Fort Conrad

Baker Massacre
Power's Post

MARIA'S RIVER

Yeast Powder Flat Rock

Pen d'Oreille Lvgs

Pen d'Oreille Coulee

Pen d'Oreille Sprgs

Snow
Sample's Flats

Bague d'Otard
Goosebill

Knees Spring

TETON RIVER

Clearings of the Teton

Dry Fork of Teton
Elbow

Chip Creek

Mose Solomon's
"Old Paint Comfort"

— 18 Mi. to Benton —

Bull's Head Ridge

FORT BENTON

28 Mi. Spring

Lake Sta.

Frozen Hill

— Benton-Helena Road —

Sun R Lvg's

SUN RIVER

Great Falls

Big Falls

Belt Creek

Highwood

Shankin Creek
(Chouteau)

FIREWATER *n* – "Term used by Indians to describe brandy given them in exchange for furs; good liquor blazed up when poured on a fire, diluted liquor quenched it." (*Montcalm,* 1757)

"It is very hard for us Indians, who have not the sense of the white people to know when we have had enough of the strong fiery water."
(*Long,* 1791)

"They doubted not, from what they had seen of the effects of fire-water, that it was the very Devil and would not touch it."
(*British Colonial Argus,* 1833)

"Some tribes would stand for a smaller quantity of spirits than others, but the sophisticated Blackfeet demanded something that would ignite if you put a match to it—firewater. It was colored with black tea to look more devilish yet."
(*Longstreth,* 1927)

Source: Walter S. Avis. *A Dictionary of Canadianisms.*
Toronto, ON: W. J. Gage Ltd., 1967, p. 259.

Introduction

I upon the 24th inst. visited the Piegan Camp and soon learned that three kegs of whiskey amounting to 15 or more gallons had just been brought upon pack horses by two white men (one of whom is known by the Indians as Curley Head) and was then being traded to the Indians. I found that I was powerless to move in preventing the fearful and disgusting spectacle of the drunken orgie [sic] which soon followed. Practice too vile and disgusting to be described, I witnessed through the night in the Piegan camp, the sole result of drunkenness. The chiefs have no power to prevent the Indians from drinking this worst and most vilely adulterated whiskey, and many of them & squaws too indulge to excess, when follow scenes of madness and frenzy, accompanied with the lowest, most brutal and disgusting practices imaginable, and seldom ends without serious loss of life.[1]

So wrote Lorenzo Lyman, a citizen of Helena, Montana Territory, in January 1874. He was one of many travellers who witnessed the tragic spectacle of Blackfoot Indians being decimated by the insidious effects of the whisky trade that swept through their hunting grounds between 1870 and 1875. In those six years, hundreds of Indians died as a result of the noxious trade, either killed in drunken quarrels, shot by whisky traders, frozen to death while drunk, or felled by the poisonous effects of the whisky itself. Chiefs lost their authority, people were afraid to meet each other on the trail, and everything that the Blackfoot owned went for whisky. Many soon became ragged mendicants, with no horses to hunt the buffalo, no warm robes to cover themselves, and no lodges to protect them from the winter storms. Wives were killed in drunken frenzies, lifetime friendships were destroyed over a keg of whisky, and children suffered abandonment and neglect.

Alcohol in any form had been unknown to the Blackfoot prior to the arrival of the first French and British traders in the late 1700s. As a result, they had no experience to draw from that permitted them to find a reasonable place for intoxicants in their social and religious life. Because of its delusionary effects, they initially equated it with visions and supernatural experiences, thus placing it in a category far removed from the reality of its effects; and exercising moderation ran counter to their own practices of excessive behaviour in warfare and ceremonialism.

At first, the use of alcohol was restricted to twice-yearly visits to Hudson's Bay Company (HBC) or North West Company (NWC) trading posts. This resulted in binge drinking for a few days and for the rest of the year the Blackfoot remained sober. From these early influences, however, a pattern emerged that made the Blackfoot easily susceptible to the siren songs of the Montana traders when they began to pour unlimited supplies of whisky into their camps in exchange for buffalo robes. Those who knew the Blackfoot could hardly believe how rapidly they were swept into the maelstrom of alcohol, violence, and death. Once wealthy with large horse herds and aggressively independent in their vast hunting grounds, they were quickly reduced to objects of pity and disdain. As the great chief Crowfoot said, "The whiskey brought among us by the Traders is fast killing us off and we are powerless before the evil. [We are] totally unable to resist the temptation to drink when brought in contact with the white man's water. We also are unable to pitch anywhere that the Trader cannot follow us."[2]

The inception of the whisky-trading era and the emergence of Whoop-Up country (in what is today southern Alberta) as a cesspool of devastation was brought about by several factors, the most important being the failure of the Canadian government to introduce any form of law enforcement after it acquired Rupert's Land (i.e., the western prairies) from Great Britain in 1869. A land without law is a land ripe for exploitation. Another factor was Montanan John J. Healy, an exploiter par excellence. Almost by accident he discovered the rich profits to be made by selling whisky to Indians in a place that was completely beyond the reach of the law. As a Montana newspaper commented, "No U.S. detective or spy dare invade their quiet rendezvous; nor is whisky ever confiscated when it gets to that 'happy hunting ground.'"[3]

After Healy and his partner, Al Hamilton, grossed some fifty thousand dollars for four months' work in the British possessions,[4] every Indian trader and opportunist in the Fort Benton area of the Montana Territory wanted to share in the bonanza. Soon names such as Whoop-Up, Slide Out, Standoff, and Robbers' Roost became part of Montana's lexicon and those who participated in the illicit and debilitating trade became identified as local heroes, or at least colourful adventurers willing to risk their lives among the wild Indians north of the border. People became familiar with such names as John Healy, Al Hamilton, Joe Kipp, John "Liver-Eating" Johnson, John "Waxy" Weatherwax, and "Dutch Fred" Wachter. They also were aware that I. G. Baker & Co. and T. C. Power & Bro. had become the two most important businesses in Fort Benton and that their owners were becoming rich through the sale of alcohol.

Few raised their voices in protest against the whisky trade other than officials of the United States Indian department and law enforcement officers, and they were viewed as people with vested interests in seeing the trade squashed. Complaints from the Canadian side, particularly by Methodist missionaries, were perceived to be biased criticisms by those under the influence of the HBC, acting in its corporate interests. Montana newspapers acknowledged the lawlessness of the whisky traders but usually were uncritical in their comments.

At the time of the whisky trade, the Republicans were in power in Washington, D.C., and federal government officials wanted to suppress the trade; however, Montana Territory was controlled by the Democrats, who seemed to do everything in their power to prevent this from happening. But when there was money to be made, supporters of the whisky trade cut across party lines. While most of the traders seemed to have been Democrats, often with Southern sympathies, the wholesale suppliers of whisky were active in both parties.

Isaac G. Baker was a reluctant participant in the whisky trade during its early years, but found he had to sell alcohol to stay in competition with his rival, T. C. Power & Bro. (Montana Historical Society, 940-671)

In the six years that the whisky trade ran rampant in both the British possessions and Montana Territory, it made fortunes for some, destroyed the lives of others (both Native and white), and, on a positive note, was an important factor in the creation of the North-West Mounted Police (NWMP). Good or bad, it was a significant period in the history of the West and in Canadian-American relations on the western prairies. In many ways, a study of the whisky trade is more a study of Montanans than Canadians, even though most of the events took place in Canada. The line of communication and transportation for the trade was from the Montana towns of Fort Benton and Sun River northward into Canada, into an area utterly devoid of Canadian settlers or traders. The HBC stayed away and the Canadian government was nowhere to be seen, so the southern plains and foothills became populated by Montanans. True, some traders were originally from Red River, Quebec, Germany, or the Isle of Wight, but by the time they entered Whoop-Up country, they were part of the Montana scene.

The southern Alberta prairies have been pictured as unknown to the white man before the arrival of the NWMP in 1874 but this obviously is not true. By that time, whisky traders and wolfers had traversed much of the region, trading posts had existed where the settlements of Calgary, Fort Macleod, and Lethbridge now stand, and the trails made by the traders became the wagon roads and later the highways of Alberta.

In Montana, the huge Blackfeet Reservation, which should have been a safe haven for the South Peigans (the Blackfoot nation was made up of the Siksika, Bloods, North and South Peigan tribes), became instead a highway to the British possessions and a place where the Peigans could be exploited and decimated by the illicit trade in alcohol. Those Indians seeking refuge in Whoop-Up country were beset by whisky traders in their many forts; those looking for sanctuary on the Blackfeet Reservation were besieged by traders working off the backs of wagons. In short, there was no escape for the Blackfoot until the NWMP came west to stamp out the trade in Canada and until the buffalo were destroyed in Montana.

This book has been almost half a century in its creation. When I began going among the Bloods in the early 1950s, I was told stories about the whisky traders, sometimes by mixed-blood descendants of traders who were now members of the tribe. I also was aware that my wife's maternal grandfather, Flying Chief, had been adopted by whisky trader John Healy as a young lad, and that her paternal great-grandfather, William Gladstone, had been the carpenter who built Fort Whoop-Up. My appetite was further whetted when her uncle gave me a drawknife, plane, and square that Gladstone had used in building the fort. From that beginning, I gradually assembled information on the whisky trade, publishing the earliest results of my research in 1952 in a chapter, "American Traders in Southern Alberta," in the booklet *Historic Sites of Alberta*. And one of the first articles I ever wrote was entitled "Howell Harris and the Whiskey Trade," published by *Montana Magazine of History* in 1953.

Over the years, the files grew but I had other books to write and other projects to complete. Then, at the beginning of the new millennium, I was awarded a grant (the first in my life) by The Alberta Foundation for the Arts to do a book on the whisky trade. This enabled me to travel to or be in contact with important sources in Montana, Washington, D.C., Winnipeg, Ottawa, and other centres, and to put the finishing touches to the years of research so that I could get on with the writing.

The three most important sources for this book were the records of the Montana Superintendency of Indian Affairs for 1868–75 in the U.S. National Archives; the Thomas C. Power Papers in the Montana Historical Society; and Montana newspapers for that period. Ironically, although the Power Papers provide a wealth of information on the business structure of the whisky trade, they also reveal Power himself as an aggressive and somewhat unscrupulous businessman. Had the papers of whisky traders Isaac Baker or Charles Conrad survived from that period, they may have presented a similar picture, but we'll never know.

For personal reminiscences, the most valuable were those of John LaMott, John Healy, George Houk, Charles Rowe, William Gladstone, and Howell Harris. All had a remarkable degree of consistency. Also, many people and institutions have helped and guided me over the years. Those who stand out from the Native community are John Cotton, Jim White Bull, Harry Mills, Laurie Plume, Jack Low Horn, Percy Creighton, Chris Shade, Frank Red Crow, and most notably, my father-in-law, Senator James Gladstone. Valuable assistance in research was provided by Lindsay Moir and Doug Cass in the Library and Archives of the Glenbow Museum, Calgary; Rick Martinez in the National Archives & Records Administration (NARA), Denver office, and Richard Fusik in the Washington, D.C., office; and by the staff of the Provincial Archives of Manitoba, including custodians of HBC records. Thanks also go to Brian Shovers and the staff at the Montana Historical Society, Helena, including Jody Foley, Ellie Argukimbau, and Angie Murray, as well as to the Special Collections staff in the library of Montana State University, Bozeman. Among the many other people who were involved or shared an interest in the topic are Margaret Kennedy, University of Saskatchewan; Carly Stewart, Lethbridge Historical Society; Stan Gibson, Okotoks; Jack Dunn, Calgary; and Patricia McAndrew, Bethlehem, Pennsylvania.

This book is not intended to be an inventory of the whisky forts, their locations, and their dates of construction. Many discrepancies and variations exist in the memories of those who participated in the trade, so wherever possible, documented sources such as contemporary newspapers and reports are used. In those many instances when one must rely on reminiscences alone, although they show a high degree of accuracy, they are not infallible. Accordingly, the story is told in the most logical and orderly fashion based upon the information available.

Finally, I would like to pay particular tribute to my wife, Pauline, not only for the work she has done in transcribing notes and documents, but also for having the patience to put up with a writer for a husband for almost half a century.

Hugh A. Dempsey

Thomas C. Power was a merchant in Fort Benton and the main force behind the illicit whisky trade. The local sheriff described him as a "hard case." He is seen here with his son, Charles. Why someone was cut out of the picture is a mystery. (Montana Historical Society, 944-433)

1. Beginnings of the Liquor Trade

When the first Europeans began trading with the Blackfoot on a regular basis in the late 1780s, their companies were already engaged in a life and death struggle for supremacy in the fur trade. The Hudson's Bay Company (HBC), formed in England in 1670, was vying with the Montreal-based North West Company (NWC) to see which would get the most beaver pelts and other furs for fashion-conscious Europe. For the first century, when it had no competition, the HBC had not dealt in liquor and had imported just enough wine, brandy, and rum to serve the needs of its own officers and men. In 1770, for example, only 250 gallons were imported for the entire HBC.[1] The Quebec traders, on the other hand, were descendants of the French voyageurs and *coureurs du bois* who had been using liquor in their trade for generations.

When the two companies first met head-to-head in the West, the Nor'westers dominated through their excessive distribution of alcohol, both as gifts to bring the Indians to their forts and as items of trade. In 1787, an HBC trader at Manchester House commented that the Peigans "are now the quietest Nation in the country, except the Blood Indians, and I make no doubt will continue so till the Canadians [NWC] gets amongst them, which is the ruin of every Nation by debauching their women and destroying themselves with poisonous rum."[2] The HBC believed that, to survive, it had to follow its opposition, and by 1785 it was bringing in more than 2,000 gallons a year to its depot at York Factory. By the time the Blackfoot trade was underway, its imports at that post were almost 8,000 gallons annually, supplemented by the products of the company's own still at York Factory.[3]

Prior to contact with Europeans, alcohol had been unknown to the Blackfoot and to virtually all North American tribes. By the time the trade began in the West, tribes along the eastern seaboard were being dominated by the deadly brew, but the Blackfoot were not immediately drawn to it. As Edward Umfreville stated circa 1789, "These people are not so far enervated by the use of spiritous liquors, as to be slaves to it; when they come to trade they drink moderately, and buy themselves necessaries for war, and domestic conveniences."[4]

There was no word in the Blackfoot language for intoxicants, so they called them *Napiohke*, which may be translated as "White Man's Water." And because it was perceived to be a form of water, the Blackfoot at first refused to pay for it. Why pay for water, even magic water, when every river and lake had all they could drink for nothing?

If the HBC and NWC were to garner the Blackfoot trade, they knew they had to make the Indians dependent upon alcohol and then supply it in greater quantities than their opposition. As a result, spirits were given as gifts by both companies until their goal was achieved. In 1794, a Nor'west trader at Fort George, on the North Saskatchewan River, described just how successful they had been. "The love of Rum is their first inducement to industry," he wrote. "They undergo every hardship and fatigue to procure a Skinfull of this delicious beverage."[5] He further described how alcohol had become an integral part of the trading process:

> On entering the house they [the Blackfoot] are disarmed, treated with a few drams and a bit of tobacco, and after the pipe has been plyed about for some time they [relax] from their usual taciturnity in proportion to the quantity of Rum they have swallowed, 'till at length their voices are drowned in a general clamour. When their lodges are erected by the women they receive a present of Rum proportioned to the Nation & quality of the Cheifs [*sic*] and the whole Band drink during 24 hours and sometimes much longer for nothing—a privilege of which they take every advantage—for in the seat of an Opposition [HBC] profusion is absolutely necessary to secure the trade of an Indian.[6]

Both companies handled primarily rum and brandy, called "high wines," which were laboriously brought by water routes, either from England or Montreal, and carried in concentrated form in large wooden kegs. At their destinations, the spirits were diluted with water, on the ratio of seven to one for the Blackfoot.[7] When the Indians came to trade, they took away the liquor either in skin bags or in small kegs provided by the companies.

By 1811, the trading procedure had become well established. In that year, trader Alexander Henry commented: "Spirituous liquor, now seems to dominate them [the Peigans], and has taken such hold upon them that they are no longer the quiet people they were. They appear fully as much addicted to liquor as the Crees."[8] Henry told how two messengers would arrive at his trading post to announce that the rest of the tribe was on its way. These men were each given tobacco and a glass of liquor. When the main body of Indians arrived, the chiefs were invited into the fort where they went through a pipe-smoking ritual followed by the distribution of free liquor. Henry continued:

After the first round we give them each half a gill of Indian liquor, beginning always with the principal chief, who is about as ceremonious in taking a drink as he is in smoking. He dips his finger into the liquor and lets a few drops fall to the ground; then a few drops are offered above; but he drinks the rest without further delay.[9]

After smoking and drinking for about half an hour, each chief was given a quart of liquor to take back to his camp. Others who wanted liquor then went to the fort to trade "bits of meat, tongues, or other trash"[10] so that they could drink all that day and into the evening. Next morning they were all relatively sober to begin the serious trade. They continued to buy some liquor, but most of their furs, robes, dried meat, and horses were exchanged for metal objects, utensils, cloth, and other European goods.

The disastrous effects of the liquor on the Blackfoot while they were at the trading posts and immediately upon their return to their camps cannot be questioned. As W. F. Butler commented, "Knives were wont to flash, shots to be fired—even now [1870] the walls of the Indian rooms at Fort Pitt and Edmonton show many traces of bullet marks and knife hacking done in the wild fury of the intoxicated savage."[11] It wasn't more serious only because the Blackfoot usually came to trade but twice a year—in the spring and fall—and had to endure a dangerous ten-day journey from their own hunting grounds. As a result, they would usually have a debauch at the trading post that might last two or three days, take a few kegs back to their camps, and then remain sober until their next visit.

In 1806 the British parliament introduced a bill to halt the sale of liquor in the Indian territories of British North America. However, the NWC successfully convinced parliamentarians that if the legislation was passed the British "would lose three-fourths of their trade because Americans on the plains would supply the Indians."[12] Interestingly, the Americans made exactly the same claims against the British; obviously, neither side was willing to take the initiative to halt the trade. And so the liquor traffic continued unabated in the British territory until 1821, when the NWC and the HBC were amalgamated as the HBC, and competition within the area was thus eliminated. The following year, HBC governor George Simpson announced, "We have taken steps as will tend to wean the Indians from their insatiable thirst for Spiritous Liquors by passing a resolution that no more than half the quantity usually allowed be given as presents."[13] In 1825, in order to further reduce expenses and the stigma attached to liquor trafficking, the company decided that the use of alcohol would be gradually discontinued entirely. The process began in the North, where the transportation of goods was expensive and the Indians were in no position to protest against the change. On the plains, however, the large bands of heavily armed Blackfoot, Cree, and

Assiniboine continued to receive rum and brandy, presumably to maintain their goodwill and to retain their trade. The HBC's only concession to reducing the trafficking in the plains region was to instruct traders to issue liquor as gifts but to ban its exchange for furs.

By the 1830s, the use of rum and brandy had been stopped in such places as York Factory, Fort Churchill, Cumberland House, and Rainy Lake. In 1836, the HBC passed a regulation that "the use of spiritous Liquors be gradually discontinued in the few Districts in which it is yet indispensable" and "gradually to wean the Indians all over the Country from the use of spiritous Liquors to which they are so much addicted."[14] The ban probably would have been extended to the trading posts serving the Blackfoot, except that the Americans had become established among the Peigans on the Upper Missouri in 1831 and they did not hesitate to traffic in whisky. Given this competition, the HBC felt it had no alternative but to continue to supply liquor. Although used primarily as gifts to cement trade relations, rum and brandy remained an integral part of the British-Blackfoot trade until their use was finally discontinued in 1862. In that year, "the last drop of rum at Edmonton House was served out to the Indians in December."[15]

During the decades of excessive distribution by the fur traders, liquor created havoc among the tribes as people killed each other in quarrels or had serious feuds and disputes. White Fat, a Blackfoot, recalled going to Fort Edmonton where his people traded their buffalo robes for blankets, tobacco, clothing, powder, and other objects. Liquor was also distributed in small kegs. "The older people were the ones who got the liquor; younger ones didn't care for it," he recalled.[16] When they got back to their camp on the Red Deer River, they had enough liquor for everyone to drink, and sing, and party all that day. This particular debauch led to a Blackfoot named Many Shields being stabbed to death during a drunken quarrel, and the next day his relatives sought out the killer and murdered him. Such tragedies during drinking bouts were not uncommon.

On another occasion, a Blackfoot who had always abstained from using alcohol, because he knew he could not handle it, was cajoled into taking a sip of alcohol by his new son-in-law, who was unaware of the man's inability to drink. "After he drank a little," recalled One Gun, "it was just as if he drank a lot. He went out of his mind."[17] The man became extremely violent as he staggered through the camp, fighting with people and threatening them, and trying to find his wife in order to kill her. At one point he grabbed the tail of a stallion and it kicked him in the face, knocking him down and rendering him temporarily senseless. Then, bloody and out of control, he staggered to his chief's lodge, and when the man refused to smoke with him he tried to murder him. At this point, the crazed man's two sons intervened and killed their father.[18]

During the first half of the nineteenth century, the only non-Indian community of any size on the western prairies was Red River Settlement at Fort Garry, the present location of Winnipeg. Free traders living there, mostly Cree Métis, began to challenge the authoritarian control of the HBC; besides trading for furs, some also imported liquor from Minnesota Territory or brewed their own spirits in the settlement, which they traded to local Indian tribes and took as far south as the Sioux in the Dakotas. In the 1860s, other traders followed the river routes from Red River to Fort Edmonton where they carried on a limited liquor trade with the Blackfoot. However, this was a precarious business, for not only was liquor a volatile article of trade, but the Blackfoot and Cree were inveterate enemies. On one occasion, a Blackfoot war party under the leadership of Eagle Ribs was on its way north when it stumbled across a Cree Métis trading party. They attacked the string of Red River carts, plundered them, and destroyed all the illicit liquor. "The whiskey was destroyed," said a Blackfoot elder, "because they were on serious war business."[19]

In order to control the use and sale of alcohol, the governor and council of the district of Assiniboia decreed in 1858 that no one could distill their own spirits without a permit from the HBC. They then turned their attention to liquor being brought in from Minnesota. According to a petition they received, "The whiskey imported from the United States is of the worst quality, containing ingredients which are positively poisonous, and therefore ruinous to health."[20] Thus, regulations were passed in 1859, restricting any spirits adulterated with vitriol, turpentine,

A typical bull train out of Fort Benton in Montana, such as this one, serviced Whoop-Up and the other northern posts. Such convoys travelled only a few miles per day. (Glenbow Archives NA-98-11)

strychnine, *cocculus indicus*, tobacco, or any other poisonous substance. The law also stated that "it shall not be lawful to sell any intoxicating liquor to any person popularly known as an Indian" and levied a fine of £10 for each offence.[21] However, the council had no effective means of stopping the traders once they had smuggled the liquor out of the settlement. When Lord Southesk, a Scottish earl, toured the western prairies in 1859, he noted: "It is only when the Indian is in communication with free traders that he becomes a regular drunkard."[22]

The British government, far away from the scenes of debauchery and lawlessness, had always favoured a complete prohibition of liquor in the Indian territories, but over the years it had been influenced against direct action by commercial interests, primarily the HBC. A similar situation existed in the United States, where the federal government opposed the sale of whisky to Indians but ultimately could not effectively control it. In 1832, a year after the Missouri River trade opened with the Blackfoot, the American government proposed a complete ban on the importation of liquor into Indian country. Not unexpectedly, the traders were strongly opposed and used British competition to justify their position. "If the Hudson's Bay Company did not employ ardent spirits against us, we would not ask for a single drop," stated John Jacob Astor.[23] He added:

> Our new posts on the Missouri river above the Mandans must yield to the superior attractions of our opponents, unless the government will permit us like them to use spiritous liquors; and the friendly relations we have at last succeeded in establishing with the Blackfeet (those inveterate enemies of the Americans) at so much expense and personal hazard, must inevitably be destroyed.[24]

In spite of protests from the fur traders, the prohibition law passed on 9 July 1834, and strong efforts to have it modified went unheeded. In disgust, trader Ramsay Crooks complained that the government, in banning the sale of liquor, was sending the Blackfoot north where rum was "abundantly and cheerfully furnished by the British."[25] This, of course, was a gross exaggeration, for the British were in the process of reducing liquor distribution in their territories and would have welcomed any move to completely eradicate the trade. One might speculate whether the situation would have been different for the Blackfoot if the Americans and British had come together and agreed to a complete ban. In reality, it probably wouldn't have made any difference. Before long, independent American traders on the Upper Missouri and the Métis at Red River would have begun smuggling whisky to compete with their larger rivals.

Once the American traders realized that the ban would not be relaxed, their next move was to find ways to circumvent it. As a result, as historian Hiram

Chittenden stated, "The fur trade was characterized during all these years by the crime of smuggling with every incident of fraud and trickery known to that business."[26] Although a few shipments of whisky came overland from Minnesota, most were smuggled on the steamboats that plied the Missouri River. Within a short time, the movement of liquor became so blatant that, in 1842, Andrew Drips was appointed Indian agent for the Upper Missouri with specific instructions to suppress the illicit traffic. However, in two years, he made not a single arrest. Whenever he went to a trading post, the whisky was buried, or placed *en cache*, and remained there until he left. None of the traders would cooperate with him, for they all relied upon whisky as a major stock in trade.

In 1843, trader Honoré Picotte wrote to his superior from Fort Pierre: "You see plainly that we must lose the Blackfeet and Assiniboine trade next year unless we have liquor. I therefore request you use all your influence to send us some of that article next year, say four or five hundred gallons in canteens, kegs, even in bottles."[27] And, although officials searched all boats as they passed Fort Leavenworth and Bellevue, through a combination of intrigue, bribery, and imagination, the whisky still managed to flow into Blackfoot and Assiniboine country in large quantities.

In one instance, the American Fur Company (AFC) even imported a distillery to produce a frontier variety of corn whisky. In 1833, Kenneth McKenzie, chief factor at Fort Union, had distilling equipment sent up the Missouri River on the steamboat *Yellowstone*, together with a supply of corn purchased in Iowa. Once the still was operational, the trader proudly wrote: "I have established a manufactory of strong water. It succeeds admirably. I have a good corn mill, a respectable distillery, and can produce as fine a liquor as need be drunk."[28] Unfortunately for McKenzie, the whisky-producing distillery had a short life. A visitor to the fort reported the infraction to the superintendent of Indian Affairs in St. Louis and the still was quickly silenced. When asked to explain the illegal activity, McKenzie blithely contended that the equipment was really intended for Red River, in the British possessions, and he was simply experimenting with it while he waited for the owners to pick it up. Of course, nobody believed him.

Charles Larpenteur, who traded with the Assiniboine, Cree, and Blackfoot at Fort William, described the American process of distributing intoxicants to the Indians.

> The liquor trade started at dark, and soon the singing and yelling commenced. The Indians were all locked up in the fort, for fear that some might go to Fort Union, which was but 2½ miles distant. Imagine the noise—upwards of 500 Indians, with their squaws, all drunk as they could be, locked in the small space.[29]

If the Indians became too rowdy, the traders sometimes spiked their drinks with a powerful narcotic, such as laudanum, to render them unconscious. Others were dragged outside the fort and left to sober up on the bare ground. But the fort was a dangerous place when filled with intoxicated Indians, so more often than not the traders dispensed the liquor at the gates and the Indians returned to their own camps to drink.

In the spring of 1836, this practice had a deadly result for a band of about thirty lodges of Blackfoot who went to Fort McKenzie to trade. An Assiniboine observed them on the trail and, noting that they had plenty of horses and appeared to be well supplied with furs, guessed they were going to the fort. He organized a war party that followed them and watched from a distance as they went to their camp loaded down with kegs of whisky. The Assiniboine warriors listened to the Blackfoot shouting and singing all night, until they knew they were all too drunk to defend themselves. "When it was near daylight," observed a trader, "the order was given for the rush, and so well was it executed that in a very short time few were left alive in camp, and all the horses were captured with ease—as we learned, upward of 300 head."[30]

In spite of the murders and other tragedies that accompanied this traffic in liquor, one American trader tried to claim that its use was beneficial to the Indians. "Mr. [Edwin] Denig declares that the drinking of whisky does Indians no harm whatsoever," wrote clerk Rudolph Kurz, speaking of his superior at Fort Union. Kurz continued:

> To be sure, here as elsewhere, brawls and murders not infre-
> quently occur as a result of drinking, but wild Indians think
> nothing of such things as that. On the other hand, they were
> more reliable, more industrious, and cared more for their
> personal appearance at the time when Uncle Sam allowed them
> to barter for whisky …, for the simple reason, universally
> accepted as true, that people work more diligently for their
> pleasures than for the necessities of life. They find in whisky,
> Mr. Denig says, a keen incentive to work.[31]

But Kurz was not convinced. Rather than selling a "harmless" item of trade, he saw the traders being motivated by the huge profits made in the illicit business—as high as 400 per cent. He further stated that the traders did not want to see the Indians settle down and become farmers, for this would cut into their profits. "They are not concerned about the Indians' morality or advance to civilization," he wrote, "because that state of things would interfere with their trade—do away with their means of earning a livelihood. As long as there are buffaloes to kill fur traders are going to take a resolute stand against the civilization of Indians, not openly to be sure, but in secret."[32]

Pierre Chouteau, Jr., and his American Fur Company (AFC) gradually gained dominance over the fur trade of the Upper Missouri as other firms, such as Pratte & Cabanné and the Union Fur Company, fell by the wayside. The AFC dealt in liquor to compete with opposition traders, but because the AFC was financed by leading businessmen and was fulfilling government contracts to distribute annuity goods, Chouteau tried his best not to get caught. However, he was embarrassed both personally and politically in 1846 when four of his leading agents—Alexander Culbertson, James Kipp, Francis Chardon, and Honoré Picotte—were each fined eight hundred dollars for bringing illegal alcohol into Indian country. At the same time, U.S. district attorney Thomas Gantt was convinced "that the Company and its agents [were] for a long time past reaping exorbitant profits from the most flagrant violations of the law."[33]

Their cases remained before the courts for the next three years, during which time Chouteau successfully avoided having his trading licences revoked and reached an understanding with the authorities. The AFC also stopped trafficking in liquor, but its agents became so desperate to service their Blackfoot and Assiniboine customers they considered importing alcohol from the British colony at Red River. In 1847, during this three-year period of prohibition, the company ventured farther upstream to establish Fort Benton near the mouth of the Teton River, and when the self-imposed restriction on alcohol use ended, this fort became the main outlet for whisky to the Blackfoot Indians for the next quarter of a century.

A Peigan elder, Many Tail Feathers, described how his people traded at Fort Benton.

> We had many buffalo robes to trade so we came to the Teton River where we made great camp. Andrew Dawson, the factor at Fort Benton, sent the chiefs presents of tobacco, coffee, hard bread, and sugar. The chiefs invited the minor chiefs in to smoke and have a feast. Next day we packed our horses and travois with buffalo robes, furs, dried meat, and skins. As the chiefs approached the fort, the men inside rolled the cannon out and brought out their flag. Then one of the white men invited Many Horses, head chief, and the minor chiefs, to come forward. Our head chief was taking a present for Dawson who was coming outside. When the two men shook hands, the cannon was fired in a friendly salute. Then the men at the fort brought a huge copper kettle of whiskey outside the gate and passed cups of it to the circle of chiefs. Afterwards, the chiefs were invited inside where the factor dressed them all in fine clothes and gave them each a gallon of whiskey.

When this ceremony was over, a few of us were allowed at a time [to] go inside to trade. We bought guns, ammunition, and tobacco, mostly. We gave 10 robes for a flintlock gun, eight robes for a No. 10 size keg of powder and a sack of balls, and four robes for four plugs of tobacco. A knife was worth one robe and we gave four robes for a gallon of whiskey. We could have all the whiskey we were able to buy but only the old, mature people drank. They dressed up in their full outfits, started to drink, and went around singing and dancing.[34]

Although whisky was sold by the AFC, it was not its main stock in trade during the 1850s and 1860s. Like the HBC, the AFC gave it as a gift to bring in their customers but sold it only in limited quantities. As informants agreed, it was mostly the older people who bought the liquor from both the American and British forts. And, as around the British forts, the use of liquor resulted in debauches and tragedies around Fort Benton, while periodic drinking in the Blackfoot's home camps resulted in violence and bloodshed. Still, it was not a major disruption of normal daily life, for once the whisky was gone, the imbibers might have to wait for months before having another taste of the "White Man's Water."

From the beginning, the liquor trade was a profitable business, regardless of its consequences. Major companies, such as the Hudson's Bay Company and the American Fur Company, tended to dominate the trade simply because they had the resources to do so. In distant London and Washington, politicians may have decried the disastrous traffic, but as long as there was money to be made, whisky trading would continue to survive. By the 1860s, with the withdrawal of the HBC from trade and with the dissolution of the AFC, the opportunity arose for free traders and opportunists to enter the scene. Unlike the large companies, these traders made no attempt to restrict the scale of their business, often dealing with whisky as their main stock in trade. The result became a formula for disaster.

2. *The Turbulent Sixties*

The 1860s saw great changes in the economics, politics, and settlement of the Upper Missouri region, which in turn had a major impact upon the Blackfoot Indians. The decade set the stage for the unbridled flooding of their camps with whisky, creating misery and chaos and thrusting them into the roles of outcasts in a land they once controlled and identified as their own.

Some of the events that led up to this tragic situation started in the 1850s, but had little impact upon the Indians at the time. In 1855, in order to make it possible for contractors to build a railway from St. Paul, Minnesota, to Puget Sound, Isaac I. Stevens, newly appointed governor of Washington Territory, was given the task of negotiating a treaty between the United States government and the Blackfoot and other tribes along the route. He convened a huge council at the mouth of the Judith River, about 100 miles downstream from Fort Benton, and brought the Blackfoot into direct negotiations for the first time with representatives of the "Great Father" in Washington, D.C.

During the council, attended by the Peigans, Blackfoot, Bloods, and bands from across the mountains, the treaty commissioners spoke eloquently about peaceful relations between the tribes and the future benevolence of the government. In the proposed treaty, the Indians were to give up their vast hunting grounds in exchange for reservations and the provision of yearly annuities. This document, signed on 17 October 1855,[1] would ultimately affect the sale of liquor to the Blackfoot. Most important of its provisions were Articles 4 and 5, which described the Blackfoot hunting grounds as a huge reservation encompassing almost the entire part of Montana Territory east of the Rocky Mountains and north of the Missouri River. (Under federal legislation passed in 1834, such a reservation was automatically designated as "Indian territory" where the sale of intoxicants was prohibited.) Another provision made it illegal for any Indian to bring liquor into his hunting grounds.

A second event to affect the Blackfoot was the sale of the American Fur Company's (AFC) forts on the Upper Missouri in 1865. Like the Hudson's Bay Company (HBC), the AFC had provided some measure of stability to the region, distributing only enough liquor to meet its competition. Its forts were taken over by A. F. Hawley and James B. Hubbell under the name of the North West Fur Company (NWFC), but it held them only until 1869 when all but the Fort Benton establishment were sold to the Fort Leavenworth, Kansas, firm of Durfee & Peck. This latter company followed questionable business practices, including the illegal importation of rifles, and was engulfed in notoriety and scandal.[2] By the late 1860s, the steadying influence of the old established traders was gone, and the Blackfoot were left to the mercy of an assortment of small and middle-sized trading firms such as I. G. Baker, T. C. Power, Carroll & Steell, and the NWFC, all intent on reaping profits as quickly as possible. Generally speaking, these traders were unwilling to make the kind of long-term commitments required to assure any stability in the trade.

Another major change in conditions along the Upper Missouri was the discovery of gold in 1856, which, over the next few years, brought hundreds of prospectors to the area.[3] Unlike the fur traders, these men had no business to conduct with Indians and considered them to be "pests" who stole their horses, interfered with their prospecting, and bothered them in their camps. Prospectors did not hesitate to trespass upon Blackfoot lands in their unquenchable thirst for gold, and in the inevitable confrontations that followed, deaths occurred on both sides.

Towns such as Virginia City and Helena arose, where saloons were opened to serve the thirsty miners. The liquor they sold came up the Missouri River by steamboat and was held in warehouses in Fort Benton, the head of navigation, until it could be hauled overland to the gold-mining region to the west. Fort Benton, then, became not only the centre of the Blackfoot trade but also the location of Montana's liquor storage depots—an unhappy combination.

Montana Territory's rough frontier mining population, combined with whisky trading, horse raiding, and Indians being dispossessed of their hunting grounds, finally exploded in a series of incidents, beginning in 1865, that the local people called the "Blackfoot war." Numerous confrontations led to hostility, anger, bloodshed, and ruthlessness on the part of both the Indians and the settlers in the Fort Benton area. One of the earliest incidents occurred in the spring of 1865 when a few young Bloods stole horses belonging to residents of Benton. The local citizens retaliated by murdering a Blood chief who happened to come into town, unaware of the raid. When the Bloods heard about the killing, a huge party set out for the American fort to gain redress; en route, they encountered eleven woodcutters and, in the ensuing battle, killed them all.

During the winter of 1865–66, the confrontations continued after four North Peigans were murdered by drunken miners at Sun River simply to validate the "bombastic bravado and boastings" that had marked the miners' evening of carousing.[4] When the Peigans learned of the senseless killing, an angry war party led by Bull Head swept into the Sun River area, destroying the government farm, killing one of its employees, slaughtering the cattle belonging to the Catholic mission, and murdering the herdsman. From there they went to a ranch on the Dearborn River where they killed a nephew of Kit Carson, the famous frontiersman.

A short time later, another group of Peigans attacked a trading party of Gros Ventres and killed two traders, Hunucke and Lagris, who were travelling with them.[5] In response, a number of Fort Benton citizens sent a petition to the Montana Territorial governor demanding that a force of five hundred men be organized "to chastise them so severely that they will never be any more trouble."[6] Interestingly, two of the men who signed the petition—Alfred B. Hamilton and Joe Kipp—were actively involved in the whisky trade. When the government failed to act, the Bentonites, led by Frank Spearson, responded by murdering the first Blood Indian who came to the village. "He was killed," observed a visitor, "and shoved under the ice, where his feet stuck out for several days."[7]

In the autumn of 1866, a number of Bentonite ruffians attacked eleven Peigans who were crossing the Missouri River at that point. One Indian was killed and scalped, while the others fled in terror. On the following day, the same gang pursued a party of Peigans about 6 miles from the settlement, killed six of them, and triumphantly carried their scalps back to town.[8]

A Blood camp on the Whoop-Up flats. Note the stones used to hold down the edges of the teepee at the right. (National Archives of Canada PA-21788)

Many of the confrontations that took place between Montanans and the Blackfoot during the late 1860s were the result of horse raids, not Indians wanting to start a war. As trader Alexander Culbertson stated, "These depredations have been committed by a portion of the young rabble, over whom the chiefs have no control."[9] Yet their actions, particularly when a simple horse raid turned deadly, were blamed on the whole nation, and especially the South Peigan tribe.

The incidents continued during 1867, starting in the spring when a freighter named Lowe was killed and robbed, his body peppered with bullets—four in the chest, two in the shoulders, and one through the forehead. Exclaimed a Montana newspaper, "Every spring and fall since the settlement of Montana began, these same bands of Indians have kept their war parties along the Helena and Benton trail, and during each season they have succeeded in scalping from three to a dozen victims under similar circumstances to the one we have just registered."[10]

That winter, a Peigan war party killed a man named Charles Scott, then tried to raid the stables of Wells, Fargo & Co. but were driven off by gunfire.[11] A few weeks later, Nathaniel Crabtree, a woodcutter on the Missouri River, was killed by some Peigans, who held a victorious scalp dance within full view of the soldiers at Camp Cook. The Peigans then appropriated twenty-three army horses and nine mules before returning north. Soon after, Peigans raided a mining camp at Confederate Gulch and exchanged shots with some of the miners.[12] About the same time, other horse raids were made at Lincoln Gulch and Thompson's Bar.

The press referred to the Blackfoot as murderous savages when reporting these incidents, but the viciousness occurred on both sides. For example, when three Blood horse raiders were pursued and killed by Bentonites, a townsman known as John the Tailor brought back "the whole skin of the head of one of them."[13] A Peigan woman, the wife of Split Ears, recalled another time when Bear Chief and his family went to Fort Benton. "The whites there began shooting at them," she said, "and they fled up to the Island. The whites killed all but one old woman."[14]

Conditions further deteriorated in the summer of 1868, when Mountain Chief, head chief of the Peigan tribe, went to Fort Benton to ask the Indian agent to remove some whisky traders from his reservation. As soon as he left the Indian agency office, the elderly chief was attacked by two men who struck him and fired shots at him, causing him to flee for his life. Although the agent tried to swear out a complaint against the men, the justice of the peace resigned rather than issuing it, and the sheriff quit rather than having to act upon it. When the Peigans heard about the indignity to their chief and the inaction of government officials, they immediately set out to seek revenge. In Blackfoot culture, revenge did not necessarily need to be levied against the individual who had caused the insult, but merely someone from the same tribe or, in this case, white people.

To avenge their chief, the Peigans took eighty horses from settlers near Diamond City, a Montana mining town, and although they were pursued by an angry posse, they successfully escaped to their own camps. In retaliation, traders and settlers at Sun River ambushed twenty-one Peigan youths and took them prisoner. They were then turned over to the army at Fort Shaw, where they were held as hostages until the stolen horses were returned. The superintendent of Indian Affairs, who concurred with the action, freed three of the boys and sent them back to their camps with the message that the other hostages could be traded for the missing horses. About two weeks later, the Peigans came to Fort Shaw with thirty-two horses, and the prisoners were released. However, as they rode away from the fort, one of the freed prisoners tried to kill the white man who had captured him. Other settlers rallied to his defence, and when an interpreter tried to intercede, he was almost killed. Finally, with a military escort, the Peigans returned to their own camps.

Many of the problems in the "Blackfoot war" resulted from the trafficking in whisky in and around Fort Benton. In the summer of 1866, for example, Little Dog, head chief of the Peigans, was killed on the trail from town by drunken members of his own tribe. A visitor was disgusted by what he saw in Benton and suggested that "a Vigilance Committee would find a good field for operations in this section—especially among the whiskey traders."[15] These men usually bought small amounts of liquor, either from the saloons or one of the trading companies, and sold it to Indians on the outskirts of town after nightfall.

By 1867 the illicit trade had extended to a number of points along the Missouri River, fed by the increasing presence of steamboat traffic. According to special Indian agent Nathaniel Pope, "It is a well known fact that every year since steamboats first came up the river, more or less trading has been carried on by officers of the boats and frequently by the passengers, whiskey and ammunition being the principal articles traded for robes."[16] In addition, he complained about men who worked as woodcutters or wolf hunters along the river and traded whisky obtained from the steamboats. He added:

> They were mostly renegades from Montana, a lawless set of men living like savages, going and coming without let or hindrance and far more dangerous than Indians ..., who do not hesitate by all means in their power to secure a stock of robes from the Indians whom they look upon as legitimate prey ... they cannot realize the pernicious effects of their illegal traffic, they laugh at the laws and it matters little to them who suffers for the misdeeds so long as they can flourish.[17]

Some government officials and legitimate traders demanded that action be taken to halt the whisky traffic. Not only was the liquor itself a problem, but often those who traded it were coarse frontiersmen whose cavalier attitude towards human life sometimes resulted in the needless deaths of Indians, followed in turn by their tribe's desire for revenge. The senseless killings in and about the village of Fort Benton contributed to the growing hostility between Indians and whites. As stated by one Peigan who lived through that era, "The whites and Indians were fierce against one another and would fire at each other on sight."[18]

By 1868, the illicit trade had expanded beyond Fort Benton and the Missouri River. Trader James Hubbell complained during a trip to Washington:

> The Whiskey traffic has never been carried on so boldly among any of the tribes of the North West as at present among the Blackfeet. Parties go out to meet the Indians on their way in to trade & of course the Indians will give them the Blankets off their backs for a half pint of diluted alcohol & no efforts are made by the Agent to stop it.[19]

He said the traders were getting permission to visit the Blackfeet Reservation ostensibly to recover stolen horses, but once out of town, they picked up their supply of cached whisky and traded it to Peigans for buffalo robes.

The Indian commissioner instructed the Blackfoot Indian agent to enforce the liquor laws, but the official claimed this was impossible. Explained agent George Wright:

> I have tried hard to prevent this whiskey trading to the Indians, but was powerless. The U.S. Depy. Marshal has been and now is a resident here [Fort Benton] and he has done nothing for me, as he was afraid if he made any arrests his customers would snub him in the spring, when he opens his own whiskey Saloon. The Sheriff and other officers have acted badly in not assisting me, and whether they did or did not trade any liquor to the Indians, I am positive they received whiskey during the winter in five and ten gallon kegs and half bbls. by Wells Fargo and Cos. express ... Under the circumstances it is providential there has been no massacres at this place from drunken Indians.[20]

Another factor to affect the Blackfoot during this decade was the creation of Montana Territory in 1864 amid the animosity and divisiveness left by the Civil War. According to some sources, when the Missouri State Guard under General Sterling Price was defeated by the Union army in 1862, many of its members deserted and found their way to Montana where they established communities at such places as Dixie, Confederate Gulch, and Jeff Davis Gulch. Ultimately, these refugees, reinforced by Irish-Americans and pro-Confederate Northerners, became the nucleus of the Democratic Party in Montana. As stated by a journalist in typical nineteenth-century hyperbole, the ex-Confederate soldiers came

> fleeing before our victorious hosts, the shattered hordes of Price, anxious to seek in this mountain country an asylum of safety. From the north there came about the same time … numbers of cowards and copperheads, bullies and blacklegs, whose blatant bravado and deeds of blood constituted them the siders and abettors of their Southern fugitive allies in forming at that period the dangerously disturbing element of society.[21]

With the creation of the new territory, virtually all federal appointments were given to faithful members of the Republican Party, but when the citizens of the area voted in their first election, all but one of the delegates to the Territorial Assembly were Democrats, as was the Territorial delegate to Congress. This meant that any attempts by the governor, federal judges, marshals, and other Republican appointees to uphold federal laws seemed to be opposed at every turn by the Democratic Territorial representatives.

Under federal law, the governor also became commissioner of Indian Affairs, and all appointments of agents and staff were strictly along party lines. At the same time, many of the traders dealing with the Indians, including whisky traders, were avowed Democrats with local public opinion clearly on their side. To many Montanans, the marshal and judges represented federal (i.e., Republican) interference with their Territorial affairs, while the traders were seen as independent entrepreneurs who laughed in the face of federal authority. As a result, there was very little public support for an active repression of the whisky trade. Many Montanans didn't care one way or the other about what happened to the Indians, but they did care about local citizens being prevented from carrying out their business practices, even if that included furnishing liquor to the Indians.

As part of its mandate, the Territorial government began levying taxes and issuing business permits. Some traders concluded that by licensing them, the Territorial government was permitting them to sell whisky, regardless of federal regulations. This led to confrontations between the two levels of government, with a local judge in one instance ruling that a Territorial permit allowed its holder to sell whisky despite federal regulations to the contrary. As a newspaper commented, "It is hard to force merchants to pay a Government and Territorial license for selling an article which is certain to be seized in case it is found in transit."[22]

To add to the complicated situation, even the federal government had interdepartmental problems regarding the legality of liquor sales. In 1864, it passed the Internal Revenue Act, which empowered the Internal Revenue department to issue licences to those who paid an appropriate tax. This was interpreted by some traders as a federal carte blanche to sell whisky to Indians. Reported a disgruntled Indian agent, "... the Govt. made a Collector of Internal Revenue up here who issues licenses to parties to trade as Merchants, by virtue of which licenses these parties claim the right (& with reason) to trade with any & all who come along."[23] When a liquor dealer was arrested for illicit sales, he claimed the federal licence was, in fact, a permit to sell the product for which he was paying a tax. The matter went all the way to the United States Supreme Court, which ruled against the dealer, stating that the licence was simply evidence that the tax was being paid and not a permit to carry on an illicit business. To clarify the matter, the law was changed in 1866 so that no reference was made to a licence being issued, just to the tax being paid.[24] However, some traders continued to use the licence as an excuse to sell liquor.

By the late 1860s, the legal powers of the federal government may have prevailed, although sometimes more in theory than in practice. In 1868, Territorial governor Clay Smith responded strongly to a suggestion that the 1834 prohibition law—known as the Intercourse Law—was now a "dead letter," as claimed by some traders.[25] He stated that "the act of Congress to regulate trade and intercourse with the Indian tribes, and to preserve peace on the frontier," and its amendments in 1862, were still very much in effect.[26]

A Supreme Court decision held that: "The policy of the law is the protection of those Indians who are, by treaty or otherwise under the protection and pupilage of the government, from the debasing influence of the use of spirits." The purpose of the 1862 amendment was: "To make parties liable, if they sell to Indians under the charge of a superintendent or agent, wherever they might be."[27]

Governor Smith cited the text of the Intercourse Law as follows:

> That if any person shall sell, exchange, give, barter or dispose of any spiritous liquor or wine to any Indian under the charge of any Indian superintendent or Indian agent appointed by the United States, or shall introduce, or attempt to introduce any spiritous liquor or wine into the Indian country, such person, on conviction thereof before the proper district court of the United States, shall be imprisoned for a period not exceeding two years, and shall be fined not more than three hundred dollars, provided however, that it shall be a sufficient defence to any charge of introducing or attempting to introduce liquor into the Indian country, if it is proved to be done by order of the War Department, or of any officer duly authorized thereto by the War Department.[28]

Governor Smith went on to say that any suspected boat, wagon, or other conveyance could be searched without a warrant in Indian country, and if liquor was found, the vehicles, horses, and goods could be seized. If the culprit was a licenced trader and was convicted, his licence would be revoked. The law also gave Indians the right to destroy any liquor found on their reservation, and that in any ensuing court case, Indians could serve as "competent witnesses." This was a departure from the norm where Indians were considered to be wards of the government and could not give testimony in court.

After citing this legislation, Governor Smith instructed all federal marshals, deputies, and district attorneys "to take immediate and energetic measures to suppress the liquor traffic with the Indians in this Superintendency, and especially at and about Fort Benton."[29] If this legislation had been effectively enforced, it would have meant a quick end to the whisky trade, but it was not to be. There was too little local support, too much bribery and coersion, too many desperate men willing to defy the law, too much animosity towards the Blackfoot, and too much money to be made from the illicit trade.

3. *The Merchants*

wo merchants dominated Fort Benton and became the primary suppliers to the whisky trade: Isaac G. Baker and Thomas C. Power. These men controlled the Indian trade during the decade or so when it was important to northern Montana's economy and when the whisky they dispensed was the most destructive force imaginable to the Indians of the Montana and Canadian prairies.

In 1864, Isaac Gilbert Baker, a forty-five-year-old native of Connecticut, went to Fort Benton as the new chief trader for the American Fur Company (AFC). Baker had been in the business since he was a young man, trading on the Upper Mississippi and along the Missouri. Even before Baker set foot in the town, his business acumen was tested when low water halted his steamboat at Cow Island, some 120 miles downstream from the fort. Without hesitation, Baker rode to Benton where he arranged for freight wagons and a crew to collect the goods and transport them overland so that the company would have the much-needed supplies for the coming season. Among the shipment were two hundred barrels of whisky, an indication, perhaps, of the direction that Baker's interest would follow during his early years on the Upper Missouri.[1]

A year later, Baker witnessed the final closing of the AFC, when the old adobe fort was taken over by the North West Fur Company (NWFC). Although offered a position with the new firm, Baker declined and chose instead to open his own store. He saw the potential for profits in the Indian trade, in warehousing, and in forwarding shipments from the steamboats to the mining camps farther west.

He hired a team of builders, including William Gladstone, an ex-Hudson's Bay boat builder who would later construct Fort Whoop-Up. They completed the store over the winter of 1865–66, in time to receive a large assortment of goods delivered by steamboat in the spring.[2] In that same year, 1866, Isaac took his brother, George A. Baker, into the firm as a minor partner, forming I. G. Baker & Bro. Later, it expanded to become I. G. Baker, Bro., & Co., and finally I. G. Baker & Co.

Responding to Baker's competition, the NWFC branched out from Benton and established Fort Hawley, an outpost 125 miles downstream, to garner the trade of the Gros Ventres during the winter of 1866–67. Not to be outdone, I. G. Baker built an outpost in the same vicinity. According to James Bradley:

"This was ... the beginning of the outpost trade which subsequently assumed quite extensive proportions, becoming, in fact, the only successful method of dealing with the Indians."[3] And, one might add, it was the easiest way of trafficking in alcohol without constant interference from the local marshal or Indian agent.

Tom Power was twenty-eight years old when he arrived in Fort Benton in 1867 with a supply of goods. Born in Dubuque, Iowa, where his father was a farmer and general merchant, Power attended Sissinawa Mount College in Wisconsin where he completed a three-year course in civil engineering. In 1860, he joined a survey party in Dakota Territory and when they visited Fort Benton during an expedition, Power immediately saw the business opportunities offered by the community.[4] In the spring of 1867, he brought a stock of merchandise up the river by steamboat, and when he arrived in Fort Benton, Isaac Baker loaned him a large tent to store his goods until more permanent quarters could be found. At that time, Benton was little more than a single street facing the river. "There were just two store buildings and a few huts and cabins," recalled Power.[5]

Baker's assistance to a potential business rival may seem strange, yet the two men maintained a unique blend of co-operation and competition throughout their entire Fort Benton careers. In later years they jointly built a local hotel, a hardware store, a bank, and a steamboat, and loaned goods to each other in times of shortages. At the same time, they used every stratagem within their means to get the best of the other in business deals, such as getting government contracts and obtaining licences to operate as Indian traders, and in trying to garner the largest share of the Indian trade.[6]

In 1868, John W. Power joined his brother and, with an investment from John M. Sweeny, the firm of T. C. Power & Bro. (later T. C. Power & Co.) was established.[7] The firm built a store at the end of the block in which the Baker company was located and soon launched into the Indian trade.

At that time, the Blackfoot Indian agency was located at Fort Benton, so the two firms had regular and frequent contact with the agent, George Wright. Occasionally, these connections were thought to be too close, as annuity goods intended for distribution to the Blackfoot sometimes ended up in Baker's or Power's store. For example, in early 1867, a local resident saw four bales of blankets that had been taken from the Indian department storage and sold to Baker for eight hundred dollars. The witness added:

> During the winter of 1866–67, about December 1866, I saw Major George B. Wright, Agent for the Blackfoot Indians, furnish William Hamilton and Nelse Narcisse with what I judged to be twenty-five hundred dollars worth of Indian annuity goods which were taken to the Blackfoot camp and traded for

robes by the said Mr. Hamilton and Nelse Narcisse, who
brought back three or four wagons loaded with robes. About one
hundred robes were counted out to him (Maj. Wright) and he
told me they were his share. I helped him sort the robes and saw
them carried to the store of Mr. I. G. Baker by a negro called
Henry, who was in the employ of Maj. Wright. Maj. Wright told
me he had sold these robes and got money for them.[8]

Another Bentonite said that in the autumn of 1867 he had removed several
cases of goods from the Indian agency warehouse and given them to Tom Power
to pay off a debt owed by the agent's brother. After the goods were delivered,
"Mr. T. C. Power paid me the sum of $75.00 which was due me from Maj. Geo.
B. Wright, a private debt."[9]

It should not be surprising, therefore, that the agent may have turned a
blind eye to any illegal trafficking in whisky done by Baker or Power. Indeed,
special Indian agent Nathaniel Pope observed that Agent Wright "has permitted
persons to trade indiscriminately and I can learn of no attempt having been
made to conceal the fact that whiskey was sold and traded to Indians last winter
in broad daylight."[10]

There can be no doubt that Isaac Baker was directly involved in the whisky
trade, presumably with the full knowledge of the Indian agent. As trader J. B.
Hubbell complained:

I informed Agent Wright that Mr. I. G. Baker, a merchant at
Benton, was about starting an "outfit" to be traded in the
Indian Camp & to which I protested. He assured me he would
not allow it, but if he did allow them to go he would not allow
them to take over 100$ worth of Goods for presents. ... had it
not been for a Deputy U.S. Marshal overtaking them & finding they had Whiskey, forced them to return, their Goods
would have been traded.[11]

However, an examination of Baker's records showed no whisky sales to local
traders, and the suspicion was voiced that such transactions were entered on the
books as some other commodity or else entered in a separate set of ledgers.

In 1868, the Bakers engaged two veterans of the Confederate army, William G.
and Charles E. Conrad, as clerks in their Fort Benton store. The young men,
twenty and eighteen years of age, respectively, hailed from a plantation in Virginia.
Both had served with the Virginia State Militia, and Charles had spent two years
with Mosby's Raiders, a guerilla-type body that had raided behind Union lines,
destroying supply depots and communication lines.[12] As employees of the Baker

company, Charles (who was described as "tall and athletic" and completely fearless) usually constructed and operated the outposts, while William (who "tended toward corpulence") concentrated on the office end of the business.[13]

Later that year, Isaac Baker ordered John LaMott to take a load of freight north from Fort Benton to meet Charles Conrad, who was trading with the Peigans. LaMott does not say if he was carrying liquor, but he probably was. In any case, he ran into trouble as soon as he crossed the Teton River, when he was set upon by intoxicated Peigans who began to harass him and to demand food. LaMott broke open a barrel of hardtack biscuits and scattered them on the ground and as the Peigans stopped to pick them up, he hurried on to Bull Bear Springs, where the Indians caught up with him.

LaMott stopped to camp for the night, and after dark when Conrad arrived, they quietly hitched up the oxen and crept away. The Indians caught up with them at dawn, harassing them again and trying to make them turn the freight wagon towards their own camp. They finally parted at Dead Indian Coulee, and a short time later, LaMott and Conrad reached the Marias River.

Charles E. Conrad joined I. G. Baker & Co. as a trader in 1868, but through his aggressive actions he and his brother became partners in the firm, later taking it over and becoming millionaires. (Montana Historical Society, 941-779)

Once there, the two men found that the nearby villages were infested with traders—most presumably selling liquor—including Carroll & Steell, the NWFC, and T. C. Power. The Peigan chiefs became so disgusted that they began to run the traders off the land. They tried to kill Joe Spearson, who was working for the NWFC, and took all his trade goods. Then they sent Carroll & Steell's outfit packing, shot at Joe's brother, Frank Spearson, turned back Captain Nelse and Charlie Duvall who were coming from Fort Benton to trade, and finally "they run the Powers outfit out."[14]

The Baker team was the only one left but even they didn't last long. Conrad and LaMott went to Full Bear's camp to trade, and while they were there, a number of young Peigans burst into the chief's lodge and threatened to kill them. Full Bear intervened, waving a revolver at the intruders, and when they finally left, the chief told Conrad and LaMott to pack up and go. When the traders refused, "These old Indians loaded up our stuff. In spite of us they loaded it in the wagons and went and got the cattle and made me yoke up and made us go … and told us not to stop until we got to Benton."[15]

Little wonder, then, that a leading Blood chief should present himself before the Indian Peace Commissioner later that year and complain: "We want the new traders to act like the old men who traded long ago, when there was nothing but peace and quietness. When we come to trading posts we do not want to be interfered with. We want good traders so that we may buy and live."[16] Peigan chief Mountain Chief stated: "We do not wish these pale faces to come to our villages. If we desire to trade, we will go into their forts, dispose of our robes and leave. There is nothing in common between us."[17]

To gain some control over the trading situation, the federal government decided late in 1868 to permit two firms to operate trading posts on the Blackfeet Reservation, beginning with the 1868–69 season. According to trader S. C. Ashby: "This was due to the fact that the Indians coming to the Fort Benton bottom would get drunk and sell their robes and furs for whisky. Those government people evidently believed that by making the trading post at some distance from Fort Benton that they would lessen the chances of the whisky traders."[18] The government also believed that placing licences in the hands of two traders, subject to cancellation if found selling liquor, would encourage the Peigans to trade with them. Such companies would have permanent posts with a large stock of goods, as opposed to the itinerant traders who worked off the backs of their wagons. In addition, licenced traders would be more likely to report any illicit sales of liquor that were cutting into their business.

One licence was given to I. G. Baker for a post on the Marias River, and the other to the NWFC for a post to be operated by John Riplinger on the Teton River, near the present town of Choteau.[19] Each firm posted a bond of five thousand dollars as a guarantee to follow the terms of the agreement. Tom Power was closed out of the Blackfeet Reservation, but did get a licence to trade with the Crows.

S. C. Ashby was engaged by Baker to build and take charge of the Marias River post. "We located the establishment on the Marias River just below what is known as the Willow Rounds, about a hundred miles northwest of Fort Benton," he said. "Mr. Baker remained with me until we had the buildings up and the trenches dug for the stockade."[20] With a crew of twenty-five men, the work was soon completed, and by early winter the fort was inundated by hundreds of Bloods, Siksika, and North Peigans who came down from the British possessions. Prior to that time, they had been obliged to make the ten-day journey to Fort Edmonton or Rocky Mountain House, or risk being intercepted by whisky traders if they tried to go to Fort Benton. Finally, the pressure of business at the new fort became so heavy that William Conrad was sent to take charge.

Although the trade was brisk, government hopes that such a post would discourage the whisky trade proved to be groundless. "As soon as we were located so that people could learn where we were," said Ashby, "the whiskey traders from Sun River and every place else began to congregate."[21] They set up camps within a mile or two of the fort and soon intoxicated Indians began to harass Baker's employees. The Indians would circle the post, shooting overhead and yelling such threats as: "You miserable dirty white dogs. You are here with your cattle eating our grass, drinking our water, and cutting our wood. We want you to get out of here or we will wipe you out."[22]

On another occasion, Father Camillus Imoda, a Jesuit priest, was staying at the fort when a group of intoxicated Bloods came in, led by Calf Shirt. The chief took exception to the presence of the priest and was about to shoot him when William Conrad hit the man's arm and the ball was fired harmlessly into the air.

Prices charged for goods at the outpost depended on their popularity, not on their real value, according to Ashby. For example, a card of brass buttons or string of brass beads worth twenty-five cents might be exchanged for a buffalo robe worth fifteen dollars. When selling flour or sugar, the measuring cup was dipped into the barrel but the contents were never pressed down. As a result, the profits at the post were impressive, even if no whisky was sold. When the season ended in the spring of 1869, Ashby claimed that the fort had done forty thousand dollars worth of business.

But all did not go well for the I. G. Baker company that winter, largely because of the strange situation created by the treaty of 1855. The treaty of 1855 between the Blackfoot tribes and the United States government had designated the Missouri River as the southern boundary of the Blackfeet Reservation. Thus, Fort Benton, on the north side of the river, was legally within the confines of the reservation, and the sale of liquor should have been prohibited in town. But the matter was never pursued by federal authorities, so as the community expanded, liquor warehouses and saloons were located in Fort Benton. Responding, no doubt, to its lack of success in controlling the whisky trade, and with the belief that Baker and others were the main suppliers, orders came directly from

Washington, in November 1868, for the army to seize the entire stock of liquor from Baker and the other traders in Fort Benton. According to a reporter, the NWFC had already disposed of most of its "immense stock," but a considerable amount of liquor was seized from T. C. Power and from Carroll & Steell. "But," said the reporter, "it remained for I. G. Baker & Bro. to do the real handsome. They turned out enough liquor to run a first-class gin-mill a year."[23]

In response to the raid, Isaac Baker sent an indignant letter to the commissioner of Indian Affairs. He wrote:

> I am aware that the laws governing trade and intercourse prohibits the introduction into the Indian Country of spiritous liquors, and would gladly submit to the requirements of the law, provided it was regarded as being in force, but events of the past few years have actually overruled the law, or in other words, necessity has made the law inoperative.[24]

Baker claimed that because he paid an internal revenue tax he was entitled to sell any merchandise he wished and that the Internal Revenue Act took precedence over the Intercourse Law of 1834. The Commissioner of Indian Affairs sought a legal opinion and was informed by the secretary of the Interior, O. H. Browning, that the Intercourse Law and its amendments "are undoubtedly in force within the territory in which the Indian title has not been extinguished."[25] Ultimately, however, the confiscated liquor was returned to the Benton merchant on a legal technicality.

Meanwhile, John Riplinger completed the NWFC post on the Teton River, and like the Baker post on the Marias, it remained entirely free of liquor in order to maintain its trading licence. However, Riplinger found it difficult to compete with the whisky sellers who invaded virtually every Peigan and Blood camp along the Marias and Teton Rivers.

Abel Farwell, a licenced trader with Durfee & Peck among the Gros Ventre and Assiniboine, complained that during the winter of 1868–69 he collected only twenty-five hundred buffalo robes, while whisky traders at Fort Benton got twenty-six thousand robes. "There are more Barrels of Whiskey taken to Fort Benton than sacks of Flour," he wrote. He continued:

> Our country is filled with wagon traders from Fort Benton, peddling whiskey among the Indians. These traders go to the camps of the Indians and there dispose of their goods, never taking anything with them to feed the Indians. The result is the Indian will exchange his furs for their whiskey and nic nacks [sic] and when winter sets in they come to me poor, to be taken care of.[26]

In another attempt to gain some control over the situation, federal authorities in Washington made a number of changes in the local administration of Indian Affairs. Agent Wright was dismissed late in 1868 and replaced by Nathaniel Pope; the Territorial governor surrendered the position of superintendent of Indian Affairs and W. J. Cullen was given the position as a full-time task; and the ineffective marshal, Neil Howie, was replaced by William T. Wheeler. Meanwhile, work was started on a new Blackfoot Agency on the Teton River, far away from the negative influences of Fort Benton. In his first report early in 1869, Agent Pope observed that "the whiskey business is carried on at Benton & in this locality to a fearful extent," and that Sun River traders had recently taken 40 gallons to a Blood camp on the Marias.[27] He said that virtually all the merchants in Benton were trading whisky, including the so-called "best men," and specifically included T. C. Power and Carroll & Steell in this group. He said that Tom Power was openly hostile to Superintendent Cullen and that this was "the best possible evidence that you [Cullen] have tried to interfere with their illegitimate business & have worried them somewhat."[28]

The flooding of the Blackfeet Reservation with whisky during 1868 and 1869 created a considerable upheaval among the tribes, as well as in their relations with white settlers. As stated by Superintendent Cullen:

> This unlawful and wicked trafic [sic] is being carried on by a band of bad men, mostly from Fort Benton and Sun river ... There is hardly an Indian camp in that part of the country which is not now being reached by these whiskey Traders; and a number of bloody fights among themselves while drunk, are reported, and the white men and Traders in their country who refuse to furnish them with whiskey are threatened with violence. This bad state of affairs has but recently sprung up among these Indians, and is believed to be entirely owing to the introduction of poisonous whiskey by bad men who not only rob them of all their means of support for their families, but are demoralizing the Indians to an alarming extent.[29]

The Blood and Siksika, who usually wintered on the British side of the line, were concerned that the whisky trade and the accompanying violence would result in innocent Indians being killed by white settlers. As a result, the Blood tribe spent more and more time in the British possessions and went south only to take their robes to the licenced trader at the new agency. One exception was Calf Shirt's band, which insisted on remaining on American soil where they were constantly visited by whisky traders.

In 1869, a series of confrontations erupted that was really a continuation of the so-called "Blackfoot war," but made much more serious by the infusion of

alcohol. As an official stated, "Much of the trouble that has disturbed the fron-
tier [is attributed] to the prevalence of drunkenness among the Indians."[30]
It started when seven Peigans pursued a Diamond R wagon train, en route from
Fort Benton to Helena, and in a running gun battle, wagon master James
Watkins was wounded in the hip, while he in turn shot at the leader of the party
and killed his horse.[31] Yet this incident may have been more complicated than it
first appeared, for a reporter noted that "the chief of this hostile faction is an
Indian called Crow Top, a scoundrel of the first water, who was punished severely
and justly last winter at Benton by a white man."[32] It is possible that the attack
was based more on personal revenge than on open warfare.

Another flare-up occurred in mid-July when two government herders were
attacked and killed near Fort Benton. When one of the dying men was brought
into town, three local residents, George Houk, Henry Kennerly, and Peter
Lukins, went on a rampage of revenge.[33] Houk stormed into the home of
William Gladstone, dragged out an elderly Peigan named Heavy Charging in the
Brush, and murdered him in the street. With him was a fourteen-year-old boy,

*William S. Gladstone, or "Old Glad," was the carpenter who built Fort Whoop-Up and other whisky forts.
He is shown here with his granddaughter, Nellie, in the 1870s. (Private collection)*

who was also killed. The older man, a brother of head chief Mountain Chief, had come to town to deliver a message. Rampaging through the village, the ruffians found three other Peigans, also members of Mountain Chief's band, and lynched them;[34] two were identified as Bear Child and Rock Old Man. Afterwards, the bodies were left hanging from a scaffold with a note pinned to one of them saying, "There are three good Indians."[35]

According to Charlie Rowe, who witnessed the events: "After the murders had been committed, the people began to fill up with whiskey for good, and the town was a pandemonium until daylight. They marched and fought and sang and screamed until they were hoarse and finally wore themselves out."[36] The murders became even more abhorrent when Isaac Baker discovered that the herders had not been killed by Peigans, but by River Crows from farther south.[37]

Understandably, the Peigans were furious about the murder of one of their respected elders and the execution of the four others, causing the *Helena Weekly Herald* to ask the editorial question, "Are we to have an Indian war?"[38] In early August, a huge Peigan revenge party of some three hundred warriors surrounded a government wagon train at Eagle Creek, and in a three-hour standoff, killed most of the oxen. During the fight, another wagon train hove into view and the Peigans tried to prevent it from joining the beleaguered freighters. A young man in this train, Sam Paxton,[39] believed he could pacify the warriors so he rode out to meet them. After a short discussion, he returned to say that the Indians wanted tobacco and provisions. He carried a box of tobacco and a sack of flour back out to them, but as he approached, they shot him dead. The freighters, well armed with repeating rifles, then drove the Peigans away, and upon joining the other train learned that only one man had been wounded. Meanwhile, four Peigans had been killed and two wounded.

Anger about the incident increased when it was learned that one of the Peigan leaders was Pablo Starr, a mixed-blood member of Mountain Chief's band, who had been a trader for I. G. Baker. "Are the people of this Territory forever to suffer these Indian butcheries, merely to allow a few rich traders to grow richer?" asked the *Helena Weekly Herald*. "The trader piles up his robes from 'friendly Peigans' dressed perhaps with the same murderous knife that tore the bleeding scalp from the head of some unfortunate white man!"[40]

The raids continued over the summer, particularly along the Benton–Helena road where a total of thirty-seven horses were taken from the various Wells Fargo mail stations.[41] Other horses were stolen from Joe Cobell, George Houk, and W. L. Stocking. In addition, Peigans attacked a military haying party near Fort Shaw, but were driven off by four scouts who had been sent along for protection.[42] Many residents blamed these raids on Mountain Chief's band, presumably because of his brother's murder. But the Indian superintendent had a different view: "I consider the Whiskey trader the cause of all the present troubles with Indians in Montana."[43]

The incidents had the frontier in an uproar, with settlers demanding more military protection. The citizens of Helena sent a petition to Colonel P. R. de Trobriand, commanding officer at Fort Shaw, requesting that two hundred cavalry be employed to drive all Indians back to their reservations and that troops be stationed at mountain passes. The officer tried to calm the situation, stating: "There is actually no Indian war in the Territory. Depredations are committed, even murders are perpetrated, but by whom? By a handful of roaming thieves and murderous red vagabonds, belonging principally to the Piegan tribe."[44]

But the murder of Malcolm Clarke on 17 August 1869, at his ranch in Prickly Pear Canyon brought matters to a head. Clarke had been a trader with the AFC and had married a woman from Mountain Chief's band. When he turned to ranching, he became one of the most influential men in the Territory and had business and personal relationships with such luminaries as rancher Granville Stuart and lawyer W. F. Sanders.

There are two versions regarding the motive for his murder, both involving Pete Owl Child, a son of Mountain Chief and nephew of Clarke's wife. In one version, Owl Child had some horses stolen from Clarke's corral by white men, and to make up the loss, he tried to take some from a nearby rancher. However, he was driven off and when Clarke heard about it, he whipped the young man in front of his friends and caused him to be disgraced.[45] The second version is that Clarke attempted to seduce Owl Child's wife, and when the young man protested, he was publicly beaten.[46] Whichever story is true, there is no doubt that Owl Child had a grudge against the mercurial rancher. On the evening of 17 August, Owl Child visited the ranch with twenty-five companions, including Bear Chief, Black Weasel, Eagle Rib, and Black Bear, and murdered Malcolm Clarke and seriously wounded his son, Horace.

Clearly, the killing was an internal family quarrel, but it came at a time when many Montanans were convinced they were facing an Indian war. At a protest meeting held in Helena and attended by such political leaders as Sam Hauser, Martin Maginnis, and N. P. Langford, a resolution was passed to raise a volunteer company, equipping them with arms and paying a bounty for every scalp they took.[47] A short time later, a U.S. grand jury was struck and was told by witnesses that nine or ten western Montanans had been murdered and more than three hundred horses stolen within the previous two months. The jury was informed that the Blackfoot tribes had moved all their women and children into the British possessions (which wasn't true) and obtained modern guns and ammunition from British traders (also untrue). "This is a declaration of war on the whites of Montana by these Indians," concluded the jury, "and some measures should be adopted for the purpose of meeting the emergency."[48] The matter was then turned over to military authorities for their consideration.

Meanwhile, the flow of whisky continued unabated on the Montana frontier. The existence of licenced traders did nothing to discourage the "wagon traders" whose only real stock was whisky or some form of flavoured alcohol. As the winter trading season of 1869–70 was about to begin, trader John Riplinger predicted that his trading efforts would be almost a lost cause. As he stated:

> To my certain knowledge there has been brot here from Benton & Sun River more than 60 Gals Whiskey. The Indians are going & coming from here and other camps below to Benton all the time. They dont go into town for it, they are met out on the Teton by the Bentonites and there get what they want, the same at Sun River … There is no use talking to them. They are nothing but a lot of unreasonable dogs; they have no sense; they dont want to understand what is good for them.[49]

He reported that a Peigan named Left Hand had taken four 5-gallon kegs of whisky from Fort Benton to Big Lake's camp on Milk River and that two parties of wagon traders had left Bob Tingley's store with 20 gallons of whisky for the Peigan camps on the Marias. Also, Blood chief Calf Shirt had obtained 20 gallons of whisky at Benton and had been persuaded to move his small camp lower down on the Marias to the mouth of Shit Creek, where he could be furnished with whisky all winter. Added Riplinger: "The Indians have been drunk nearly all the time since they came to the Marias and the prospects are that they will be drunk all winter. They pay no attention to hunting Buffalo while they can get Liquor … Something must be done to check this whiskey trade."[50]

A month later, he reported that all his dire predictions had come true. "The Camps below & above me are full of whiskey," he said. Riplinger continued:

> Last night at 11 o'clock Clarke Tingley passed here with a wagon & a half Bbl. of Liquor. He is in a Blood camp about two miles above me and has Traded about 100 Robes since he arrived … The Indians are Drunk all the time. The camps below all have liquor traders in them. We are doing nothing here; all Indians that don't trade their Robes for Liquor here in Camp go to Benton to Bakers & Powers as they report that Baker trades Liquor to them after dark.[51]

In the hopes of improving his trade for the NWFC, Riplinger decided to build a new post farther down the Marias River at Red Coulee, close to the British border. He employed William Gladstone to build the fort and hired a number of people who had been on the fringe of the whisky trade, such as Thomas Healy and Lee Keiser. Another figure in his employ was the tragic Alexander Culbertson, once one of the most influential traders with the AFC, but now drinking heavily while he mourned the loss of his fortune through bad investments, and his wife's subsequent unfaithfulness.[52]

Riplinger's decision to build a new post closer to the British border was a harbinger of things to come. Many Montana traders would, in fact, extend their trading activities into the British possessions during the 1869–70 trading season.

John J. Healy, shown here in 1883, was half-owner of Fort Whoop-Up and partnered with Alfred B. Hamilton in the British possessions. (Montana Historical Society, PAC 98-100.4)

4. Off to the British Possessions

There were several reasons why Montana traders extended their activities across the forty-ninth parallel into British territory in 1869–70. One was the fear that Washington meant it when it said it would close down the United States whisky trade. The seizure of I. G. Baker's liquor supply, the refusal to consider the validity of inland revenue licences, the insistence that the 1834 Intercourse Law was still valid, the strict directives of the Territorial governor, and the appointment of William T. Wheeler, a strong Republican who was not in the pocket of any of the whisky merchants, as marshal were all indications that perhaps the federal government was prepared to act.

Another factor was that the turbulence of the late 1860s had caused many Blood and Siksika to remain north of the border and to trade with the British, rather than risking their lives in Montana Territory. Certainly the Hudson's Bay Company (HBC) did all it could to keep its customers north of the line. Late in 1869, trader John Riplinger said, "The Blackfeet Indians will not be here this winter. They started this way with the Bloods but got word from the Mountain Post [i.e., Rocky Mountain House] to Return there to trade …"[1] This was confirmed by the HBC chief factor at Fort Edmonton who stated that "most of the American Indians being at war on the other side come to this side to trade."[2] The Bloods, in particular, were excellent customers in providing buffalo robes, but the only way for the Montana traders to deal with them was to venture into their hunting grounds.

A third impetus to move north of the line likely came from the aggressive Tom Power. He had been frozen out of the legitimate end of the Blackfoot trade, and although he may have outfitted a few wagon traders, he must have been chagrined by the profit of forty thousand dollars taken by the Baker firm at the Teton River post. He was astute enough to realize that if that kind of money could be made without the use of alcohol, a trading post beyond the jurisdiction of the United States government offered almost unlimited possibilities.

A fourth reason concerned the quest for gold. A number of miners had prospected along the foothills and were convinced that there was a lode to be

Alfred B. Hamilton, John Healy's partner at Fort Whoop-Up, left the whisky trade in 1873 to become a licenced trader. He later established the town of Choteau, Montana. (Montana Historical Society, 957-275)

found somewhere in the neighbourhood of the Porcupine Hills. In this area, stated a reporter, "prospects have been heretofore obtained and believed to be rich mines."[3] Encouraged by these reports, veteran miner John McClellan organized an expedition in the summer of 1868, consisting of twenty-seven men financed and outfitted by I. G. Baker, Carroll & Steell, and others in Fort Benton. These prospectors travelled from Sun River across the upper waters of the Teton and Marias Rivers and camped for several days on the shores of Waterton Lakes. From there, they searched westward into the mountains and then proceeded north to the Oldman River. Somewhere along the Porcupine Hills, stated McClellan, "for the first time since the commencement of the expedition was gold discovered, five or six colors to the pan being obtained from the top dirt."[4]

One member of McClellan's expedition was Joe Healy, brother of trader John J. Healy of Sun River. Joe was not interested in the Indian trade, but was dedicated to the quest of finding gold or other precious minerals along the chain of the Rocky Mountains. After Joe returned from his gold-seeking venture, he probably convinced his brother that a trading post in the British possessions would be an ideal base to continue the search for gold. At the same time, it would give John Healy an outlet for his increasing role in the sale of whisky to the Blackfoot. Accordingly, in 1869 the Healy brothers, together with Al Hamilton, formed the Saskatchewan Mining, Prospecting & Trading Outfit for the express purpose of moving across the line into the British possessions.[5] The two principal partners in this venture, John Jerome Healy and Alfred B. Hamilton, were to dominate the northern whisky trade for the next five years.

John Healy was born in Ireland in 1840 and raised in Brooklyn. He enlisted in the 2nd Dragoons in 1858 and took part in a campaign against the Mormons in Utah Territory. When he took his discharge he turned to prospecting and joined the gold stampede to Oro Fino in Washington Territory in 1861. The following year, he was among a group of miners who discovered gold on the Salmon River in the present state of Idaho. Healy then crossed the Rockies to Fort Benton where he spent the summer building mackinaw boats for the American Fur Company (AFC). Later that year he made a brief visit to New York to see his parents, and while there he married Mary Frances Wilson. He came back to Montana with his wife in 1863 but was lured north by stories of major gold discoveries on the North Saskatchewan River. He spent the summer around Fort Edmonton but left in anger when the HBC refused to sell goods to the miners, as these supplies were meant for the Indian trade. Healy continued to search for gold until 1865 when he was placed in charge of the government-owned farm at Sun River.

After the Sun River farm was destroyed by North Peigans in 1866, Healy opened his own store at Sun River, where his brother Joe had previously built a prospector's cabin. The family was joined a few years later by brothers Thomas and Michael. Healy's store served travellers along the trail from Benton to Helena, but his main customers were the Blackfoot Indians to the north and the Pend d'Oreilles who annually crossed the mountains to hunt buffalo on the plains. Very early in his merchandising career, Healy learned of the profits to be made in selling whisky and became one of the main suppliers out of Sun River.

His partner, Alfred B. Hamilton, a nephew of I. G. Baker, was born and raised in Missouri. He went to Fort Benton in 1865 where his uncle put him in charge of the AFC post while it was being transferred to the North West Fur Company (NWFC). Hamilton then became a "wagon trader" for Baker at Peigan camps on the Marias River. When the NWFC received a licence to build a post on the Blackfeet Reservation in 1868, Hamilton became an employee; at the end of the season, he moved to Sun River. There he went into partnership with John Largent, a local merchant, and a year later he became a junior partner in the firm of Healy Hamilton & Co. At the time of his trip to the British possessions in 1869, Hamilton was a member of the Territorial legislature. Known to the Blackfoot as *Inuispi*, or "Long Hair," he was married to a Peigan woman named Lucy, the daughter of Iron Breast.

Both Healy and Hamilton were ardent Democrats and quickly ingratiated themselves with the Territorial and federal representatives. The delegate to Congress, James Cavanaugh, was a fellow Irishman and a close friend of Healy's. Despite Cavanaugh's party affiliation, he exerted considerable influence in Republican Washington because of the strong mandate he had received from Montana electors in 1867 and because he was a man "of keen wit and great personal magnetism."[6] Healy and Hamilton were also friends of Martin Maginnis, owner of the *Rocky Mountain Gazette*, who in 1873 was elected as a delegate to Congress. And probably one of their most influential friends was Sam Hauser, described as "a kingmaker and a stringpuller per excellence" for the Democratic Party and a man with extensive Washington connections.[7] As owner of the First National Bank of Helena, Hauser had direct business dealings with Healy and Hamilton.

Support for the Democratic Party among the whisky traders was strong, if not overwhelming. Besides Healy and Hamilton, trader Joe Kipp was such an active member that there was a group known as the "Joe Kipp Democrats."[8] Other supporters were "Dutch Fred" Wachter, J. M. Arnoux, Moses Solomon, and C. A. Broadwater. Broadwater owned the largest freighting company transporting supplies for the liquor interests; on the supply side were Charles and William Conrad of I. G. Baker, Southerners and strong supporters of the party. Not surprisingly, many Montanans felt that the Democratic Party had "a monopoly on illicit liquor traffic with the Indians."[9]

But the Republicans were in power in Washington, and this fact was not lost on merchant Tom Power, who became an active and vocal supporter of that party in Montana. He served as a delegate to the Republican Territorial convention and developed valuable contacts in Washington on several visits to the capitol. In the political arena, he was ably supported by George A. Baker, brother of I. G. Baker, as well as by Matthew Carroll and George Steell, of Carroll & Steell. Consequently, the three leading mercantile firms in the Territory had direct lines to the bureaucrats and mandarins in Washington.

Before Healy and Hamilton could establish a post in the British possessions, they had several obstacles to overcome. The first was money, as they had neither the cash nor the resources to take on such a project without help. Initially they went to Carroll & Steell, but that company refused to back them. Then they saw George Baker, of I. G. Baker & Co., but he too refused to help them, in spite of the fact that Al Hamilton was his nephew. Baker was known for his dislike of the whisky trade and, as early as 1867, had been urging the authorities to put a stop to the illicit traffic, despite the fact that his own company was involved.

The last resort for Healy and Hamilton was Tom Power, and this time the gods seemed to shine upon the pair as they stumbled into an unbelievably lucky situation. Power, in anticipation of getting a lucrative licence to trade with the Assiniboines, had brought in a large stock of goods. However, just days prior to the Healy and Hamilton visit, he learned he had been turned down, lamenting to the Indian superintendent, "What is to become of me?"[10] He revealed that he had twenty thousand dollars in Indian goods on hand and the refusal "could be ruinous for me."[11] As he faced the possibility of financial disaster, Healy and Hamilton came to his store looking for goods! True, they wanted them on credit, but there was as much money to be made from charging high interest rates as there was in selling the goods themselves.

By the time Healy and Hamilton left the store, they had Power's commitment to provide them with eight thousand dollars worth of Indian trade goods.[12] By a mere twist of fate, both parties had been rescued by the circumstances of the moment. As a fellow trader commented in disgust, Tom Power "has generally been at the head or foot of most of the whiskey trade, while the reputations of [Healy and Hamilton] does not leave a doubt as to what their intentions are on the matter."[13]

Another problem facing Healy and Hamilton was gaining permission to cross the border—not from the British but from the Americans. In 1869, the territory north of the forty-ninth parallel was still under the control of the HBC and as such was British territory. Steps were underway to transfer the region to the new Dominion of Canada, but negotiations had not yet been completed. In any case, neither the British nor Canadian government was in any position to restrict access to its territory. The nearest judicial authority was at Fort Edmonton, almost 400 miles north of the border, and it consisted of nothing more than the chief factor being a justice of the peace with no military or police to back him up.

What Healy and Hamilton needed was permission from the United States government to cross the huge Blackfeet Reservation so they could enter the British possessions. The reservation encompassed the entire route from Sun River to the forty-ninth parallel, and it was clearly governed by the terms of the 1834 Intercourse Law. The area was also the centre of much of the lawlessness and illegal trafficking in whisky that was plaguing the federal authorities.

In November 1869, Healy and Hamilton tried to cross the reservation without the necessary papers, but Indian agent W. B. Pease seized their wagon and turned them back. Although he found no whisky, they did have ammunition among their supplies, and the agent was concerned that taking a large amount of powder and shot through Blackfoot country would be a dangerous enterprise.[14]

What happened next is a mystery, but the result was that on 1 December the Honorable E. S. Parker, commissioner of Indian Affairs in Washington, sent a telegram to Alfred Sully, the new superintendent of Indian Affairs for Montana, stating: "J. J. Healy & A. B. Hamilton desire to pass through the Blackfeet country north. Give them the necessary permit if no objection known to you."[15] This telegram was probably in response to a request from someone in authority, asking that these two members of the Saskatchewan Mining, Prospecting & Trading Outfit be allowed to cross the reservation on their way to the British possessions. The finger of guilt seems to point to Territorial delegate [i.e., Congressman] James Cavanaugh, not only because of his friendship with John Healy but also because a year later he was the man who tried to have the permit renewed for another year.[16] As the telegram appeared to be a directive, rather than a request, Sully had no recourse but to reply that he had no objection and to issue the necessary permit after Healy and Hamilton posted a bond of ten thousand dollars.[17]

There were some restrictions on their travel. The bond guaranteed that the Healy & Hamilton firm would not "trade with any person, neither White men, Negroes or Indians in this Territory after they leave Sun River Settlement" and that they had "no intention to infringe the laws regulating trade and intercourse with the Indians." On that basis they were

> permitted to pass through the Blackfoot Country and Cross the Northern boundary line of the United States of America at a point within about 30 miles of St. Mary's Lake. They are also privileged to take with them a party of from 20 to 30 men and six wagons loaded with supplies, provided there is no spiritous liquors in the Wagons, except a small quantity which may be taken safely for Medicinal purposes.[18]

What was meant by a "small quantity" of liquor wasn't stated, but it was obviously defined liberally by Healy and Hamilton.

Needless to say, those trying to suppress the whisky trade were outraged. Marshal Wheeler stated flatly that the mining aspect of the application was "intended as blind under which to sell liquor & everything else they choose to Indians." He added that "Genl. Sully & Agt. Pease say they have to let them go because of *orders* from Washington. Bah!"[19] J. B. Hubbell, co-owner of the NWFC agreed. Protesting to Washington, he stated:

> Genl. Sully issued a public notice warning [certain] parties not to go into the Indian Country under penalty of having their Goods & Robes confiscated, whereupon they managed to get a permit *from Washington* to pass *through the Indian Country to the British line* for the purpose of prospecting & mining. This is all humbug … Marshal Wheeler … has no doubt about the intentions of the Saskatchewan Mining & Prospecting Outfit … Genl. Sully or the Agent Lieut. Pease don't realize the class of men they have to deal with & nothing but years of contact with them in a civil life enables a man to appreciate them [italics in original].[20]

Yet there are indications that gold prospecting was indeed intended to be a significant part of their activities. In fact, during the years that followed, Joe Healy used his brother's fort as a base for his prospecting expeditions.

Although Tom Power funded Healy & Hamilton's northern project, he handled it in such a way that his hands appeared to be clean. Instead of directly financing the expedition, Power simply loaned the partners money; they, in turn, used the money to buy the goods they needed from him. In making the loan, Power used a standard promissory note that showed the date, due date, and carried the statement, "I promise to pay to the order of T. C. Power & Bro. …," followed by the amount, rate of interest, and signature of the borrower.[21] The first such note was issued on 1 December, the day when Healy & Hamilton's approval came from Washington. It was for $5,565.93 at an interest rate of 1 per cent per month, the money likely being earmarked for the capital costs of constructing a fort, as well as for obtaining equipment, hiring staff, and buying supplies. A second note was issued on 16 December for $113.25 at the same rate, another on the same day for $450.23 at 5 per cent per month, and finally a note on 21 December for $591.89 at 1¼ per cent per month. By May of the following year, when the robes and pelts came in from the north, Healy & Hamilton's loan of $6,721.30 had grown to $8,376.89 through Power's prohibitive interest rates.[22] So Power made a profit not only on the goods he sold to Healy & Hamilton and on the robes and pelts he bought from them, but also in loaning the funds necessary to carry out the project.

One might speculate that the $450.23 note at the usury rate of 5 per cent interest per month, or 60 per cent per year, was for the purchase of whisky, a risky product with a fast turnover rate. As Double Anchor whisky was selling in Fort Benton for $1.75 a gallon, and other brands for the Indian trade were even cheaper, such an order would have amounted to at least 250 gallons of whisky.[23] Of course, such liquor sales seldom appeared in Power's sales books, likely being entered in a private account book. Healy claims he took only 50 gallons on that first trip "not so much for the value of the goods it would bring in, as thereby to secure the Indian trade."[24] But as this statement was made after the suppression of the whisky trade, it is highly suspect.

With a permit in hand and supplies provided by Tom Power, the partners made active plans to openly move across the line as quickly as possible. Normally, such an enterprise would have set out in October but they had to wait until December when the permit was in place and the funding assured. A number of traders and labourers joined the enterprise; besides Healy and Hamilton, there were interpreter Joe Spearson; labourers Pat Haney, a man named Jose, and Jerry Potts; freighter Bob Mills; and perhaps Joe Healy and John Largent.[25] Also accompanying them was Joseph Wei, who was apparently trading on his own and acting as a fur buyer for Tom Power.[26] He may also have been there to keep an eye on Power's investment in the Healy & Hamilton enterprise.

Another member of the trading party was Martin Donovan, wagon master for freighter Hugh Kirkendall. On 14 December 1869, Donovan had been camped with his wagon train on the Dearborn River when he was raided by a war party of Bloods, led by White Man's Dog. The Bloods succeeded in running off thirty magnificent mules that formed one of the finest freighting teams in the Territory of Montana. All were branded HK in a square on the left side of the neck and were worth at least $250 each.

Unwilling to give up such a large investment without a fight, Kirkendall went to the Indian agency on the Blackfeet Reservation and discovered that the animals had been taken across the line into the British possessions. He was told that White Man's Dog was a Blood who lived with the South Peigans but had gone back to his people after the raid. Kirkendall also learned that Healy and Hamilton planned to go north, so he asked Superintendent Sully for permission for his wagon master to accompany them and to remain in British territory for the winter where he would try to recover the mules.

Not only was Sully agreeable, but he suggested to authorities in Washington that Al Hamilton be engaged by the United States government to investigate the rumours of stolen horses being bought by the HBC. "Mr. Hamilton will, if you think it worthwhile," said Sully, "hunt up the facts of the case while he is in the Saskatchewan area for the winter, provided he can be remunerated for his trouble. If entrusted with this duty I feel sure Mr. Hamilton will act faithfully in the matter."[27] That a known whisky trader, preparing to debauch a major segment of the Blackfoot nation, was being treated like a respectable businessman not only indicates the influence someone wielded in Washington, but also reflects the extent to which local authorities were willing to go to avoid displeasing their superiors.

Members of the expedition left Sun River about 28 December 1869, and were still on the trail on New Year's Day.[28] So, to be precise, Healy & Hamilton's fort was not established in 1869 (as historians have claimed) but in January 1870. Before leaving, the traders engaged Big Plume, an influential Blood chief, to accompany them on their journey. Big Plume normally traded with the NWFC but, according to trader John Riplinger, he decided to go with the Healy & Hamilton expedition "to protect them and stay with them."[29] The trip was uneventful until they reached the Marias River where they met a band of twenty Bloods under the leadership of Bull Back Fat, head chief of the tribe. These people were starving so the traders fed them and took them along with them until they found buffalo. From there, Bull Back Fat accompanied the traders for the rest of their journey.

After three weeks they arrived at the confluence of the Belly and St. Mary Rivers, the site of their fort, reaching there just after the middle of January. It is possible that the site was chosen by accident and that they really wanted to go farther west. Hamilton indicated this in a letter he wrote during the winter: "Here we are in winter quarters about one hundred and sixty miles north of Sun river crossing. We were overtaken by severe cold weather and so were compelled to stop here … We will not be able to prospect a great deal before spring."[30] But there is no question that trading was a major part of their plan, for he added, "The chances are that we will make a good trade, as there are plenty of Indians around us and buffalo in sight every day."[31] The site was a favourite wintering place of the Blood tribe. It was known to the Blackfoot nation as *Akai'niskwi*, or "Many Died," because of a tremendously high mortality at that location during the smallpox epidemic of 1837–38. In later years, that name also was applied to Healy & Hamilton's fort. "Many Died" seemed appropriate.

The trip north itself was without incident. As Hamilton recalled:

> The Indians were to my knowledge friendly, because in the winter of that year we travelled in the Indian Country where these Indians roamed without being molested, in fact some ten of them travelled with us from the Missouri River, Montana, to where we located across the Canadian line. We hunted buffalo together.[32]

Upon arrival at the site, Healy sought out Many Spotted Horses, a leading chief of the Blood tribe who normally wintered at the forks of the rivers. After giving him three hundred dollars in gifts, Healy received permission to build a trading post in the chief's wintering camp and also to use the trees for construction and for firewood. Such permission was always sought by knowing traders, both to gain allies and to acknowledge ownership of the land.[33] Healy also followed the common practice of taking a "winter wife" from the tribe, despite having Mary Frances at home in Sun River. "Healy was married to Many Spotted Horses' daughter or sister," confirmed a Blood elder.[34] According to North-West Mounted Policeman Cecil Denny,

> As nearly all these traders had married Indian women, according to the Indian custom, that is by purchase, and in many cases, the women were connected with some of the leading chiefs, they had a certain influence through these women with the Indians themselves.[35]

By the time the traders arrived that January, the weather had turned bitterly cold, and the men were living in leather teepees until more permanent accommodation was available. While the traders were felling trees and preparing to build their fort, events were taking place on the Montana frontier that were to have a considerable effect upon their success. Ever since the murder of Malcolm Clarke, local settlers had been agitating for some direct action to "punish" the Peigans. Fuel was added to the fire when James Quail was killed on the outskirts of Helena, and even though later evidence indicated that he had been murdered and robbed by a white man, the damage had already been done. And when further incidents of horse raiding occurred, including the theft of Kirkendall's mules, the military was prepared to take action.

In late December, Colonel de Trobriand from Fort Shaw learned that the Peigans were camped on the Marias River, and that Mountain Chief was at a location known as the Big Bend. In his camp were his sons Pete Owl Child and Black Weasel, who stood accused of the murder of Clarke. In an attempt to find a peaceful solution, Indian Commissioner Sully travelled to meet with the Peigans on 1 January 1870, but "found the Indians very much intoxicated, and some of the head-men so overcome with the effects of liquor that it was impossible for them to meet me."[36] Sully spoke to the few who were sober and warned them that the government would not allow any more lawless acts on the part of the Peigans and, if necessary, the army would pursue wrongdoers all the way into the British possessions. The chiefs were advised to turn the accused men over to the authorities and return the stolen stock, but Sully was not optimistic, reporting: "I hope my mission to the Piegans and Bloods may be a success, yet I am not over-sanguine; two or three weeks will determine."[37]

Then, on 16 January, a report was received that Healy and Hamilton's party had been attacked by North Peigans on Eagle Creek.[38] This proved to be untrue but was used as a further reason for military action. Stated General James A. Hardie: "Warnings and negotiations had failed ... It was the universal belief among the citizens and military that there was no hope of a cessation of hostile acts on the part of these Indians unless the strong arm of the government made itself felt upon them."[39] On the basis of information on hand, General Phil Sheridan telegraphed Fort Shaw on 15 January: "If the lives and property of the citizens of Montana can best be protected by striking Mountain Chief's band, I want them struck. Tell Baker to strike them hard."[40]

On 23 January, a military expedition under Colonel Eugene M. Baker reached the Big Bend of the Marias and attacked a camp they believed belonged to the "hostile" Mountain Chief. Instead, it proved to be the village of a friendly South Peigan leader, Heavy Runner. But it made no difference, for even as the chief ran from his lodge, waving a letter that proclaimed him a peaceful chief, the bullets were flying and the cavalry were streaming into the village. By the time the attack was over, 173 Peigans had been killed, mostly women and children. The soldiers also captured more than 100 women and children, as well as some 300 horses. The camp itself was destroyed, the horses taken back to Fort Shaw, and the prisoners turned loose in the bitterly cold weather. They and others who had escaped the onslaught travelled northward across the border, seeking refuge in the British possessions. Alexander Culbertson, who was trading on the Belly River at the time, reported that "a very large number of squaws and children died on the way, from the severe cold weather, and from Small Pox which they had at the time."[41]

The attack, known as the Baker Massacre, created a great controversy in the United States, with people in Montana strongly supporting the action and Easterners condemning it. Speaking in Congress, delegate James Cavanaugh defended the killing of women and children by saying, "Papooses become warriors and the women too, take the war path."[42] Others claimed that the only Montanans criticizing the action were the whisky traders, who had lost some of their best customers and now faced hostility from the Blackfoot tribes. Although the military action was roundly condemned by many politicians and newspapers, no action was taken against Baker or his superior officers.

For a time, fears were expressed that the Peigans would retaliate by attacking white settlers. The *Rocky Mountain Gazette* published a rumour from Fort Benton (later proven to be untrue) that "Mountain Chief, who was last heard from on Milk river, has declared war and vengeance against the whites ... It is said the Indians will make an attack on this town if they can concentrate sufficient force."[43] In fact, the only confrontation that took place occurred at Healy & Hamilton's camp on the St. Mary River. A short time after the massacre, a Blood woman hurried into the lodge where Healy, Hamilton, and Pat Haney were cooking a meal and exclaimed that a large party of South Peigans led by the head chief, Cut Hand, was approaching the camp.

"Cut Hand is here," she shouted. "He will trade only for powder and ball. When he gets enough he will kill you three white men, as well as the other five at the stockade."[44]

At that point, Martin Donovan, wagon master for Hugh Kirkendall, wandered by and when he heard the news, he asked for something to eat. "If I'm going to cash in," he said, "I want a full stomach to die on."[45]

The traders' lodge was located about 50 yards from the fort, but only part of the stockade had been erected and none of the buildings were finished. Healy decided to take refuge in the partially completed trading post and the others followed. They broke open the ammunition boxes and each man was stationed to provide the best defence against possible attack. Healy, Hamilton, and the labourer Jose went into the trading room, where everything was finished except the roof. They fastened the door and waited. About fifteen minutes later there was a knock on the door. After some hesitation, they opened it, but only wide enough to know that, instead of confronting an angry Peigan chief, the men were faced by Bull Back Fat, the Blood chief they had met on the trail.

> "Friends," he said. "You know the white soldiers a short time ago cleaned out of the Piegan camp over on the Marias. There were no warriors in that camp, for it was a 'sick camp,' and the able-bodied men were out hunting for meat for their wives, babies and old people. The white soldiers came in the night and slaughtered the sick old men and women, the mothers and the babies as they slept or hunted them down in the snow and killed them. The hearts of all the Blackfeet, the Piegans and Bloods are filled with bitterness against the whites for this. Cut Hand and his Piegans have come here to kill you.
>
> "But you men have been kind to us and you are our traders. We Bloods were hungry when you met us and fed us. We are grateful. Now five hundred of my warriors have joined our party. The Piegans will have to kill us before they kill you. They outnumber us greatly, but they are our cousins, and I do not believe they will force us to fight. If they do, we will die fighting for you white men. Open the door and look out."[46]

When Hamilton opened the door, he saw that the stockade was entirely surrounded by Blood warriors, some armed with guns, others with bows and arrows. A short distance away stood scores of angry South Peigans, gathered into small groups. Bull Back Fat told the Peigans to start their trade, but he insisted that it must remain peaceful. They were admitted into the makeshift trade room two at a time where they threw down their robes and demanded powder and shot. Healy and Hamilton began by asking one buffalo robe for forty rounds of powder and ball, but as their supply dwindled they raised the price to two robes, and finally to four robes. So eager were the Peigans for ammunition that they did not argue. Neither did they ask to trade for blankets, tobacco, calico, beads, or even whisky. When it was over, Healy and Hamilton had taken in some sixteen hundred buffalo robes, as well as a quantity of furs and elk hides.

James M. Cavanaugh was the Democratic Party representative to Congress for Montana Territory during the whisky-trading era. (Library of Congress, LC-BH83-2581)

Afterwards, Bull Back Fat addressed Cut Hand. "You have finished trading with these white men," he said. "Now go and go peacefully. You have come to kill these white men. You will have to kill me and my men first. If I find that later you molest these friends of mine, I will attack your camp. You will be the first I will kill."[47]

That was Pat Haney's story. Hamilton provided a less dramatic version of the Peigan visit, omitting the confrontation:

> During that winter, I think it was the latter part of March, a party of Piegan Indians numbering about one hundred came to our place to trade buffalo robes. This was after the Baker Massacre. Previous to that time we had heard through the Blood Indians of the Baker Massacre on the Marias River in Montana. I learned through our interpreter, Joseph Spearson, that some of these Indians had escaped from the soldiers on the Marias. I saw one Indian called Wolf Leader who was unable to talk; he had been shot through the Jaw. Our Interpreter told me that this Indian was shot by the soldiers during the Massacre. These Indians told me through our Interpreter about the massacre and that their chief, Heavy Runner, and some of his Family had been killed by the Soldiers.[48]

Later, when cooler heads prevailed, the Peigans realized that the traders had taken no part in the massacre. In June of that year, Cut Hand was the first of his tribe to sign a petition, begging the United States government for peace.[49] He also appealed to federal authorities in Montana to stop the sale of whisky on his reservation; this didn't happen, and four years later he was murdered near his home by an intoxicated fellow Peigan.[50]

In order to determine the attitude of the Peigans, Father Camillus Imoda, a Jesuit priest, decided to travel to the Belly River (and probably to Healy & Hamilton's fort) in the British possessions in March 1870, where he met with their leading chiefs, including Cut Hand, Mountain Chief, Boy Chief, and White Calf. They all said the same thing: they wanted peace. Father Imoda reported:

> Being called by the Mountain Chief into his lodge, he spoke at length of these late misfortunes and of the desire he and his people have of making now a lasting peace with the whites ... He said he had been stripped of his Lodge and made poor. But he is satisfied that his young men have been beaten, and thinks that now they will mind their chiefs and not go anymore to trouble the whites.[51]

After Healy and Hamilton's confrontation with Cut Hand, the traders set to work to complete their fort. The finished structure was a simple one, about a 60-foot-square design often used on the American frontier, and was named Fort Hamilton in honour of the junior partner. One might ask why it was not named for John Healy. Clearly, Hamilton was the much more respected figure, both among Montanans and the Blackfoot, being a member of the Territorial legislature, and in a permanent marriage to a Peigan woman; in general, he was considered to be an honest and upright individual. Healy, on the other hand, was a pugnacious entrepreneur with a penchant for fighting and boasting.

The north side of Fort Hamilton consisted of a log building, 60 feet long and 10 feet wide, divided into three rooms. The back of this building formed the north palisade and all doors and windows faced into the square. These rooms likely were the living quarters for the traders and their men. The south side consisted of two buildings, one measuring 30 feet long and divided into two rooms, and the other a single room 15 feet long. Between them was a gate in the

Chief Bull Back Fat of the Bloods posing with his family in front of their "Big Striped Teepee" in 1878, with the edge of Fort Whoop-Up visible in the background. Photograph by W. E. Hook. (Hook View Company)

palisade wall that provided the only access to the fort. These two buildings likely held the trading room and storage rooms. The east and west sides of the fort consisted of a solid row of palisades that completed the square and created a central compound in which horses could be kept in times of danger.

Although not specifically talking about Fort Hamilton, John Healy provided the following description of a trading fort.

> A simple one is constructed with two rows of log houses 100 feet apart, chinked and mudded, with a dirt roof. The open space at the ends is stockaded by logs set four feet into the ground, 12 to 16 feet above ground, a plate pinned along the top to hold them firm … The gate is a large double one framed of heavy timber, fastened with a large beam across on the inside. One half of the gate has a smaller gate which is kept open during the day with a watchman on guard to close it on the approach of an enemy. This smaller gate will permit a man on horseback to enter and is also closed with a level and lock.[52]

Healy also described a typical trading room. "It was a long room," he said.

> Along one side ran a high counter breast high to an Indian. Behind on a raised platform stood the trader, while on a shelf underneath within easy reach were weapons that he might need at a moment's notice. Behind all were shelves with the blankets, cloths, and other trade goods. Sometimes only one Indian at a time was allowed into the room.[53]

George Houk was a freighter who spent some time at Fort Hamilton over the winter. After interviewing him, a reporter wrote:

> The medium of exchange was whiskey, with a bottle unit as the price of a buffalo robe. From this unit the prices were graded: two black calf skins represented the price of one buffalo skin, a white calf skin ran to the same price, and a cowhide fetched $1, five being the equivalent of a buffalo robe. The exchange was profitable to the whiskey-traders, for at that time whiskey, which escaped customs dues in the way it was trafficked in, cost $20 a keg of five gallons, with five bottles to the gallon, making the price of a bottle of whiskey 80 cents … When Houk says that the buffalo robes were sold by the whiskey-traders to a New York firm for $6, it can be estimated that there was no little

HUGH A. DEMPSEY

profit in the exchange made with the Indians. The profits grow when Houk relates that in two months the traders at Fort Whoop-Up obtained 15,000 robes.[54]

The winter trade exceeded all of Healy and Hamilton's expectations. In spite of a short season, trade was so brisk that by March, more supplies were needed. According to Houk:

During the winter ... the camp ran short of whiskey and a Dutchman named Joe Wye [sic] was sent back to Fort Benton for more. He was accompanied by Bob Mills and took two or three teams. Joe was well known in Benton and his friends were much concerned about his welfare in the strange northland. When asked as to what he was doing "up" there, Joe, who was quite a gambler, replied, "Oh, we're just whoopen-on-em-up," meaning that they were whooping up the whiskey trade with the Indians and making good money at it.[55]

The expression caught on, and from that day forward, Fort Hamilton was more commonly called Fort Whoop-Up.

Tom Power's account book shows that someone—possibly Joe Wei—picked up supplies for Healy & Hamilton on 3 March. As usual, whisky is not mentioned, but there are two big expenditures for blankets, as well as for vermillion paint, brass wire, and coal oil. John Healy also made a quick trip to buy gun caps, chewing tobacco, ticking, and a dozen bottles of highly alcoholic Jamaica ginger.[56]

Meanwhile, Martin Donovan had had very little luck in recovering Kirkendall's missing mules. Shortly after his arrival, the wagon master learned that a number of the animals were in the nearby North Peigan and Siksika camps, and he tried to recover them. Negotiations began when the traders sent a message for the chiefs to come to the fort for a feast, paid for by Donovan. According to Hamilton, "They would not tell us how many of Kirkendall's mules they had but said a great many of them had been sold to the Hudson Bay Company."[57] They did not offer to return the ones they had, and over the next several weeks, Donovan was chagrined to see Indians riding up to the trading post on his boss's mules. In February, the wagon master accompanied the traders when they visited the camps and there he recognized several mules with the distinctive HK brand. Finally, shortly before the trading season ended, he was obliged to give blankets and presents in order to buy back three of the mules. The rest were never recovered.

With the arrival of spring in 1870, Al Hamilton revealed some romance in his soul when he gave refuge to a pair of young lovers. The drama began when a

55

North Peigan named Cut Cheek fell in love with the young wife of Crow Eagle, the tribe's leading chief, and the couple ran off together. Their absence was quickly noted by the enraged husband, who set out either to capture the pair or kill them. Realizing that they were being pursued, Cut Cheek and his partner ran to the gates of Fort Whoop-Up and begged Hamilton to give them sanctuary.

The trader took pity on them, letting them in and promising that no harm would befall them. He ordered the cook to prepare them a meal, then hid them in a cellar, covering the trapdoor with a pile of buffalo robes. "The white man had been well aware of the risk he was taking when admitting the two lovers," commented a man who witnessed the event, "but having once allowed them to enter beneath his roof, and having besides promised them protection, he was now determined to shield them at all hazards."[58] A short time later, Crow Eagle arrived with ten men and demanded the surrender of the lovers, for their trail clearly led to the trading post. Hamilton acted surprised, declaring there were no lovers there, and invited them to search the fort if they wished. They accepted his offer, probing every nook and cranny, but never moving the stack of robes. At last they stormed out of the fort in anger and posted guards along the river valley all day in the expectation that the pair would emerge, either from the fort or from the surrounding brush.

At nightfall, the fort was locked and the lovers permitted to come out of their subterranean refuge. Next morning, there were no signs of the Peigan warriors, so Cut Cheek and his woman decided to make a run for the river. But no sooner were they out of the fort when the North Peigans reappeared, riding down the nearby hill and crossing the river flat. With no time to go back to their haven, the lovers darted into a small grove of bushes and watched while Crow Eagle and his followers made another search of the fort. Again they were unsuccessful and again they posted men along the valley, but this time they remained on guard day and night. On the second day, one of the traders noticed where the couple was hiding and casually wandered by, dropping a roll of cooked meat for the hungry pair to eat. The same procedure was followed again on the third day. Finally, the warriors left but Cut Cheek, convinced that they would be hunted down, begged Hamilton to let them stay. Hamilton was just preparing to go to Sun River for supplies, so he agreed to take the young man with him, but the woman would remain at the fort until their return. By that time he hoped that Crow Eagle would have either accepted the situation or moved off to his hunting grounds.

Hamilton and Cut Cheek made the trip to Sun River in five days, rested for a week while the supplies were being assembled, then set out again, with another white man accompanying them. A week later they reached Nine Mile Butte, where they stopped for the night. Hamilton and his companion unrolled their bedrolls on the prairie while Cut Cheek curled up under the wagon to sleep.

Some time after midnight, the Peigan was aroused by a suspicious sound and in the pale moonlight he saw an Assiniboine war party, creeping forward to kill the sleeping men and take their horses. Moving rapidly, he scooped up one of the Winchesters near the beds of his sleeping companions and opened fire. The raiders quickly retreated and Hamilton and his partner jumped up to find out what was happening. According to the storyteller:

> Guard was kept for the remainder of the night, and with the first streak of daylight they rapidly left the dangerous locality behind. It was a long drive that day, but the presence of hostile Indians in the country demanded it, and the small party were glad when they found themselves within the shelter of the Fort in the evening.[59]

In gratitude for saving their lives, Hamilton helped settle the Indian's romantic problems by presenting Crow Eagle with horses as a settlement for the loss of his wife. As for Cut Cheek and his beloved, they decided to stay with the traders and made their home at Whoop-Up for some time.

By the end of the season the business at Fort Whoop-Up had exceeded all expectations. In only four months, Healy & Hamilton had surpassed the annual trade of most licenced traders in Montana. They had disposed of most of their supplies, including their whisky, and had experienced no major confrontations with their customers. As affirmed by wagon master Martin Donovan, "We travelled through the country without molestation; the Indians did not bother us; when they would come along they visited our camp and were friendly always."[60] It had been a most successful season.

Their season had been successful in large part due to the impact of the Baker Massacre upon their business. First, a number of Peigans and Bloods who would normally have traded on the Blackfeet Reservation in Montana remained in the British possessions for fear that they too might be killed if they returned. As a result, much of the business that might have gone to licenced traders went to Healy & Hamilton instead. Second, the massacre eliminated much of the hostility the Blackfoot tribes had shown to white settlers. The young warriors were less likely to prey upon Montanans if there was a threat of military retribution on their women and children. Healy & Hamilton's success that winter would spark the whisky traders' rush to the north.

5. *Rush to the North*

Over the winter of 1869–70, the illicit whisky trade flourished in northern Montana, with the pedlars always being on the alert for the federal marshals. Wagon traders slipped out to the Blackfeet Reservation, while saloon keepers and other merchants in Fort Benton ventured out of town after dark to sell whisky directly to their Indian customers. Indian Superintendent Alfred Sully commented that Benton,

> while it has some very respectable inhabitants, is infected with a set of very low people, who during the winter depend on the trading of whiskey with the Indians for their support, and I am sorry to say that some of the more respectable portion of that community purchase from the low whiskey traders, the robes and furs they get in trade from the Indians.[1]

The "low whiskey traders" referred to such men as Tom Power, Isaac Baker, and other merchants.

The only success the Indian department had that winter in suppressing the liquor traffic was to arrest a trader named Curley and to confiscate his single barrel of whisky. However, even that had limited success, for when the barrel was put with some freight bound for Fort Benton, its contents began to disappear. When Superintendent Sully learned of this, he rushed a man out to meet the train and, indeed the once-full barrel was now partly empty. An investigation determined that a man on the train had sold it by the cupful, so the authorities promptly seized the twenty-eight buffalo robes he had traded for, as well as his horse and wagon, and brought the remainder of the barrel into Benton under tight security.[2]

In the spring of 1870, the *Helena Daily Herald* gave its readers the first public report of the success of Fort Whoop-Up and its winter trade. The editor wrote:

> It will be remembered that last winter, Messrs. Al. Hamilton and John Healey, two of Sun River's enterprising citizens, having received authorization to go beyond the border to trade for robes, departed with their outfit of Indian goods into the

British Possessions. These gentlemen recently returned from the expedition, bringing with them a large number of robes and peltries of various kinds. Mr. Largent, whom we had the pleasure of meeting at Sun River, on Saturday, informs us that his trip had not been altogether unpleasant or entirely unsatisfactory in its pecuniary benefits. We judge, from all we could learn, that this venture will net Messrs. Hamilton and Healey upwards of $50,000—not so very bad for a six months' cruise among the Lo Family across the border.[3]

The item immediately gained the attention of just about every whisky trader and supplier in the Benton and Sun River areas. Isaac Baker was probably green with envy when he saw the money being made by Healy Hamilton & Co., especially when his brother had turned down the chance to participate, and now

A previously unpublished view of Fort Whoop-Up as seen from a nearby hill. The details are poor because it is copied from an old lantern slide, likely taken by W. E. Hook in 1878. (Montana Historical Society PAC 98-100)

most of the profits were going to his competitor Tom Power. In response, Baker tried to get a permit to go north under the same subterfuge as that used by Healy and Hamilton. In May 1870, he wrote to Superintendent Sully asking "permission to pass through the Blackfoot Country with ten men and six teams and provisions, to and across the northern boundary line of the United States at a point north of Fort Benton for the purpose of exploring and prospecting the country."[4] Sully passed the request along to Washington, at the same time professing ignorance about the real purpose of Healy and Hamilton's earlier trip. "It is said," he commented, "that Healy and Hamilton did trade on the Saskatchewan with the Indians belonging in the British Possessions. How true this is I do not know, as the place they are reported to have traded is beyond my jurisdiction."[5] However, because of the unsettled conditions created by the Baker Massacre, officials in Washington believed the Indians would be "suspicious of any expedition of whites among them" and refused Baker's request.[6]

Although most of the wagon traders didn't have the capital to build their own forts in the north, they could get credit from Power or Baker and use Fort Whoop-Up as their centre of operations. By the beginning of the 1870–71 season, more than one hundred men had found their way north of the border, either as traders or wolf hunters. With their presence, the trickle of whisky during the first season became a flood the following winter.

Meanwhile, I. G. Baker and T. C. Power had to face another serious matter, one that could mean possible financial disaster. During the winter of 1869–70 a terrible smallpox epidemic had swept the northern plains, killing more than two thousand Blackfoot, seven hundred Gros Ventres, and almost as many Assiniboines and Crees. Concerned about its possible spread to the major cities of the East, the federal government prohibited the shipment of all buffalo robes and animal skins purchased from tribes where the disease had been prevalent. Officials believed that smallpox could be spread by handling robes that had been prepared by sick women or taken from the beds of smallpox-ridden Indians.

A directive came from the Department of War on 23 April 1870, just as the winter robes and wolf skins were coming in. On that day, Baker and Power were notified that all shipments of infected robes from Fort Benton were banned. "As it will be impossible to distinguish peltries so infected from those not so infected, by any known means of inspection," stated Captain N. W. Osborne, "it will be impossible to justly certify that any peltries coming or going from localities which have been visited by small pox during the collecting seasons."[7] Only robes given a clean bill of health from the army's medical officer could be shipped, and this he wasn't prepared to do.

Baker was in the East at the time, but Power was at home and immediately reacted to the situation. The directive specifically mentioned Fort Benton, so he contacted his traders stationed at Camp Cooke and at the mouth of the

Musselshell River, both downstream, and told them to ship all their robes and pelts in case the restrictions were extended to them. They were put on the first boat south and consigned to traders Durfee & Peck at Fort Leavenworth, Kansas. As he waited to see if they got through, Power wrote to one of his New York creditors, making only a partial payment on his outstanding account and stating: "Gentlemen, do not blame me for not remitting the whole for we are in a bad fix. Over forty thousand dollars worth of Furs & Robes lying in warehouse and not allowed to ship on account of being reported as infected with smallpox."[8] A short time later, he wrote that "there is no more danger of contagion in our Benton robes than there is from the shirt on your back ..."[9] Yet others weren't so sure. A man who was at the Musselshell post when the robes were being shipped said everyone there was panic-stricken because of the epidemic, and added, "Infected robes which found their way east are said to have caused the outbreak of smallpox which occurred the following year in Philadelphia and other points."[10]

But Power's robes slipped through, and he got the money to pay off some of his debts. Isaac Baker, on the other hand, tried to go through regular military channels, but time and again, his applications to ship robes were rejected. When he received some furs from the north, which he claimed were disease-free, he was still turned down because they were being stored in his warehouse together with infected robes. When Tom Power tried to send some wolf skins that he claimed were not diseased, he was turned down for the same reason. In frustration, Power fumed that his goods were being held "at the whims of the Medical Officer of the Army."[11]

Finally, Baker went to Washington in early August, and after holding meetings with officers in the Department of War, he managed to break the log jam. Within a month he was permitted to make his first shipment of more than three thousand buffalo robes, two thousand wolf skins, and assorted elk and deer hides. A month later, Tom Power was allowed to send some seven hundred buffalo robes and six hundred wolf skins from his supply of robes and pelts. His stock included Healy & Hamilton's robes from Fort Whoop-Up, which had been lying in Power's warehouse all summer.

During this time, Healy Hamilton & Co. were making plans to expand their activities in the north. By the early winter of 1870–71, they hoped that matters had settled down enough since the Baker Massacre that Washington might be amenable to renewing their trespassing permit, in spite of the earlier refusal to I. G. Baker. Accordingly, Territorial delegate James Cavanaugh wrote to the secretary of the Interior and put the request to him on behalf of the two whisky traders.[12] But his timing couldn't have been worse. A few weeks earlier, Secretary Delano had received a scathing report from the secretary of the Treasury, accusing the Department of the Interior of having "allowed parties to take wagon loads of liquors in the Indian country, simply requiring bonds of them not to trade in our lines."[13] Upon investigation, Delano received the embarrassing confirmation that "permission to pass through the Indian Country with their goods was given to Messrs. Healey and Hamilton."[14] He offered a half-hearted apology to the secretary of the Treasury, placing all the blame on his Montana superintendent (even though Sully had been acting on orders from Washington), and blithely added, "the Officers of this Department are expressly enjoined to enforce the laws regulating trade and intercourse with Indian tribes."[15]

Under these circumstances, Delegate Cavanaugh received a quick, brusque, and blunt rejection of Healy and Hamilton's latest request. "If the carrying of merchandise in the Indian Country for the purpose mentioned by you be forbidden by law," said Delano, "this Department cannot authorize it."[16] However, the only impact of this refusal was that the partners would continue to do what they had been doing, but without a permit.

In spite of this temporary setback, Power was more than willing to issue a new promissory note so that Healy and Hamilton could build a larger and more easily defendable fort. They had been lucky in their first season, but they were experienced enough to know that a steady flow of liquor was sure to create confrontations and violence. In addition, the season had already shown that the old fort was inadequate. Not only was it home to Healy, Hamilton, and their traders, but wagon boss Martin Donovan had boarded there all winter, and

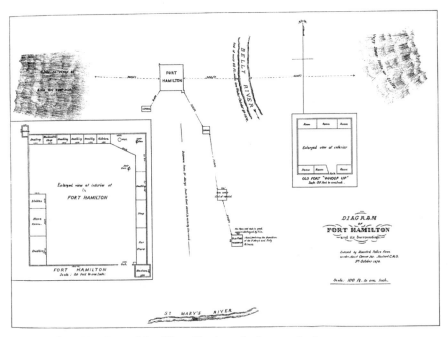

Diagram of Fort Hamilton and Fort Whoop-Up, drawn by the NWMP in 1874.

Joseph Wei had used it for the base of his activities. In the coming year, they expected a number of Bentonites to stay at Whoop-Up, to buy whisky and trade goods from Healy & Hamilton, and to sell robes to them.

Healy and Hamilton hired William Gladstone, former Hudson's Bay Company (HBC) carpenter, to build their new fort. He left Fort Benton in June 1870 with a crew of forty men, mostly Canadian Cree half-breeds, and when Healy and Hamilton arrived for the fall trade, the fort was already partially completed. It would take two years to finish but was livable for the winter. The old building, still called Fort Hamilton by some, was used as a fur warehouse and as living quarters for labourers and interpreters.

According to Healy, the new fort was built with six thousand cottonwood logs, with bastions at each corner, and equipped with a rifle cannon on wheels and two smooth-bore cannons. "The entire Blackfoot nation could not touch us," he remarked.[17] A visitor commented:

> We found that the fort, like all other forts on this river, was built of logs enclosed by a palisade, in length about a hundred and fifty feet, and the same in breadth; the roof is composed of mud, which put on when wet forms a hard cake and will last for years. The cracks in the logs are filled up in the same way, and altogether the fort was very comfortable, coal being used for fuel.[18]

A North-West Mounted Police plan drawn in 1874 shows that the fort measured 130 feet by 140 feet, with solid rows of buildings on the north and east sides, bastions at the northwest and southeast corners, and a building, 75-feet long, extending from the southwest corner along the west side. The latter was divided into stables, a store room, and a dwelling. The building on the north side held four dwellings, a blacksmith shop, and a kitchen, while on the east side were a dwelling, a shop, and a fur store. The northeast corner had a small courtyard, enclosed by an inner palisade and containing a well. This was for a second line of defence, in the event that the main fort was overrun. The backs of the buildings formed the fort's outer walls, and the spaces between the buildings were enclosed with palisades. All doors and windows faced inward towards the square, the only access being through the main gate.

The fort was obviously designed with the expectation that there would be trouble ahead and that violence would be the norm rather than the exception. John Healy admitted as much when he said, "If the sale of whiskey and ammunition has excited the Indian to deeds of bloodshed and enabled him to gratify his desire for plunder and butchery, the traders themselves have usually been the only victims."[19]

While construction of the fort was underway, the political climate in Montana was changing. Criticisms of the Baker Massacre had caused President

Ulysses Grant to rethink the existing policy of having army officers serve as Indian agents and superintendents, and steps were taken to have them replaced. Accordingly, in September 1870, General Alfred Sully was removed from the position of Indian superintendent for Montana and succeeded by Jasper Viall, a Republican stalwart from Iowa, while the Blackfoot agent, Lieutenant William B. Pease, was replaced by M. M. McCauley. However, pressures were brought to bear to have McCauley removed because he was a Democrat, and he was replaced in January by Jesse Armitage, a local Republican.

One of Viall's first actions was to hire Charles D. Hard as deputy marshal, with the specific duty of suppressing the whisky trade. Although an active member of the Republican Party who regularly rubbed shoulders with Tom Power, Hard's sense of justice far outweighed his political affiliations, and he soon became a thorn in the side of the whisky traders and suppliers. In fact, one of Hard's first actions was to seize a wagonload of buffalo robes and beaver skins being taken from the Gros Ventre camps to Fort Benton on behalf of T. C. Power & Bro. and to arrest the traders. When Power produced a licence permitting him to trade with the Crows, Hard pointed out that this was the wrong tribe and that his actions were illegal. "I think we have the best of T.C.P.," Hard wrote to Viall, "and hope to keep it. You will hear from him. Look out for him for he claims to be very smart."[20]

When Power's men were convicted of illegal trading, this set off a heated controversy in the Montana press, with the Republicans praising the decision and the Democrats condemning it. The *Rocky Mountain Gazette*, edited by John Healy's old friend Martin Maginnis, claimed that the whole concept of "Indian country" was vague and indefinite, pointing out that white people who settled on reservation lands north of Sun River received patents, while another branch of government was arresting unlicenced traders for conducting their business on the same type of lands. It also condemned the government practice of allowing only licenced traders to buy robes imported from Fort Whoop-Up. Such an action, stated the editor, was done solely to create a monopoly in the trade "to satisfy the greed of a few individuals," and would "largely divert that trade from our Territory, and drive it to the Hudson Bay posts."[21] The *Helena Daily Herald*, a Republican paper, praised Jasper Viall's efforts to suppress any illegal trade and observed that "if unlimited license existed, the Indian country would be flooded with the vilest whisky, and the difficulties of apprehending the guilty parties innumerable, and that pillage, massacre, and perhaps a general war be the inevitable result."[22] The editor believed that the monopolies held by licenced traders like Tom Power were beneficial and pointed to the HBC as a prime example of how such a monopoly could be an instrument of peace.

A couple of days after the arrest of Power's men, George Baker approached Deputy Marshal Hard and said his company would be pleased to discontinue the sale of whisky to persons suspected of being involved in the illicit trade, if Tom Power would do likewise. Apparently, Isaac Baker and his brother were having second thoughts about the illicit trade, but they had to sell whisky if they were to compete with T. C. Power. In fact, this was their second attempt to close off the trade. In 1867, just after Tom Power started in business, I. G. Baker suggested to military authorities that all whisky supplies be seized in the fall, held over the winter, and returned to suppliers in the spring. This would effectively cut off the Indian trade, which occurred during the winter, but leave the wholesalers free to supply mining towns and white communities during the summer. Colonel J. V. D. Reeves, however, rejected the suggestion as being illegal.[23]

When Hard went to see Tom Power about voluntary restrictions, he received no encouragement from the whisky-dealing merchant. "Thos. C. Power & Bro. is still defiant," said Hard, "and I really cannot see my way to reach him, only can recommend that his License be suspended. He is a hard case and something should be done with him."[24]

George Baker also surprised Hard when he announced that his company had purchased some robes from men who had been trading across the line and, as such, he was prepared to pay $263 in customs duties. As Viall indicated, this was "the first money ever collected as duty on robes brought across the lines from Brittish [sic] Territory."[25] A few days later, Tom Power wrote to the collector of customs, making the same offer to pay customs duties.

> We have in our possession perhaps about six hundred Robes that might be claimed to have come from the British Possessions which we purchased here and at our Post on the Marias River in this country. We stand ready to pay the duties and if properly instructed we can hereafter make the proper parties stand the duties by deducting it when we purchase their Furs & Robes.[26]

Meanwhile, Deputy Marshal Hard was concerned about the burgeoning trade in the British possessions, and told Viall, "I shall look for the Healy & Hamilton outfit from Sun River."[27] However, the prairie was wide and the deputy marshal was alone, so it was a simple matter for Healy and Hamilton to load their legitimate supplies on bull trains at their Sun River store, use fast four-horse teams to pick up the whisky where they had cached it, and make their way successfully to Whoop-Up for the winter of 1870–71.

When they arrived, Healy and Hamilton found that other Montanans had been drawn to the site and an entire community had sprouted up around the fort. In December, a journalist noted that "a large crowd of prospectors, hunters, plainsmen and traders from Benton" had left for the north. He continued:

These have founded a village in that beautiful country, on the well-wooded and fertile banks of a river near St. Mary's Lake ... This town, which is north of the British line, is called by the original and classic cognomen of "Whoop Up," which means thirty houses, and is the base of operations for the inhabitants, who, with American enterprise, have started stores, ranches, and carry on trading, prospecting and hunting in that beautiful country, of which they are the pioneers.[28]

This community was referred to in 1871 as Hamiltonville,[29] and Joe Wei was described as the "Mayor of Whoop-Up city."[30] Among those who traded near Whoop-Up that winter were John Neubert, Charlie Thomas, and a man named Monks, as well as Joseph Wei and his partner, Herman Brinkman, outfitted by T. C. Power and acting as fur buyers on its behalf.

Healy and Hamilton's teams arrived at the fort in the early autumn of 1870, ready to do business. Some of the South Peigans were still on the British side, fearful about returning to Montana Territory, and by fall they were strung out in camps along the St. Mary River. The main Blood bands also were nearby, most being north and west of Fort Whoop-Up along the Belly River. From there, these tribes were able to carry out their winter hunts, returning with large quantities of robes and preparing them for sale to the traders. Sometimes the robes were exchanged for much-needed goods such as ammunition, knives, blankets, and tobacco, but often the craving for whisky was too great to resist. And as the whisky flowed, so followed the violence, debauchery, and death.

There were two reports of liquor trafficking at Whoop-Up during this period, both by Canadians and both shocking. Jean L'Heureux delivered one report to the traders at Rocky Mountain House, stating:

In the two years that they have been established [i.e., 1870–71] 12,000 gallons of liquor were sold to Indians for 24,000 robes, representing a value of more than $150,000 ... More than 112 persons have perished in these orgies and horrors. Mothers forgot the maternal instinct under the influence of drunkenness and let their infants fall from their breasts for starved dogs to devour under the dulled eyes of the unfortunates.[31]

Although this may seem like an exaggeration, L'Heureux was living with the Blackfoot at the time.

The second report came from the Reverend George McDougall, a Methodist missionary and a strong prohibitionist. He quoted from a letter he had received from a man who had spent two months at Whoop-Up during the winter of 1870–71: "No language can describe these drunken orgies; more than sixty Blackfeet have been murdered; and if there can be a transcript of hell upon earth, it is here exhibited."[32] George McDougall then added his own comments about

> the poor Blackfeet, who for months, and that on Dominion soil, have been pillaged and depopulated by American alcohol traders ... If multitudes of unprincipled men, to avoid the laws of their own country, can at pleasure cross our lines and establish scores of low grog-shops, then from the Missouri will roll back on us such a flood of intemperance and demoralization as shall make the fairest part of this North-West one vast field of blood and contention.[33]

His predictions, although impassioned and strident, proved to be accurate; yet, in spite of the rapidly deteriorating condition, the matter did not come to the official notice of the Canadian government for another year.

In addition to their whisky trafficking, the traders were no sooner settled into their winter quarters at Whoop-Up when they were witnesses to, and perhaps participants in, the last great Indian battle on the Canadian frontier. The trouble arose because of a fight six months earlier, in which Peigans had roundly defeated a large group of Assiniboine, near the Cypress Hills. When it was over, seventy Assiniboines had been slain while the Peigans lost only one man.

Later in the season, the Assiniboines called their allies together to attack the Blackfoot tribes in force. Piapot, leader of the Young Dogs (a group of mixed Assiniboine-Cree warriors), and Cree chiefs Big Bear and Little Pine joined Little Mountain and set out from the Qu'Appelle Valley for Blackfoot country. They gathered at the Red Ochre Hills on the South Saskatchewan River in late October, then travelled westward, passing the Cypress Hills and making a war camp at the mouth of Little Bow River. From there, scouts were sent out to find their enemies somewhere in the vicinity of Fort Whoop-Up. They expected to locate a few Blood camps and had no way of knowing that Mountain Chief and the other South Peigans were wintering near the fort. After discovering a Blood camp on the river bottom about 3 miles upstream from Whoop-Up, the scouts reported that it would be an easy prey and an appropriate target for their revenge.

Just before dawn on or about 1 November 1870, the Assiniboines and Crees arrived at the brow of the hill overlooking the river. Below them, in semi-darkness, was a camp of eleven Blood teepees under the leadership of Chief Mountain. When the attack began, a larger camp across the river heard the gunfire and quickly raced to the defence of their beleaguered comrades. At dawn, each side made a discovery: the Bloods became aware of the huge size of the revenge party they were facing, and the Assiniboines and Crees saw that their enemies were not in the numbers they had expected. Stated Mike Mountain Horse, "At break of day warriors from the Blackfoot camps north and south could be seen approaching on horseback, in twos and threes, over hills and knolls, chanting their war songs in anticipation of battle."[34]

As soon as the fight began, a Blood messenger was sent to the South Peigans for help. On his way, he stopped at Fort Whoop-Up and told the residents what was happening. One of the first to leave the post and join the fray was the trader Jerry Potts; he was accompanied by a freighter named Howell Harris. According to a man who visited the fort a short time later, a number of the Bloods ran to the fort for protection but were refused admittance. Instead, about 250 of them crowded into the corral. He claimed that "the trader dare not admit them within the protective walls of the fort. Notoriously treacherous, the Blackfeet would have been unsafe allies."[35]

The South Peigans were quickly roused to action when they heard of the fight. Big Brave, a twenty-two-year-old warrior, recalled:

> The people were just getting up in the morning when the news came that the lower camp had been attacked by the Crees. I got my best horse; it was a gray horse. My father led his band in company with Big Lake who that summer had been elected a big chief. We rode up over the ridge while in the plain below the battle was raging. As we rode down the hill slope, I began to sing my war song.[36]

When the Assiniboines and Crees saw how they had misjudged their enemy's strength, they tried to flee. They moved out of the valley onto tableland that stretched 4 miles across a wide bend in the Oldman River. They retreated to the northeast, fighting a rear guard action against the Bloods, who were now streaming up from their camps along the river, and fleeing from the Peigans, who were coming from the south. The Assiniboines and Crees finally reached a long coulee that extended out from the Oldman River and each group took up a strong defensive position. Some of the Bloods occupied a short coulee immediately to the south of the Crees, and these two coulees became the main focus of the battle for the next four hours.

Jerry Potts had joined the battle by this time, and while reconnoitring around the edge of a ridge that faced the river, he saw the Assiniboines and Crees as they began slipping away. Realizing that this was the beginning of a general retreat, he signalled to his compatriots to charge the coulee. When they did, the withdrawal became a rout. The Assiniboines and Crees rushed into the river by the score, and the Peigans and Bloods stood on the banks, firing at them with their Winchester and Spencer repeating rifles until the river ran red with their blood. The battle had become a slaughter. "You could fire with your eyes shut and be sure to kill a Cree," said Jerry Potts.[37]

Although many of the fleeing Indians reached the opposite bank of the river, they did not escape the fury of their enemies. Warriors rode across the stream and continued the slaughter. During the melee, a party of Assiniboines and Crees tried to make a stand but they were surrounded and about fifty of them were killed. Another group of ten took refuge in a grove of trees where they dug trenches; they would have been annihilated except that Mountain Chief said there had been enough killing and it was time to go home.

After the battle, the Peigans and Bloods counted the dead on both sides. According to John Cotton, "42 Bloods, Piegans and Blackfeet were killed. They thought this was a catastrophe but felt better when they found that 173 Crees had been killed."[38] The winter counts, a calendar system kept by the tribal elders, recorded the historic event as "*Assinay/itomotsarpi/akaenaskoy* – Assiniboines/when we defeated them/Fort Whoop-Up."[39]

Because of the battle's proximity to Whoop-Up, the question arises as to whether any of the American traders took part. Howell Harris admitted to having been an eyewitness to some of it, but claims he was not actually a participant. American sources, on the other hand, state flatly that the whisky traders did join the fray on the side of the Blackfoot. The first press report, published in a Montana newspaper in December 1870, stated, "There were about twenty white men encamped in the neighborhood and they joined in with the Bloods and Piegans …"[40] Two weeks after the fight, A. J. Simmons, Indian department official among the Assiniboine in Montana, wrote:

> The Blackfeet and Piegans were encamped near St. Mary's … across the line in the British possessions; about fifteen white men most from Fort Benton in this Territory were with them trading whiskey and other articles for robes and furs. About November first the camp was attacked by a war party of Assinaboines [sic], who fired into the lodges, killing it is said, fifty three men women and children belonging to the Blackfoot and Piegan camp. The white men now joined with the latter and together they killed about ninety of the Assinaboines, allowing but a very few to escape to tell the tale.[41]

Simmons was concerned that the actions of the traders would cause the defeated Indians to seek revenge and that there would be more trouble "so long as worthless irresponsible white men go among them, pass through their reservations to British territory, trade whiskey and participate in their warfares."[42] Others saw the traders at

Whoop-Up being in danger because of the battle. A Bentonite commented that the Assiniboines wanted to "totally annihilate the town of 'Whoop Up,'" which, however, they will find a hard nut to crack unless these Indians take it by surprise."[43] But, like so many other newspaper reports of the period, the comments were based upon gossip and speculation, and no such attack ever occurred.

During the winter of 1870–71, the United States authorities intercepted only one illicit shipment to the British possessions. In mid-December Marshal Wheeler captured two wagonloads of supplies between the Teton and Marias Rivers on the trail to Whoop-Up, three men were arrested, and the whole outfit was seized. It consisted of four barrels containing 100 gallons of whisky, three sacks of flour, a sack of coffee, and sundry articles. Also confiscated were two wagons, four mules, and three horses.[44] The men were jailed in Helena, but Superintendent Viall was concerned they might never come to trial; they were, he reported, "backed by men of wealth and influence who boast of their ability to evade the penalties of the law, and defy the rules of the Department's prohibiting the sale of whiskey to Indians."[45] Neither the arrested men nor their backers were ever identified, and when the accused came to trial, they were released because the indictment was incorrectly worded, stating that they had been selling whisky to Indians, rather than being in possession of it.[46] As a result, their whisky was restored to them and presumably found its way to Whoop-Up.

During the trial, Chief Justice Henry L. Warren caused some consternation among government officials when he stated that, in his opinion, the men would have been released even if the indictment had been correct. He said that the accused were clearly taking the whisky to the British possessions, and that under the 1855 treaty, white people had the right to cross Indian country if they had no intention of actually trading with the Indians of that reservation.[47] If that view was sustained by the courts, Superintendent Viall was convinced that all control over the whisky trade would be lost, both on the Blackfeet Reservation and across the line. In a letter to Washington, he expressed his views.

> Assisted by the u.s. Marshall for this District, the military, and employees in the Indian service, the whiskey trade has been about broken up within my jurisdiction. This caused a settlement north of the line, within British territory, called "Whoop-up," which is occupied almost wholly by our citizens, engaged exclusively in trading whiskey to Indians of the tribes, which is purchased at, and taken from Fort Benton, M.T., about one hundred miles south of the line ...
>
> You will form some idea of the extent of this traffic when I state that from reliable data, four thousand gallons of spirits have been taken from Fort Benton alone to north of the line

and traded to Indians within the last twelve months, and that about one hundred and twenty-five whites are engaged in the trade. All other causes combined are not so demoralizing to the Indian, or so much stand in the way of his civilization, as this. It is a great and serious evil, an enormity that demands earnest and active measures for its suppression.

If I had authority of law for following our citizens across the line and for arresting them and seizing their outfits when found to be engaged in this traffic, or for preventing them transporting liquors from within my jurisdiction into British territory, with the evident purpose and intent to trade the same to our Indians, I have no doubt the nefarious business would be suppressed.[48]

Permission for law officers to cross the boundary, of course, could not be granted without the approval of the British and Canadian governments, and as it involved national sovereignty, such a request was never made nor would approval likely have been given. However, on the question of trespass, Columbus Delano, secretary of the Interior, stated quite emphatically that the Blackfeet Reservation was "Indian country" and that "it is the decision of this Department that said roads were not to be used in the transportation of liquor across the reserve."[49] This was at variance with Justice Warren's views, so all Viall could do was to hope the opinion of the department would prevail.

This interior view of Fort Whoop-Up shows the kitchen and living quarters on the left, and dwellings on the right. This photograph was likely taken by W. E. Hook in 1878. (RCMP photo, 1240)

In the late winter of 1870–71, a delegation of Pend d'Oreilles from across the mountains visited the Blackfeet Agency to sue for peace, and to this end held a council with such leading South Peigan chiefs as Big Lake, Mountain Chief, Generous Woman, Five Bears, and Middle Bull. All concurred that such a treaty would be desirable, so they agreed to have a formal ceremony later in the year at Fort Whoop-Up. In early summer 1871, the South Peigans left their winter quarters on the Montana plains and passed through the Sweetgrass Hills en route to the whisky fort. "We sent Middle Bull ahead to tell Al Hamilton that we were coming," recalled Many Tail Feathers.[50] The chief came back a short time later to announce that the Pend d'Oreilles and Kootenays were there and ready for peace. Many Tail Feathers continued:

> We moved then to Fifteen Mile Lake and from there with a spy glass we could see people at the Belly Buttes. Our people kept saying they were glad there was going to be peace. Early next morning we moved camp to Fort Whoop-Up, but the St. Mary's River was so high that we couldn't cross to the mountain tribes. Finally, Mountain Chief, Big Swan, and Strangled Wolf crossed in Hamilton's boat. The boat upset just as they started but they tried again and this time they crossed safely.[51]

With Healy and Hamilton acting as intermediaries, a peace pact was made, and as soon as it was concluded, the Peigans and the mountain tribes began swimming their horses back and forth across the river to visit each other's camps.

One man who witnessed the ceremony was Frank Wilkeson, a mining engineer exploring the area for the Northern Pacific Railroad. He stated that the Pend d'Oreilles camped across the river from the fort and, on the morning of the treaty, "they put on gay-colored calico shirts and gaudy leggins made of blankets and painted their faces with vermilion."[52] As they waited, guards were posted to protect the camp. Wilkeson continued:

> Down the river the faint barbaric music made by beating Indian drums arose. Presently the head of a column of mounted troops came into sight on the crest of the northern bluff of the river. Banners were flying, drums were sounding, and the Blackfeet warriors were chanting their marching song as they slowly advanced. They came to the Belly River, forded it, and marched past the fort to a level meadow, and there the head of the column halted. Long before the tail of the column had crossed the river their camp had been pitched. Conical lodges stood in regular rows, with wide streets between them.[53]

About two hundred Peigans then rode over to the Pend d'Oreille camp for the peace council. Speeches lasted for an hour, then a pipe was produced. "It was filled with tobacco," said Wilkeson, "lighted, and passed from hand to hand, each warrior smoking it for an instant. A shout arose on the council ground. Quickly it was answered. Women and children began to talk and laugh."[54] The treaty had been successfully concluded. The next day, John Healy invited the leading Pend d'Oreille chief to the fort. Said Wilkeson:

> Helay [sic] explained to him that the Summer trade with the Piegan clan of the Blackfeet would begin the next day, that all the Indians would get drunk, and he urged the Pend Oreille [sic] chief to gather his men and return to his main camp and to keep away from the trading post until after the Summer trade was over.[55]

The chief followed Healy's advice, and later that day the Pend d'Oreilles and Kootenays departed for the open plains, to travel as far east as the Cypress Hills for their summer hunt.

The treaty had been a peaceful one but violence was an ever-present reality at Whoop-Up, both for the Blackfoot and for the traders themselves. During the late summer of 1870, John Wren shot and killed a half-breed at the fort during a drunken argument,[56] another froze to death in a drunken stupor in the yard that winter, and in the spring of 1871, Joe Spearson, Healy & Hamilton's interpreter, was murdered.

Spearson had been unpopular with the Blackfoot for several years; the Peigans had tried to kill him three years earlier when he was trading for I. G. Baker on the Marias River. On 1 April the traders were loading the wagons at Whoop-Up when a Blood Indian named Strange Dog shot Joe Spearson in the leg. His knee was shattered and he was in great agony, but he refused to allow anyone to amputate his leg. Instead, he begged to be taken to Fort Shaw where an army doctor could look after him. A wagon was prepared and M. Foy and William "Colonel Spike" Teasdale volunteered to take him on the long journey south. However, Spearson didn't make it, for he died of his wound when they reached the Marias River.[57]

After the shooting, and fearing further trouble, the traders were hurrying to load their wagons and leave for Fort Benton when someone accidentally knocked over a lamp and set the old Fort Hamilton afire. At the same time as the traders were rushing to move the furs from the building, a dispute arose outside between a Blood Indian and his wife. In anger, the man drew his revolver and shot her in the hip. She fell beside the burning building, and as she cried out in pain, Al Hamilton hurried outside to see what was happening. The woman lay beside the wall and her husband was getting ready to shoot her again, so Hamilton jumped between them and, with rifle in hand, ordered the man to back off. As he did so, Hamilton carried the woman to safety but she died soon after from her wounds. According to one version of the incident, "The Bloods ever afterward feared the man who would fight for a woman, and they learned to respect him for his kindness, courage and power."[58] The fire itself came to the attention of the Montana press, which noted that the fort "has been burned."[59]

As with the previous year, the winter of 1870–71 proved to be a prosperous one for Healy & Hamilton, as well as for the myriad of other traders who had invaded the area. And, as with the previous year, federal officials—many of whom seemed committed to suppressing the whisky trade—were again defeated by a severe lack of resources and the partisan politics of the day. As for the Blackfoot, except for the peace pact with the Pend d'Oreilles and the Kootenays, their whole world seemed to be falling apart under the weight of the whisky traffic.

6. *The Standoff*

The summer of 1871 saw the movement of many more Fort Bentonites across the line, each hoping to cash in on the financial success of Healy & Hamilton and the wagon traders. I. G. Baker & Co. chose to move directly into the field with its own trading and supply post, rather than relying on the business of others, while merchants such as Fred Girard and Scott Wetzel and saloon keepers H. E. Bond and Moses Solomon made plans to construct their own trading posts in the British possessions. Other smaller traders included Fred Kanouse, formerly with Carroll & Steell; Charles Rowe, one-time owner of the Overland Hotel; and Jim Nabors, who had a restaurant in Benton.

The first of these new trading posts was erected by Joseph Kipp and Charles Phillip Thomas, both experienced traders with a knowledge of the area north of the border. Charlie Thomas had been at Whoop-Up during the previous winter and was aware of the profits to be made. He was married to a Peigan woman named Mary, daughter of Full Eagle, and was known to the Blackfoot as *Poka'nikapi*, or "Child Old Man."

Joe Kipp was the son of James Kipp, a chief trader with the American Fur Company, and Earth Woman, a member of the Mandan tribe. Joe had at least three Blackfoot names—*Maistowun'opachis*, or "Raven Quiver"; *Asu'koyi*, or "Bay Horse"; or simply *Kih'pa*, the Blackfoot way of saying "Kipp." The boy was educated in St. Joseph, Missouri, and when he returned from school at the age of eighteen, he was employed by the firm of Carroll & Steell. In 1868 he joined Charlie Thomas and John Wren in a prospecting expedition that took them along the Rocky Mountains as far as Fort Edmonton. On their way, they were camped near a small creek at the entrance to Crowsnest Pass when they lost their pinchers, used for shoeing their animals. As a result, they called the site Pincher Creek, and the name stuck.

After their return to Montana, Kipp became a scout for the American army and guided them on the fateful Baker Massacre. When some of the Peigans threatened to kill him for his role in the affair, Kipp chose to go prospecting again and was out of the territory during the beginnings of Whoop-Up and the northern trade.[1] On his return, he joined up again with Charlie Thomas and they decided to build a fort in the British possessions. Kipp had money of his own and Thomas had the proceeds of his trading expedition to Whoop-Up, so with these funds, plus a loan from a Fort Benton merchant, they put together an outfit in the summer of 1871.[2] However, as they assembled their trade goods in Fort Benton and arranged to buy a supply of whisky, they came to the attention of Deputy Marshal Charles Hard.

Ever since May, when Secretary of the Interior Delano had confirmed the right of authorities to arrest trespassers on the Blackfeet Reservation, Hard had been assiduous in carrying out his duties. In that same month he had seen three men convicted of selling liquor to Indians and sent to prison. "I understand," said Montana governor Benjamin Potts when writing to Washington, "no conviction has ever been made under the laws to prevent illicit trading with the Indians in this Territory before the above, although many parties have been engaged in it for years."[3] Even more amazingly, one of these men, a whisky trader

Joe Kipp, seen here in 1888, was one of the most colourful of the whisky traders, establishing Standoff Post in 1871 and Fort Kipp the following year. He was also prominent in Democratic Party politics in Montana. (Montana Historical Society, 943-266)

named Davidson, was convicted entirely upon Indian testimony. Previously, Indians had been considered government wards, not capable of appearing as witnesses, but now the rules had changed. "Several Indians were sworn," said the *Helena Daily Herald*, "and gave their testimony against Mr. Davidson, each giving a straight account of how, when, and where the deed was committed." After the man was found guilty, the newspaper added, "This is the first instance on the records of Montana where a white man has been convicted on Indian testimony."[4]

Indian superintendent Jasper Viall was pleased with the verdict and with the support he was receiving from Washington. He told his superior, "I am in great hopes now, since the decision of the Hon. Secretary of the Interior … that during the coming fall and winter I shall be able to put a stop to most of the whiskey trade fitted out at Benton."[5] This, then, was not the best time for men like Kipp and Thomas to launch their whisky-trading careers.

The partners had no difficulty in finding a crew of men to load the wagons and accompany them on the journey, however. They included Antoine Juneau, an old-time trader from Montreal; John Wren, Kipp's prospecting partner; a man named Lee (accidentally killed a short time later); and Canadian William McClure and his partner, John Johnson. The latter was better known as "Liver-Eating" Johnson, a nickname given to him after he pretended to eat the liver of a Crow Indian he had killed. At one time Johnson worked at Fort Whoop-Up for John Healy who described him as follows:

> He was a giant and a wonder in his way. I never saw a man like him. He had been a sailor and a whaler until he was forty years old and he came to me and I outfitted him. He was a man about 6 feet 2 inches and weighed about 250 pounds and did not have a bit of spare flesh on him. He was quite an offhand shot. We were corralling the Indians occasionally and he came and I quote, "I want to get my hand in. Break me in," and he would take an Indian by the nape of the neck and almost break his neck, you know.[6]

According to James Willard Schultz, Kipp's biographer, on the day that Kipp planned to leave Fort Benton, Deputy Marshal Hard suddenly appeared and wandered around the town. That night, as Hard went to the Overland Hotel, Kipp instructed his crew to hitch up the teams in the stable yard where the wagons had been cached. They left as quietly as possible, while Kipp stayed behind to throw the deputy off guard. Almost everyone in the village knew what was going on, but because their livelihoods depended largely on the liquor trade, no one tipped off the visiting lawman.

One of the wildest characters in the whisky trade was John "Liver-Eating" Johnson, seen here in the 1870s. (Montana Historical Society, 943-008)

For two days, both trader and deputy marshal loitered around the town until Kipp was satisfied that Hard hadn't learned of the departure of his wagon train. Next morning, the trader pulled out and overtook the wagons while they were encamped beside the Marias River. The following day they reached Rocky Spring Ridge and were approaching the Milk River when they saw the dust of someone in pursuit. Realizing that the law was after them, Kipp urged the teams forward but the loaded wagons were no match for the fast-moving horses of Hard and Indian agent Jesse Armitage. According to Kipp's biographer, the following conversation occurred.

> "Well, boys," said Hard, "I've got you; been a hot chase; left the fort just two an' a half days ago, but I've caught you at last."
>
> "It looks to me," said Kipp, "as if we had caught you. We've crossed the line and I will not turn back. And if you make us any trouble, or attempt to arrest us, just understand at once that you've got to do a lot of shooting."
>
> "What! Do you defy me? Me—a United States officer?"
>
> "You're no officer here; this is Canada. If it isn't, just show us the line. That's where we've got you, Hard, and you may as well stop bluffing. If we can't prove that this particular place is in Canada, you can't prove that it isn't. If you arrested and took us back, our case would be thrown out of court, and you know it."
>
> "Well," Hard said, "I'll turn back. You will be sneaking more whiskey out this way, and I'll be on hand; I'll catch you yet."[7]

The story is a good one but it probably never happened. Although Joe Kipp was supposedly the most notable member of the group, there is no evidence that he was actually there, except for his biographer's story. The only person to be charged because of the incident was Liver-Eating Johnson, who in the following year was arrested by Deputy Marshal Hard and charged with "resisting a United States officer."[8] He, and not Joe Kipp, was described as the "leader of stand off party last year."[9] Although the shipment admittedly belonged to Kipp, he may not have actually been a member of the party, but in telling the story, Schultz, his biographer, inserted him into it.

Schultz also failed to mention that the traders drew their guns on the deputy and that, in fact, they were still well within the United States. Marshal William Wheeler's version of the affair was much more succinct and to the point:

> A few days since, my Deputy, Mr. Hard and Mr. Armitage, Agent of the Blackfeet, started after a party who they learned were taking some six hundred gallons of whisky north across

the Blackfoot reservation to British America. They overtook the party and undertook to arrest them, but they (there were nine of them) each raised his Henry rifle and defied them. Of course they could not take the party, but Mr. Hard has their names.[10]

Meanwhile, Liver-Eating Johnson and his men took the whisky and trade goods farther north until they reached some bottom lands at the confluence of the Belly and Waterton Rivers, about 30 miles southwest of Whoop-Up. The fort they built there was not as large nor as strongly fortified as Whoop-Up; it was described as being "built of large logs cut and hauled from the timber bordering the river, was mud-chinked, dirt-roofed, fire and bullet proof."[11] When completed, it was named Standoff, to commemorate "standing off" the deputy marshal. Carpenter William Gladstone commented, "I was there when they gave the name to the fort."[12]

The traders' confrontation with the authorities obviously impressed the Indians, for only a month later, a Blood chief said he knew where the International Boundary was located because that was "the point where the American agent and his men stopped the chase of the wagons laden with whiskey."[13]

Kipp and Thomas soon discovered they should have located their fort a few miles downstream, past the barrier of the huge Belly Buttes, which effectively blocked them from the Bloods' winter camps. That lower region had wider river bottoms for winter campsites and heavier stands of timber. However, they did have a good trade, garnering some three thousand buffalo robes and two thousand wolf and antelope skins, and with their profits they planned a bigger post the following year, closer to Fort Whoop-Up.[14]

Meanwhile, the sale of illicit whisky had become big business and the influence of the traders and their financial backers soon became evident in Washington. In spite of Superintendent Viall and others constantly railing against the noxious effects of the Whoop-Up trade, the mandarins in Washington suddenly and inexplicably decided to allow more permits to be issued for persons to cross the Blackfeet Reservation into the British possessions. In August 1871, permits were issued to Frank H. Eastman and to Durfee & Peck, granting the firms the right to cross the reservation for the next year, likely to trade among the Assiniboine in the Cypress Hills. Interestingly, a first draft of the permits specified that they would not be permitted to transport any "contraband goods or merchandise," but this phrase was deleted in the final permit.[15]

At the end of September 1871, Isaac and George Baker were given a permit giving them the right "to travel from Fort Benton through the Indian country to the British Possessions with teams loaded with goods for the purpose of trade."[16] The firm was required to post a five-thousand-dollar bond as a guarantee it would conform to the terms of the permit. Like the other permits, it was good for one year and made no specific reference banning the transportation of liquor. With this document in hand, I. G. Baker & Co. took an active role in the northern trade by sending Charles Conrad north to erect a fort and trade directly with the Bloods. Charles and his brother, William, were becoming more and more involved in the business end of the firm and soon would become full partners. They did not appear to be as reluctant as Isaac and George Baker to deal in the retail end of the liquor sales, and with Isaac often handling the business far away in St. Louis, the Conrads' opinions seem to have prevailed.

I. G. Baker's trading post was constructed on the Belly River, a short distance above Kipp and Thomas's fort.[17] John LaMott recalled:

> Conrad built a big supply post at Stand Off Bottom … and lesser forts were built farther out in the wilderness, getting their supplies from the Conrad post. Some of the boys, ambitious to get out on their own, would take a load of supplies from Stand Off, go out to an Indian camp farther on and carry on a profitable business, both for themselves and the Company. Supply trains were kept busy on the trail between Stand Off Bottom and Fort Benton.[18]

A third whisky fort along the Belly River was built by Fred Kanouse in September 1871. Also in the party were Charles Duval, Jim Nabors, Charley Rowe, Fred Wachter, George Hammond, George Croft, Jerry Patch, O. P. Rush (an alias of N. L. Mitchell), Jerry Potts, and George Huse, a black man.[19] They set out with two teams and, on their way north, they were harassed by a band of South Peigans and then attacked by a Crow war party. When they finally arrived at St. Mary River, they tried to rest their horses, but were immediately

Fort Kipp.

By 1874, Fort Kipp was owned by T. C. Power & Bro., and when sketched by R. B. Nevitt, it housed a detachment of NWMP troops. Note that the only entrance is through the main gate and into a yard—all doors and windows faced into the yard. (Glenbow Archives NA-1434-9)

surrounded by Blackfoot Indians demanding whisky. They were forced to surrender a 5-gallon keg, and only after they had pointed their guns at the chief, Bear Shirt, were they allowed to move on.

"We passed Joe Kipp's post at Stand Off," recalled Charley Rowe, "and visited with them three days, and then we pulled for ten miles further on down the creek. We built our trading post and called it Fort Stide."[20] It had a sturdy stockade and a well inside.

After about two months, Kanouse and Rowe decided to go out wagon trading as there was too much competition along the river. With "Spotty" Whalen as their teamster, they took some goods north to the Porcupine Hills. A chief there made his teepee available to them as their depot, and they carried on a brisk business until Kanouse became involved in a dispute. The disaffected Indian gathered a war party to attack the traders, forcing them to take refuge behind

This rare photograph, taken on the Missouri River in 1866, shows five men who became prominent in the whisky trade. L–R, standing: Moses Solomon, Bob Mills, and John Largent; L–R, sitting: Joe Kipp and Henry Kennerley. (Sun River Historical Society)

rolled-up buffalo robes inside the chief's lodge. The raiders finally withdrew, but not before they had taken some of Kanouse's robes. Kanouse and his party beat a hasty retreat, and although they were pursued, a blizzard enabled them to escape. "I promised myself," commented Rowe, "that we would do our trading after that in a good house where we had some protection."[21]

Another post was built in 1871 on the Belly River, downstream from Kipp and Thomas's, by three Benton merchants: general storekeeper Fred Girard, who had taken over the business of Carroll & Steell, and two saloon keepers, H. E. Bond and Moses Solomon. Also involved were brothers Dick and Donald Berry, with Dave Mills as their interpreter.[22] Like I. G. Baker, Fred Girard had received a permit to cross the reservation.[23] Of the three principals, Solomon remained in the whisky-trading business much longer than the other two. A Polish Jew who was raised in New York and came west to prospect for gold, Solomon was described as a "Godless man" who never showed "the pallid flag of fear."[24] He opened a saloon in Benton about 1867, and later had trading posts on the Marias near the mouth of the Teton, in the Cypress Hills, and on Lee's Creek in southern Alberta.

Shortly after their fort was finished, an incident occurred that reflected the violence and lawlessness in the whisky traders' lives, not only in their treatment of Indians, but also in their relations with each other. John Weatherwax, the Berry brothers, and John LaMott were in the fort when a man named Dan Hardin, a fugitive from the law, came in.[25] In the previous year he had been indicted for selling whisky in Montana and had fled across the line. People who knew him said he was a mean character, ready for trouble when he was intoxicated, and on this occasion he had obviously been drinking.

"Dick," said Hardin as he walked up to the counter, "give me a whiskey."[26] The trader obliged but Hardin simply spilled it on the floor and asked for another. After he had done this three or four times, Hardin said to Berry, "When I get through tormenting you, I intend to kill you." He then turned and strode out of the building. Some time later, interpreter Dave Mills poked his head through the door and said, "Dick, Dan Hardin is coming." The trader just shook his head and said, "Too bad, too bad."

Berry strapped on his six-shooter, and when his adversary came in the door, they began to argue. As Hardin turned to walk out, the trader shot the unarmed man in the head and he died later that night. When the news reached Montana, no one grieved for the dead man and no action was ever taken to bring Berry to trial, either in Canada or the United States. In referring to the killing, the *Helena Daily Herald* called Hardin "quite a desperado" and "a refugee from justice."[27]

Another fort worthy of notice during this season was built by John Weatherwax on the same river flat as Fort Whoop-Up. A year or so later, the Reverend John McDougall commented on it:

Here was a fort [Whoop-Up], strongly built of cottonwood and poplar logs, and further down was another post. Whoopup itself belonged to Healy & Hamilton, and the other post to a Mr. Weatherwax, or, as the boys called him, "Old Waxy," and when we came in contact with him we thought he was well named—cool, calculating, polished, using the finest of English.[28]

Weatherwax was in the employ (and later a partner) of Scott Wetzel, a Fort Benton merchant, and was also the agent for T. C. Power & Bro. During the entire period of the whisky trade, Wetzel and Tom Power had a close working relationship that was one step short of being a partnership. Weatherwax apparently replaced Joseph Wei as Power's agent when Wei decided to open a meat market in Fort Benton. Although Wei and his partner, Herman Brinkman, remained active in the whisky trade, Wei appears to have limited his activities to Montana Territory.

One of Weatherwax's duties apparently was to keep an eye on Healy and Hamilton's enterprise for Tom Power. When a shipment of merchandise, probably whisky, was sent to the traders directly from Power's warehouse, Weatherwax was instructed to receive it at his fort on Whoop-Up flats and to turn it over to Healy & Hamilton only if the firm had enough robes on hand to pay for it. If not, he was told, "Hold till you hear from us or till such time as Messrs. H & H can raise enough furs to pay up the account."[29] It was a very businesslike transaction, considering the type of product it represented.

During the summer of 1871, Fort Whoop-Up did not close its doors in the off season. Rather, William Gladstone and his men continued with their construction work while Hamilton carried on a limited trade with the Blackfoot tribes. In August, surveyor Frank Wilkeson visited the area and recorded his experiences for the *New York Sun*. When he reached "Hamilton's Fort" on 21 August, he met with Mountain Chief, leader of the Peigans, and Bull Back Fat, head chief of the Bloods. Both complained of the way they had been treated at the Blackfeet Agency; Bull Back Fat said that all he intended to do was "to kill buffalo, drink whiskey, fight the Sioux, [and] trade where he wanted to."[30]

When speaking to Wilkeson about their own activities, the traders were frank and cynical. Wilkeson wrote:

The whiskey traders, whom I have found to be very pleasant men, told me they came here to make money. They risked their lives among these warlike Indians. They traded everything to them, but made their money on whiskey, and whiskey alone. Far from being an injury to the United States, they said they were a great benefit as they keep the Indians poor, and kill directly or indirectly more Indians of the most warlike tribe on the continent every year, at no cost to the United States government, than the more regular army did in ten years!

The Indians, they said, were British subjects and had a right to exercise all the freedom of British subjects; and if the British subjects saw fit to pay big prices for poor whiskey and get immensely drunk on the Saskatchewan plains, it is the subjects' affair, and not that of the United States.[31]

In preparation for the 1871–72 winter trading season, John Healy left Sun River for the north at the beginning of October with a large shipment of goods, including 5 tons of vegetables and large quantities of flour. He was going, he told Tom Power, to "the land where they Whoop it Up."[32] On the day before his departure, he wrote to Power:

I had a letter from Al to day. Everything lovely, about 50 packs of good Robes on hand and he writes me that the Indians are all moving towards our place. He writes for "Stimulant" in a hurry, also flour, Strychnine & H. Bread. His letter is encouraging and if we can keep our lick up we will make it warm for the Curve-back …[33]

He doesn't identify "Curve-back," but this may be a nickname for a competitor.

When Healy left Sun River, he had borrowed more than sixteen thousand dollars through Power, repayable in the spring.[34] And, like John Weatherwax, he carried with him the authorization to act as a buyer on behalf of the Power firm. The document stated that "Messrs. Healy & Hamilton have authority to draw on us in payment of good average Robes at the rate of $3.50 … each and $2.25 … each for good large wolf skins, attaching invoice of Robes &c with Drafts three days sight which will be duly honored in currency here."[35] This meant that the traders who sold their robes to Power through Healy & Hamilton at Whoop-Up would get a draft they could cash within three days of presentation to the store in Fort Benton. Power gave specific instructions to the partners as to how to make the drafts payable. John Healy was to sign them if he was at the fort, as T. C. Power & Bro. had samples of his signature, but if he was away, Al Hamilton was to sign the draft "Healy & Hamilton" and then place his own signature in red ink across the face of it. Following the issuance of the draft, all furs bought for Power were to be baled, tagged, and stored free of cost.

Weatherwax also acted as a buyer at the trading posts around Standoff, in addition to the Whoop-Up area. In early December 1871, Power wrote to him in "Stand off country, B.A. [British America]" commenting: "How are you running this cold weather? We have been all froze up the last two weeks."[36] He quoted the same prices for robes and furs that he had given to Healy, except that he would pay 10 per cent more if they took trade goods instead of a cash voucher. He instructed Weatherwax to issue the notes in the name of Scott Wetzel and the necessary money would be transferred into Wetzel's account.

Over the winter of 1871–72, the traders did a booming business, and it seemed as though just about everyone from Fort Benton was in the area. In midwinter, a resident of Benton lamented that

> the only officers of the law present in Chouteau county are two
> Commissioners and the Assessor; no Sheriff, no Coroner, no
> Justice of the Peace, no Constable. I am informed that a full set
> of officers was elected at the last election, but most of them are
> at present out at Whoop-up, trading with the Indians.[37]

The only setback suffered by the Benton merchants occurred late in 1871, when they lost some of the whisky destined for their winter trade. This whisky was being transported by the steamboat *Flirt*, when it was stopped near Fort Peck because of low water in the Missouri. At that time the fort was surrounded by more than six thousand Yanktonais, Lakotas, and Dakotas, who were objecting to the construction of the Northern Pacific Railroad. Their leaders, Sitting Bull and Black Moon, were friendly, but officials feared that if the alcohol got into Sioux hands it could create havoc. As a result, orders were given to pour the booze into the river. In all, more than 3,000 gallons of whisky and 200 gallons of pure alcohol went into the muddy waters of the Missouri. Of this, about 900 gallons had been consigned to I. G. Baker, and more than 2,100 gallons, fifty kegs and thirty packets of liquor, had been destined for T. C. Power.[38] This incident revealed once again that Tom Power was the driving force behind the illicit trade. Indian superintendent Viall had no doubt where the whisky had been bound. "I am fully persuaded," he said, "it was the intention to transport it across the line into British Territory to 'Whoop-up' for purposes of barter and trade with Indians at that point."[39]

The *Flirt* was the last boat of the season, so in order to replenish their supplies, Power and Baker were forced to use the slower and more expensive freight-wagon route from the village of Corrine, Utah, on the Union Pacific railway line, across the Rocky Mountains to Helena and thence through Sun River to Fort Benton. As a result, there were times when whisky was in short supply.

On one occasion, Joe Kipp decided to go to Helena when there was no whisky in Fort Benton. He bought 100 gallons from a Helena merchant, but his presence was noted by Deputy Marshal Hard, who was still angry over the standoff with Kipp's outfit earlier in the season. Hard learned that the trader's two wagons and horses were at the local livery stable so he kept them under close surveillance. Kipp knew he was being watched, so in order to smuggle the whisky out of town, he arranged for a local freighter to transport it to the river and place it *en cache*.

That night, Kipp loaded his two wagons with regular trade goods and had his teamsters sneak away in apparent secrecy. As expected, the deputy was not far behind. As soon as Hard was gone, Kipp went to the river where he built a raft, floated the whisky down to the mouth of Sun River, and waited for his men. As long as Kipp's two wagons were outside the boundaries of the Blackfeet Reservation, there was nothing Hard could do, as no laws were being broken. But as soon as they crossed the river into "Indian country," he swooped down to make an arrest. To his chagrin, he found no whisky and no Joe Kipp. Realizing he had been outmanoeuvred, he rushed back to Helena and was not surprised to find that the whisky trader had disappeared. Meanwhile, the teamsters met Kipp at Sun River where all the trade goods were piled onto one wagon and the whisky onto the other. Three days of hard riding took them over the border and out of Hard's jurisdiction.[40]

Because the posts at Standoff Bottom were in close proximity and in competition with each other, the managers encouraged their men to take the wagonloads of whisky directly out into the Blackfoot camps. This was a dangerous business, and although the traders usually tried to make a quick trade and get back before the heavy drinking started, sometimes they found themselves in great danger from the trouble they themselves had created.

On one occasion, John LaMott took a wagonload of whisky from the I. G. Baker post to Running Crane's camp on Oldman River, unaware that another trader had murdered someone from that band earlier in the day and that the relatives were looking for revenge. LaMott had traded away most of his whisky and was inside Running Crane's lodge when the bereaved family crowded inside and pointed their guns at him. They held the weapons against his head, and although he kept pushing them to one side, he saw very little hope of escaping. As LaMott's biographer told it:

> When the excitement was at its highest pitch, a couple of women came staggering into the lodge, singing and reeling amongst the staggering men. LaMott thought they too were drunk as they jostled and pushed the men around. One of them fell against him, giving him a deliberate push which knocked him down. He thought that his time had come, but as he struck the ground he saw that the other woman was lying right where he had fallen and she was raising the wall of the lodge slightly. Several women outside the lodge reached in and dragged the frightened man out.[41]

They took LaMott to a little lodge, and there he found all his robes and furs packed safely away. The women fixed him a bed and piled the furs over him, where he remained hidden all night. Next morning, when everyone in the camp was relatively sober, LaMott loaded up his furs and took them to I. G. Baker.[42]

On another occasion, LaMott was on a trading expedition to Lee's Creek with three Canadian Métis—Bill McClure, Bill Cornick, and Rock DeRoche— trading whisky to the Flatheads. "We kept trading right on and traded all our stuff off for liquor and everything, and started back for Belly River, Conrad's Fort, Stand Off Bottom. As [we] went along in the morning, we traveled quite a while, and we run across another camp of Indians."[43] These were Blackfoot who had been to Fort Whoop-Up and, after a binge, were on their way back to their camp. They still had robes to trade but LaMott said he was out of whisky. Seeing an empty barrel in the wagon and believing it was full, the Indians surrounded the traders and insisted they trade with them. After discussing the matter among themselves, the interpreter told the Blackfoot that the traders wanted to have their breakfast first. When the Indians withdrew a short distance away, LaMott filled three 5-gallon camp kettles with water, and when they were boiling, added handfuls of tea and "a whole lot of tobacco."[44] When it was cool he poured the mixture into the empty barrel and passed it off as whisky, trading it to the Blackfoot for the rest of the day.

Later, a man came to them and complained that even though he had consumed several cups of "whisky" he did not feel like singing, as he usually did. "Well," explained Cornick, "this isn't singin' whiskey."[45] The Indian was satisfied, and later that day the traders quietly packed up their robes and arrived safely at Standoff.

With the Kipp & Thomas post being in the same area as I. G. Baker, their traders often visited the same Indian camps. If one set of traders arrived shortly after the other had left, they could find themselves riding into a camp of Indians who were already drinking and ready for trouble. One time, some of the I. G. Baker crew were in a camp when some Indians began shooting at them from a distance and then riding away. The Indians would come back some time later and start shooting again. It finally got so bad that the traders decided to leave; however, their wagon was overloaded with robes and trade goods and the Indians could soon overtake them. When one of the men noticed a crack in a nearby cutbank, they piled everything in there, covered it up, and fled to safer ground.

They were on the trail when Bill Russell, a member of Kipp & Thomas's crew, caught up with them and told them that the Indians who were shooting at them had also been trying to intercept his boss's wagon train of whisky. The train had been about 5 miles from Baker's people and was trading whisky along the way. During the attack, the freighters had to hide behind the wagons to fight off the Indians, and when one of the men, Charlie Duvall, tried to shoot from underneath the oxen, he was kicked in the head and knocked out. Because the two trading outfits were not far apart, the Indians kept riding back and forth from one camp to the other. Baker's men reached Conrad's fort safely and later, when everything was quiet, they recovered their cache and went out on another trade.[46]

Problems also occurred around the trading posts, particularly if Indians were able to gain admittance in large numbers. This was usually discouraged, and when they were drinking, only one to two Indians were allowed within the fort at one time. Because the forts were designed with no outside windows or other ways for Indians to gain access, if there were problems outside, the traders could seal themselves in the fort until the Indians left.

As a journalist commented, the traders

> appear to have been singularly oblivious to the effects that their whiskey was producing just outside their doors … The whiskey trader would coolly close the heavy gates of his stockade, and sitting down safely and comfortably inside the fort, have no more concern at the rattle of firearms outside, the shouts of the victors, and the shrieks and moans of the wounded and dying, than he would to the snarling and howling of a band of coyotes fighting over the remains of a dead buffalo.[47]

One day while John LaMott was at Conrad's fort, he walked over to Kipp & Thomas's post and, along the way, noticed that a lot of drinking and fighting was taking place in the surrounding camps. He decided not to stay around and had just stepped out of Kipp & Thomas's stockade when John Weatherwax and Blood chief Calf Shirt came behind him. As they stood together, an Indian emerged from a nearby camp and, placing his rifle on a tripod, fired a shot at Weatherwax; when he missed, he jumped on his horse and galloped away. Calf Shirt took after him and, when he caught up with him, killed him. LaMott later learned that the dead man was Calf Shirt's nephew, but he never discovered the reason for the attack on Weatherwax.

According to the various Blackfoot winter counts, violence because of the whisky traffic increased sharply in the winter of 1871–72. Among the incidents mentioned were the murder of Three Coming over the Hill, a North Peigan; the death of Weasel Child, a Siksika, from the effects of alcohol; the stabbing of Old Man's Child by White Pup, both Siksikas; and the death of Pounder, a Blood.[48] But these were just the tip of the iceberg, for only one event, usually involving a leading chief, was recorded for each year while the scores of other deaths went unreported.

In the case of Old Man's Child, White Pup disliked him because he was a coward who would not go to war or even defend his camp. While they were drinking with White Pup's brother, they got into an argument and White Pup killed Old Man's Child. A short time later, Old Man's Child's brother was killed in another drunken argument.[49]

In another incident during this same period, a number of Siksika traded their robes for whisky when they were approached by traders with a wagonload of whisky. The Indians' drinking led to an argument between Eagle Ribs, a chief in Crowfoot's band, and Young Man, Stars Everywhere, and Cutter, all members of Old Sun's band. Young Man became so angry that he fired a shot at Eagle Ribs, wounding him in the waist, and, fearing revenge from Crowfoot's followers, the three men fled the scene. When Crowfoot learned what had happened, he went to see the wounded man and said, "I am practising to give a good example and try to stop this kind of trouble. We better take Eagle Ribs home with us."[50] There was great danger that a feud might develop between the two bands, so Crowfoot immediately went to his rival chief and they worked out an arrangement whereby Young Man, Stars Everywhere, and Cutter made a payment of horses and other gifts to Eagle Ribs as settlement for his injury.

By the winter of 1871–72, the focus of the Blackfoot people had shifted from warfare, hunting, and family life to alcohol. It was now easy to obtain, either from the forts on the Belly River or from the wagon traders who invaded their camps, and it was quickly destroying them. As Crowfoot stated:

> The whiskey brought among us by the Traders is fast killing us off and we are powerless before the evil. [We are] totally unable to resist the temptation to drink when brought in contact with the white man's water. We are also unable to pitch anywhere that the Trader cannot follow us. Our horses, Buffalo robes and other articles of trade go for whiskey; a large number of our people have killed one another and perished in various ways under the influence.[51]

But in spite of the many deaths over the winter, or perhaps because of them, the whisky traders had a banner season. The huge bull-team wagons were constantly going back and forth between Forts Benton and Whoop-Up, and Indian superintendent Viall's effort to halt the trade had resulted in utter failure. Some 40,000 buffalo robes were shipped on steamboats from Fort Benton in the spring,[52] almost all having come from Whoop-Up country. Tom Power alone made one shipment to Chicago of 16,400 buffalo robes and 5,000 wolf skins, as well as other furs and pelts.[53] The 225 tons of robes and furs in that single shipment had been exchanged for countless gallons of whisky and had resulted in the deaths of many Blackfoot.

The violence on the frontier carried over into the spring of 1872, when the robes were being brought to Benton and many traders were ending their activities for the season. During the winter, Fred Kanouse, Charles Rowe, Bob Mills, Jim Nabors, and George Crowe had a small trading post at Porcupine Coulee, likely one of the creeks flowing out from the Porcupine Hills. They shipped their robes to T. C. Power in the early spring, but Kanouse and Nabors got into an argument regarding another nine hundred robes they acquired after the wagon train had left. Kanouse claimed that Nabors had had no part in the collecting of these robes and should not have a share in them.[54]

When they closed the fort for the season, Mills used his pair of mules and a wagon to haul out the last of the robes. They passed Whoop-Up and were back in Montana Territory about 15 miles from the Marias River when another argument erupted between Kanouse and Nabors. Some say it was about the robes, others contend that Nabors wanted to take a horse and ride ahead to the river. Whatever the cause, Kanouse drew his revolver and shot his adversary dead on the spot. The next day he rode into Fort Benton but was not taken into custody. Commented the *Helena Weekly Herald* wryly, "Kanouse is Sheriff of Chouteau county, and has not up to the present time been arrested."[55]

He wasn't apprehended until the following year, when Deputy Marshal Hard arrested him in Fort Benton and took him to Helena for trial. However, the court determined that this was not a federal matter, so Kanouse was turned over to the authorities in Deer Lodge County. At the conclusion of the trial, the county judge ruled "that there was no probable cause to believe the defendant guilty, and it appearing to the full satisfaction of the Court that he was innocent, it was therefore ordered that the defendant, H. A. Kanouse, be discharged from custody."[56]

It was a fitting conclusion to a season of whisky and bloodshed.

7. *A Devastating Traffic*

The 1872–73 season marked another banner year for Healy & Hamilton, but they were not getting rich. Although Fort Whoop-Up continued to dominate the trade, money was an ongoing problem. In the spring of 1872, Tom Power assured one of Healy & Hamilton's creditors, banker Sam Hauser, that the

> prospects look fair for them to make some money and they want to do any thing that is fair and within their power to satisfy all concerned. They will know in six weeks' time what they can do and you can depend on us. We will represent the business as it is squarely between you and H & H. It all depends on a trade they expect from the Northern Indians yet to be made.[1]

Healy, however, was less than enthusiastic when he asked Power if he could arrange for an extension of his note with the bank. "I will give you credit for untold patience," Healy said, "if you will only get us out of this with honor or until such time when we will not feel the blow so much."[2] When another debt was being discussed, he commented, "I do not think that we ought to be forced to pay it when the money would be so beneficial to us at present but on the other hand I suppose the laws of mercantile honor would say pay by all means."[3]

The reports from Al Hamilton for that trading season were good, so Healy left Sun River in June to help bring in some sixteen hundred buffalo robes that had been traded from the Blackfoot in the spring. These were taken to Power's fur warehouse in Benton, but even with the sale of the robes, Healy & Hamilton still ended the season owing $2,365.56 on their note with Power.[4] At that time, the traders estimated their stock at Whoop-Up was worth $8,000, not including the fort, horses, oxen, and wagons. This stock was insured at an annul rate of 2½ per cent of its appraised value "to guard against accident."[5]

In spite of Healy & Hamilton's financial difficulties, Fort Whoop-Up remained at the centre of the commercial trade in the British possessions. Many traders obtained their supplies from the partners, sold their robes to them, and sometimes either acted as their agents or were employed by them. T. C. Power's 1872–73 account books indicated a number of people who did business at the fort, with Power paying the accounts on behalf of Healy and Hamilton. There were work orders or invoices from Mills & Rowe, William Lee, John Kennedy, Kelly & Kountz, Ben Deroche, John Evans, J. M. Brown, Tony Lachappelle, "Spanish Joe" Aranna, George Houk, Pat Haney, and many others who were known traders in Whoop-Up country.[6]

Apparently, account books specifically recording whisky sales to traders have not survived, either in the T. C. Power Papers or any extant records of I. G. Baker, with one exception. An 1872 volume, entitled "Bill Book," shows more

H. A. "Fred" Kanouse operated whisky forts at various locations in the British possessions. After the NWMP arrived, he became a druggist in Fort Macleod and later had a hotel in the Crowsnest Pass. (Glenbow Archives, NA-31-1)

than 2,000 gallons of intoxicants being sold by T. C. Power to various traders during a two-month period. Entries show Healy & Hamilton buying 564 gallons of whisky and 92 gallons of alcohol; Tom Healy getting 324 gallons of whisky; "Dutch Fred" Wachter and Fred Kanouse buying 100 gallons of alcohol; George Hammond and partner buying 184 gallons of whisky and 100 gallons of alcohol; Joseph Wei getting 58 gallons of whisky and 50 gallons of alcohol; Asa and Daniel Sample buying 309 gallons of whisky; and Charley Rowe buying 211 gallons of whisky, 30 gallons of alcohol, and 84 gallons of bourbon.[7] In all, these traders purchased 1,650 gallons of whisky, 372 gallons of straight alcohol, and 84 gallons of bourbon in just a few weeks.

By 1872–73, the trail from Fort Benton to Whoop-Up had become a major north-south artery. When surveyor George Dawson saw the trail at the international boundary, he stated: "The road where we crossed it is deeply worn & wide & shows evidence of recent & very heavy teaming being done over it. Ashe saw yesterday a party of traders going N. They had several freighting waggons drawn by mules & horses & heavily laden."[8]

Charles Schafft, a legless Civil War veteran, had been a teamster on the Whoop-Up trail and described his experience. He said there was "a sort of irregular express" between Benton and Whoop-Up and he signed on with a wagon driven by "Captain Fred."[9]

> I was told to be in readiness inside of twenty-four hours, and that we would whoop things up. Requesting one of my friends, knowing in such matters, to fix up an outfit for me to take on the prairie, he judiciously selected and put up two or three gallons of whisky and an assortment of canned conveniences, advising me to be careful in regard to drinking the water to be met with. "It's regular pizen," said he, "to them that ain't use to it."

The train consisted of horse-drawn wagons, much faster and lighter than the plodding bull teams that carried tons of freight along the trail. But Schafft was unimpressed when they set out, for they travelled "at a pace that might have compared favorably with the slow and measured march of a funeral." The wagon almost upset when going down the banks to the Teton River, so everything had to be unpacked and carried to the bottom of the hill. By this time the rest of the wagon train had left them so they camped that night beside the Teton. Next morning, just as they were starting the slow, uphill journey on the other side of the valley, they met another outfit and double teamed up the slope.

As they approached the Leavings of the Teton (i.e., the last place for water), they struck a mud hole and had to stop again to unload. After they made a few more miles they stopped for lunch, where they were joined by a Captain Nelse, who assumed command long enough to get the reluctant team onto the prairie land beyond the riverbank.

> Thanking the Captain for his courtesy, we traveled on over the smooth plain at a smart pace and overtook the outfits that night at Pend d'Oreille springs. [Captain] Fred was happy now, for other animals would assist him over slight elevations, and enable him to reach the end of his journey without much further jaw-breaking and expenditure of whip material.

They passed Yeast Power Flat without any trouble and safely reached the Marias River. While descending into the river valley, the wagon train was besieged by a violent thunderstorm, which, as Schafft said, "lashed up our team with lightening flashes and caused them to exhibit a marvellous agility in the descent to the bottom."

The rest of the journey was relatively boring as they passed Antelope Coulee and Rocky Springs before reaching the border; during that time all they saw were a few bands of buffalo bulls, some antelope, and a number of badgers. Along the way, the teamsters kept a sharp eye open for any signs that the deputy marshal, the military, or the Indian department detectives might have discovered their illegal presence on the Blackfeet Reservation. Safely on the British side, they crossed the Milk River ridge, passed Slippery Springs and Middle Coulee, and then reached Fifteen Mile Coulee, which was 15 miles from the fort.

Here, Schafft says, "we met with the first indication of violence, by finding a dead Indian lying spread-eagle fashion in the center of the road. He could not have been exposed very long, for, exposed to the rays of the sun without any cover except a fragment of Uncle Sam's blue attached to an army button, decomposition had not yet taken place." A few miles farther along, according to Schafft:

> We reached Whoop-Up. It was a large and solidly put-up trading post, the construction of which must have cost way up in the thousands. Situated as it was in a bare flat, its inmates could easily stand off any number of hostiles contemplating an attack. A small grave-yard on the outside attested the fact that not every one who came to the country was permitted to return; but no inscription told the story of those who were here laid at rest.

The season of 1872–73 in Whoop-Up country was marked by a rapid spread of the whisky trade far beyond the confines of the Belly River into other parts of the Blackfoot hunting grounds. Although the Belly River was still one of the best wintering areas for the tribes and a rich source of buffalo robes, so many traders infested the region that some found it necessary to spread out if they were going to compete. During the autumn and early winter, Montanans moved north and west to the Oldman, Highwood, Elbow, and Bow Rivers, and east to the Cypress Hills, to trade with the Assiniboines. And as they built their forts, some of the established Belly River traders constructed small outposts in the same areas, not wanting to miss any of the potential profits of the whisky business.

In the spring of 1872, Kipp and Thomas were visited by John Riplinger, trader for the North West Fur Company, who had been sent north by the Indian agent to try to convince the Peigans to come to his agency. During their discussion, Riplinger learned that the partners wanted to relocate, so he arranged to buy their fort for his firm.[10] Later in the year he loaded a six-mule-team wagon with 6 or 7 tons of flour, tobacco, coffee, sugar, potatoes, beans, and lead shot—all reportedly government property—and took them to his post on Birch Creek, and then to Standoff, which was described as "still further north in the British Possessions."[11] Riplinger placed a trader in charge at Standoff but maintained overall supervision from his post at the Indian agency. Unlike the other Belly River trading posts, it appears that Riplinger's post did not deal in whisky, instead handling the same type of trade goods as those found in his store on the Blackfeet Reservation.

Until this time, the main route of traders to the north had been along the Benton–Whoop-Up Trail, which passed just west of the Sweetgrass Hills. Because of Riplinger's frequent travels between the Blackfoot Agency and Standoff, he opened a new route closer to the foothills, and it became known as Riplinger's Trail.

Having sold their old post, Kipp and Thomas moved downstream to the confluence of the Belly and Oldman Rivers, where they built Fort Kipp. It was described as "a series of log houses forming three sides of a square. There was a cook room, living rooms, trade and store rooms. The windows of these were high, so one could not look in through them from the ground. Broad fireplaces of mud-plastered stone furnished the necessary heat."[12] The trading room had a long, high counter that divided the traders from their customers. A few feet behind the counter was a wall with two doorways, one leading to the fur storage area and the other to a room where the whisky and bulky objects were kept. The wall had loopholes so that, in the event of trouble, the men could slip into a room, bolt the door, and have a clear line of fire at anyone in the trading area. If the room was particularly crowded, a guard might be placed by one of the loopholes in case of trouble.

Work continued on Fort Kipp over the summer and was almost completed when the I. G. Baker people decided to make their move; they, too, had decided that business would be better farther downstream. Charles Conrad selected a site across the river from Fort Kipp, about 3 miles down, on a flat known as Captain Jack's Bottom. Their fort, which was about 30 feet by 50 feet in size, complete with palisades and a stone fireplace,[13] became known as Conrad's Post. About 40 miles downstream, at the mouth of Little Bow River, was a smaller, one-roomed outpost of the fort named Robbers' Roost.[14]

This outpost had a short life, however, because the young man left in charge of it was unable to control his customers. A band of North Peigans managed to get inside the shack, where they threatened him with rifles and forced him to surrender his stock of whisky. After getting drunk and abusing him, they left the outpost and the young trader took refuge in the brush. Later, he saw a friendly Blackfoot who used to work at the fort and induced him to carry word of his plight to Conrad's Post.

When Howell Harris arrived at the outpost, the young man crawled out of his hiding place. "He was so scared," recalled Harris, "that he refused to stay there alone, so the two of us started for Capt. Jack's. On the way back we were jumped by five Indians. The young chap started to run, but I grabbed his bridle reins and, reaching a buffalo wallow, tied our horses, got out my rifle and started shooting."[15] In the ensuing conflict, four of the attackers were killed. Later, the outpost was abandoned and burned down by the Blackfoot.

Conrad's Post also had its share of adventures—not uncommon on the Whoop-Up frontier. Harris recalled an incident when about eighty Indians managed to gain entry to the post, but Conrad pacified them with presents and got them outside before any damage occurred. According to Harris, this post had a short life, operating for the winter of 1872–73, then being burned down by Indians in the spring.

After the North-West Mounted Police came west, Isaac Baker claimed that his company had not traded whisky on the Canadian side of the line, commenting, "The Whiskey Traders so annoyed them and demoralised the Indians that they were obliged to remove in 1874."[16] This may have been true, but probably was not. More likely, Baker was trying to disassociate his firm from the illicit trade in order to win Canadian government contracts. However, it is true that the senior partners, Isaac and George Baker, had been reluctant participants in the wholesale whisky trade, realizing that as long as Tom Power was actively trafficking they had to do likewise or go broke. Clearly, Power was the aggressor in promoting the illicit trade, and he probably got the bulk of the buffalo robes and wolf pelts.

Tom Power never ventured into the retail end himself in the first years of the whisky trade, preferring instead to finance free traders and make huge profits from their business. According to N. C. Thum, "Both of them [Baker and Power] say they can make more by selling the whiskey and taking robes in payment than they could by trading it themselves."[17] Therefore, it remains a mystery as to why the Baker firm, whose principal owners were not strong proponents of the whisky trade, should build Forts Standoff and Kipp, and later a post on the Highwood River, while Power waited until the waning days of the whisky trade before making his move. Certainly, this anomaly could be explained if the Baker posts were whisky-free, but the statements of Howell Harris and John LaMott seem to dispute this.

In the fall of 1872, a number of other traders decided to move north and build a fort on the Highwood River. They named it Spitzee Post, taken from the Blackfoot word *spit-si*, meaning "tall trees" (i.e., Highwood). According to John LaMott, one "good-sized" fort was constructed and shared by three sets of traders including Dick Berry, for I. G. Baker; Asa and Daniel Sample and Rowland "Red" Buckland, financed by T. C. Power; and Fred Kanouse, Sol Abbott, and Jim Scott, all trading on their own.[18]

These men were a mixed lot. Dick Berry was said to have ridden with Jesse James's gang and was considered to be a hard case. According to LaMott:

> For years he had been hunted with a price on his head. After dodging about the States evading capture, frequently changing his name, barely escaping the officers a dozen times, he figured that his safest move was to slip into the new West, outside the pale of government officials, and take his own name.[19]

Berry was also notable because of his vivid nightmares and sleepwalking. Just after arriving at Spitzee Post and unloading their supplies, the traders settled down to sleep. In the middle of the night Berry suddenly jumped up and, still asleep, shouted "Indians!" and started shooting his gun. He was finally overpowered but the incident recurred so many times that the other traders were said to have built a barricade of green hides to deflect any flying bullets.[20]

The Sample brothers were born in Kentucky and arrived in Fort Benton in 1867, where Daniel opened a saloon and Asa became a wolfer. Both men turned to whisky trading in the early 1870s. As for Red Buckland, he was from Massachusetts and had prospected for gold before going to Montana. Henry A. "Fred" Kanouse was from Illinois, and after the Civil War he worked for the American Fur Company. His father, Jacob Kanouse, was a Fort Benton barrister and schoolteacher, and it is said that his son's misadventures broke the old man's heart.[21] Fred was a trader for I. G. Baker on the Marias River in 1870–71, then went north into the British trade. Known to the Blackfoot as *Kainaikwan*, or "Blood Indian," perhaps because of his preference for Blood women, he claimed to have had at least fifty Blood "wives" during his career as a whisky trader. After he murdered Jim Nabors in 1872, he spent much of his time across the line.

These men set out from Conrad's Post in December 1872 with three teams of twenty oxen each, each team hauling three wagons "loaded with whiskey, calico, flour, tea, sugar and such goods."[22] When they reached the Highwood River, they built their fort on a bench of land about a mile west of an unusual tree, which had two trunks joined together by a large branch. It was known to the Blackfoot as a "medicine tree."[23] From surface remains, it appears that the main building had four fireplaces and that another building was 12 feet high, with loopholes in the upper storey.[24] Local historians state that, some time later, a second fort was built by traders Dave Akers and "Liver-Eating" Johnson about 2 miles downstream.[25]

One day during the winter of 1872–73, LaMott went from Spitzee Post to Fort Kipp to get more supplies. On his return, he learned that Fred Kanouse, together with Sol Abbott, Jim Scott, and a crew of men, had moved north to the Elbow River to build a fort within what is now the city of Calgary. They were, explained one writer, "all well armed and with a good supply of trading stock, including whiskey."[26] Meanwhile, Dick Berry and the Sample brothers remained at Spitzee Post for the winter.[27]

In February 1873, a band of Bloods, led by White Eagle, came to the Elbow River post and were in the trading room with Kanouse and two workers, Lafleur and Horness, when an argument broke out.[28] According to John Cotton, a member of the Blood tribe, "My grandfather, Making a Fire, got into an argument with Fred Kanouse at a drinking party at a whiskey fort."[29] The Bloods, who had been drinking, reacted so strongly to the dispute that Kanouse called for Sol Abbott, who was in the back room, to come and help him. Kanouse wanted to open fire on the Indians while they were still in the trading room, but Abbott thought they could just throw them out.

He was wrong. As soon as the traders tried to push the belligerent Indians out the door, the Indians began shooting, and a man named Joe Muffraw was fatally wounded by a number of lead balls. Said John Cotton, "Kanouse took his gun and shot at my grandfather but the bullets didn't take effect. Then my grandfather shot Kanouse in the shoulder."[30]

Abbott shot one Blood through the jugular vein, and he died instantly; the others fled from the building and then laid siege to it. The cook at the fort, Donald Fisher, was in a back room and unarmed when the fight started, so one of the men locked his door to prevent the Indians from overrunning the whole fort. When Fisher found he was trapped, he took an axe and broke down the door so he could "go in where the killing was going on."[31] Kanouse mistakenly thought Fisher himself had locked the door, and accused him of being a coward who had "burrowed and hid himself in a hole he dug in the dark compartment."[32] Later, Fisher told LaMott the real story.

According to journalist Leroy Kelly, the Bloods laid siege to the fort for three days until help came from Berry and the other traders at Spitzee Post. "Examination showed that Kanouse had his shoulder blown away," said the *Helena Daily Herald*, "the muzzle of the gun having been placed against it when fired, leaving a most shocking and fatal wound. Lafleur was shot through the thigh, and Horness through the hand and side; both will probably recover."[33]

Kanouse was taken to Spitzee Post and placed in a room in Dick Berry's quarters. Gravely wounded, he was a difficult patient, and as LaMott said, "We could do nothing with him at all. Sol Abbott was the only one that could handle him."[34] Kanouse complained that Berry and the others were mean to him, yet he did not complain when Abbott used a butcher knife to dig out the small shattered pieces of bone in his shoulder. When he was fit to travel, Kanouse was taken to Fort Whoop-Up and an ambulance was sent up from Fort Benton to transport him to Helena. He arrived there sixty-two days after the shooting and was treated by Dr. J. S. Glick.[35] Upon examination, the doctor found

> that the charge had entered above the left nipple and ranged across through the shoulder, carrying away the entire coracoil process of the glenoid cavity, the tronchylus head of the humerus, also all the minor arteries, veins and sinews, leaving only the main leader and superior artery intact. The lower side of the wound was distant only five-eighths of an inch from the heart, and the whole shoulder rotten from exposure and neglect.[36]

The doctor immediately performed a long and delicate operation that saved Kanouse's arm and his life.

John Cotton was quite proud of the fact that his grandfather had shot a notorious whisky trader. "That was the last time Kanouse wanted to fight the Indians," he said.[37] The wound affected the way the trader walked, so with a touch of wry humour, the Bloods renamed him *Motsikis*, or "The Shoulder."

Artist's conception of the Healy & Hamilton outpost on the Elbow River in 1873, at the present site of Calgary. (H. Dempsey file)

Sol Abbott operated a number of whisky forts in the British possessions in the 1870s. After more bootlegging in Montana, he eventually settled on the Blackfeet Reservation, where he became a deputy sheriff. (Montana Historical Society, 940-097)

Kanouse and his crew weren't the only traders on the Elbow River that winter. When John Healy learned that the other traders were going to the Bow River country, he decided to send one of his men from Whoop-Up—Donald W. Davis, one of the most aggressive men on the frontier—to open an outpost in the same area. Davis was born in Vermont and joined the 13th Infantry in 1867, taking his discharge at Fort Shaw in 1870. He then went to work for Healy & Hamilton at Fort Whoop-Up. "D. W. Davis was my trader at this time," recalled Healy, "and was out with teams trading and establishing winter trading stations. One was on the Elbow, near the present site of Calgary ... Davis was my best man."[38]

However, not everyone recalled Davis with fondness. Tom Power found him to be a deadbeat, who in 1873 still hadn't paid off a $158 loan made when he left the army.[39] The Reverend John McDougall said he was of "the wildest type" among the traders, who promised to flood the country with whisky.[40] Something of his nature can also be seen in an 1873 letter to his father, in which he wrote, "My work is not without danger as it is trading with Indians altho I have never been hurt or scared yet had to kill 2 last winter on act of stealing horses."[41] Still, there were others who found him to be a very likeable and amiable man.

Davis selected a site on the Elbow River some distance along the stream from Kanouse and Abbott's post.[42] The Davis fort was described as a log building about 20 feet by 40 feet, with three rooms—a general living room and kitchen, store room, and trading room. The trading room was subdivided so that when an Indian came in the door he was in a restricted area about 8 feet wide and 20 feet long. In the partition was a trap door that could be quickly closed in case of emergency. The only other door in the building was off the dwelling room, and it led to an enclosed, 20-foot by 40-foot yard, where the men could exercise or relax without fear of interference.

When Donald Graham visited the fort in the spring of 1873, he found Davis in charge

> and my experience of him was that he was a very kindly, hospitable man. I told him that I did not intend to return to Edmonton, but was going to continue on to Fort Benton, Montana. He, however, advised me strongly against going on alone. The Indians met would be Bloods and Blackfeet, he said, and as they might be the worse of liquor, it would be very dangerous, to say the least. He then cordially invited me to stay at the post until their wagons came along for the furs.[43]

Liquor was the main stock in trade at the fort. A 40-gallon barrel was filled with 10 gallons of alcohol and 30 gallons of water, then coloured with burnt sugar. When the Blackfoot came to trade, each passed a 1-gallon empty keg and a buffalo robe through the trap door; the keg was filled from the barrel and passed back. During the few minutes that Graham watched the procedure, eighteen robes were exchanged for as many gallons of liquor. The second most popular item of trade was ammunition, after which the women picked out cloth or other items they wanted.

The Indians were encouraged to take their liquor back to their camps and not drink around the fort. However, if they were drunk and wanted to force their way inside, they sometimes tried to climb on the sod-covered roof. Thus, whenever a noise was heard above them, the traders "lit the candles" for the intruders, which meant firing their Winchester rifles into the ceiling.

D. W. Davis was a trader for Healy & Hamilton in 1870 and built a number of outposts, including one at the site of present-day Calgary. Davis became Canadian manager of I. G. Baker & Co., and later was elected as a Member of Parliament. (Glenbow Archives, NA-32-1)

The trading party at the fort consisted of Davis, his black interpreter, a cook, three other men, and Davis's wife. Davis was known to the Blackfoot as *Spitai*, or "Tall Man," while his wife was Revenge Walker. She was part of a headstrong and turbulent family led by Red Crow, head chief of the Blood tribe, that seemed to be constantly involved in liquor conflicts. On one occasion, Red Crow brought whisky from a trading post back to his camp and became quite drunk. While he was in a stupor, two young men decided to beat him up. "Old Maycasto is too drunk to help himself," said one, "and he has been pretty mean to us sometimes; we will tie him up and get even with him."[44] But as they made a move towards their chief, he awoke, drew his revolver, and killed one of them on the spot.

During another drinking episode, two relatives of Red Crow staggered into his teepee. When the chief offered them a smoke, one of the men took offence and fired a shot at Red Crow. The bullet missed him, but struck and killed the chief's wife, Water Bird. Red Crow shot the attacker, but the other man escaped into the darkness.[45] There was another incident late in 1872. Red Crow's uncle, Big Plume, was in his camp, midway between Spitzee Post and Elbow River, close to the big rock called *okotoks*, when some drunken Siksikas entered his camp, looking for liquor. When he tried to kick them out, they killed him.

A short time later, while camped near Spitzee Post, Red Crow became convinced that his younger brother, Kit Fox, was having an affair with his youngest wife. During their drinking, the chief voiced his suspicions, and instead of denying it, Kit Fox began to make fun of his brother's appearance, poking him in the face and calling him ugly. In anger, Red Crow grabbed him by the hair and slammed his head into the stones of the fireplace again and again until he was dead. "I'm sorry I had to kill my brother," he said, "but I had warned him not to touch my face."[46]

The murder caused a rift in the family, with sister Revenge Walker and brothers Sheep Old Man and Not Real Good moving off on their own. Towards the spring of 1873, Revenge Walker and the others went to the Elbow River to trade, and when D. W. Davis saw the woman he wanted to marry her. Red Crow arrived a few days later, and during a drinking spree, Revenge Walker learned that her brother had cheated her out of some horses; in anger, she rode over to the herd and killed some of Red Crow's horses. Fearful that the chief might retaliate, Sheep Old Man and his family moved to the Highwood River where they camped near Spitzee Post. When Sheep Old Man failed to return from the whisky fort, Revenge Walker sent her younger brother to find him. The drunken Sheep Old Man failed to recognize his brother on the trail and, thinking the stranger was after his whisky, shot and stabbed Not Real Good, causing severe wounds.

When Revenge Walker heard about the incident, she rushed to her brother's side and tended to him. When he failed to get better, Not Real Good said to his sister: "You take my advice and marry the white man who keeps the store, Davis. They must have good medicine, and I may then get better."[47] So Revenge Walker married D. W. Davis, and Not Real Good moved into the fort. Donald Graham saw him there, commenting: "His wound was dressed by Mr. Davis, and a bed made for him. He was at the post for several weeks, receiving every possible attention. He may have been quarrelsome, but he showed gratitude for the treatment received, as he sent Mr. Davis a present of a fine horse."[48]

Obviously, Indian superintendent Viall was unsuccessful in stemming the flow of whisky from Montana Territory into the British possessions during the winter of 1872–73. He did, however, manage to slow the liquor traffic on the Blackfeet Reservation down to a trickle. This was made easier because many South Peigans and the most aggressive of the whisky traders were now across the line. In addition, Viall continually pressed his marshals and Indian department employees to clamp down on the illicit traffic. When William Ensign was appointed Blackfoot agent in 1872 he implied that the existing traders were now nothing more than a minor irritation on the reservation. "They smuggle small quantities of liquor into the Indian Camps," he said, "trade it for robes and furs, and immediately decamp, conducting their operations ... quietly and quickly."[49]

Yet the situation was too good to last. In December 1872, Jasper Viall was obliged to resign after he appointed an Indian agent who was considered to be an enemy of the Republican Party.[50] When Territorial governor Benjamin Potts complained about the appointment both to Secretary of the Interior Columbus Delano and Congressman (later President) James A. Garfield, Viall's political career was finished. This must have been good news for Tom Power and his associates, for soon the whisky was again flowing freely in Montana. Less than a month after Viall's resignation, Indian department detective William Judd caught traders with 20 gallons of whisky destined not for Whoop-Up, but for the Blackfeet Reservation.[51] In addition, barrels now seemed to be leaving Fort Benton with great regularity, with nothing being done to stop them.

The new Indian superintendent was James Wright, former Secretary of State for Iowa, who frankly admitted that he had a problem.

> My predecessor succeeded in restraining the traffic in a good degree. But last Nov., as soon as it was known that he had left the Territory on business, parties at Ft. Benton furnished bad men with whiskey. These men introduced it into the Indian Country, sold it to the Indians, thus cheating them out of their Robes and furs. When it was known that Col. Vial [sic] had resigned, this traffic was greatly increased. There have been several murders among the Indians while under the influence of whiskey obtained through this channel.

These [traders] mostly obtain their whiskey on a credit at
Ft. Benton, with the understanding that it can be paid for in
Robes and furs. These as I am informed are turned into the
hands of licensed traders, receipts taken for them, which are
turned over to the whiskey vendors at Ft. Benton.[52]

Interestingly, T. C. Power & Bro. had finally become licenced traders on the
Blackfeet Reservation under the name John Power. They had built trading posts
at the Willow Rounds and at the mouth of Dryfork Creek, both on the Marias,
with Henry Kennerly and Mat Fernell appointed as traders.[53] In 1872 another
post was built right inside the government stockade, but the firm was forced to
relocate at least 400 yards away or lose its licence.

During this period the Indian superintendent sometimes enlisted the army
to help watch for persons illegally entering the reservation. Fort Shaw, the military headquarters for the district, was only 4 miles away from Sun River, so Healy
& Hamilton were regularly under surveillance. According to Healy:

At Fort Shaw were two companies of cavalry. Men were detailed
off each day to watch by the river, across from the post, and keep
watch upon my movements ... I knew personally one of the men
who were detailed to stand guard. He sympathized with me, and
one day he said to me, "Captain, if you want to get away, I may
not find you gone until you have made a good start." "No," I
said, "I will have you do nothing. I'm going to get away and I am
going to do it in spite of all the soldiers at Fort Shaw!"[54]

Healy moved his goods at night to a cache and hid his wagons in a coulee
several miles from his store. He then went to Fort Benton to send a telegram to
Al Hamilton who was in Helena.[55] In the wire, he directed his partner to meet
him at a rendezvous that was actually about 75 miles away from his intended
route. Continued Healy:

I knew this message would be reported to Fort Shaw. I then
galloped back to the post as hard as I could, brought the wagons
in, loaded the goods, and started straight for the north. I had
calculated on being followed and to forestall this I tied behind
the wagons long poles dragging behind on the ground, like the
travois of the Injuns. If they came upon my trail, they would
think it belonged to Injuns.
    Well, it happened just as I had worked it out. The cavalry
were sent off up east seventy-five miles out of the way and

before they found out their mistake I was through the gap and well on my way into Canada. So I crossed the reservation in spite of them as I said I would do.[56]

In Whoop-Up country, although the methods of trading varied according to the size of the trading posts, a number of procedures remained the same. The first was that Indians, when drinking, should not be allowed free access to the trading room, but be admitted only two or three at a time. If they were particularly belligerent, or if the trading was taking place at night, it might be conducted through a small window in the main gate.

In the trading room, the liquor was kept in a large barrel in an adjacent room and doled out by the gallon or by the cupful. The intoxicant itself varied according to the supplies available and the degree of drunkenness or sobriety of the customers. Trading in Montana in 1870, Peter Koch stated that their recipe called for a quart of alcohol, a pound of chewing tobacco, a handful of red peppers, a bottle of Jamaica ginger, a quart of black molasses, and as much water as they could get away with.[57] At Fort Kipp, traders used a mixture of alcohol, burnt sugar, oil of bourbon, and water at a ratio of four parts water to one part alcohol if the customer was sober. If slightly drunk, a ratio of six to one was used, and if thoroughly intoxicated, ten to one.[58]

Other traders added Hostetter's bitters, laudanum, blue stone (copper sulfate), red ink, and anything that would give the mixture "bite and scratch." A few of the ingredients were actually poisonous and if mixed incorrectly could result in the deaths of their customers. Although some traders used straight alcohol laced with various ingredients, others used whisky. For example, Single Anchor whisky was sold to traders for $1.60 a gallon, Double Anchor and Eldorado for $1.75, and Shawhan for $2.75, while straight alcohol was $3.25 a gallon. All of these intoxicants were cheaper than the whisky found in Helena bars, such as O'Donnels for $3.75 a gallon.[59]

In addition to whisky, guns were an important stock in trade, as were balls and powder. The traders were supposedly prohibited from selling repeating rifles, but they did. As a Hudson's Bay Company trader reported to his superior:

> As you are aware their repeating carbines have been for some years traded to the Blackfeet by the Americans; the propriety of supplying them with so formidable a fire arm in their present wild & lawless state may be questionable … I can only state that 12 Large Prime Robes can be had for 1 carbine & that they are one of the most attractive articles that constitute an American trader's outfit.[60]

At the time of writing, a trader on the Bow River had in stock thirty carbines and eight thousand cartridges. Revolvers also were popular and had a ready sale among the Blackfoot. In 1873, among a T. C. Power shipment to a Belly River fort were three Smith & Wesson revolvers, four Colts, and five Army Colts, as well as six Spencer carbines.[61]

In later years, ex-whisky traders claimed that liquor and guns weren't the only items they stocked, and this was perfectly true. If the lady of the lodge came to buy, she could choose from a large selection, including blankets, skirts, cloth, brass kettles, face paint, needles, thread, butcher knives, and axes. Men could buy shirts, trousers, caps, tobacco, telescopes, mirrors, combs, and skinning knives.[62]

But the bottom line was whisky, always whisky. It caused the traders to invade the British territory, it was a source of revenue for the traders, and it was the basis for the suppliers to become wealthy. It also caused chaos, destitution, and bloodshed among the peoples of the Blackfoot nation. As the 1872–73 trading season ended, the *Helena Daily Herald* probably summed up the situation when it spoke of the "wretched whiskey traders who ply their nefarious traffic across the line separating the Territory from the British Possession, bringing back the robes and peltries bartered by the savages for the white man's 'fire water.' This traffic is calamitous."[63]

Indian agent A. J. Simmons estimated that between two hundred and three hundred barrels of liquor—more than 10,000 gallons—had gone north that winter and that fifteen thousand robes and numerous furs had been acquired from the Blackfoot tribes. These were brought to Benton in May and June and immediately went into the warehouses of Power and Baker. The whole business was accurately described by Indian superintendent Wright as a "soul and body destroying traffic."[64]

Thus, the traders continued their move northward in the 1872–73 season, building their forts ever farther north to better compete for the profits of the whisky trade. With little or no law enforcement to suppress their activities, more and more whisky made its way into Whoop-Up country. However, the Cypress Hills Massacre in June 1873 would be a turning point. It alerted the Canadian government to the devastating and deadly effects of the trade on Canadian soil and eventually culminated in the arrival of the North-West Mounted Police in Whoop-Up country.

8. The Wolfers & the Cypress Hills Massacre

*P*arallelling and sometimes overlapping the activities of Fort Whoop-Up and the whisky trade was the business of killing wolves for their skins. For many years there had only been a limited market for wolf skins, but in 1868, the *Helena Herald* reported that the "European demand for American prairie wolf skins has already started out parties of trappers, who expect to realize handsome catches."[1] Before that time, the catch had been negligible, mostly brought into the trading posts by Blackfoot hunters. But once the demand was known, the market mushroomed until by the mid-1870s some thirty thousand skins a year were being shipped from Fort Benton, most of them coming from Whoop-Up country.

On the social scale, the wolf hunters, or wolfers, were all pretty well at the lower end of the ladder. There were, however, various classes of hunters. At the very bottom were the men who hunted wolves exclusively and had nothing to do with Indians or traders. Next came the ones who set out with a wagonload of goods, traded these at the Indian camps, and then went wolf hunting. A third type worked at trading posts and, during their free time, went out wolfing on their own; these men considered themselves to be traders, with wolfing as a sideline.

Wolfers generally were coarse, ill educated, and tough enough to survive blizzards, starvation, and angry Indians. One Bentonite admired their ruggedness, commenting, "Intense cold had kept them beneath their blankets for two and three nights while water and wood were far distant; and Indians were liable at any time to pounce down upon them."[2] Another Montanan made reference to them eating wolf meat that had been laced with strychnine, stating:

> These wolfers … lead a miserable life during their long and tedious journeys after spoils, and instances have been known of the scarcity of other food compelling them to subsist on the carcasses of poisoned wolves. I am told (but consider the story exceedingly "fishy") that the poison evaporates during the cooking process, and that wolf meat is very nutritious. He must have been a brave man who first made a feast of poisoned meat, or hunger had driven him to a recklessness of life.[3]

When they set out on their hunt, the wolfers would select a winter camp-site where there was plenty of wood and water. Once settled, they would lay out their campaign, usually deciding on a circuit of some 5 or 6 miles, along which they would kill a buffalo every mile or so to use as wolf bait. The wolfers under-took the task of poisoning the carcasses in a number of ways. One method was to roll the buffalo on its back, skin the legs and belly down to the ground, and cut open the carcass. The heart, lights (lungs), and liver were cut up into small pieces and put into a container, such as an empty 5-gallon whisky tin, and sprin-kled with strychnine. These were thoroughly mixed and then the pieces rubbed over any of the exposed meat on the buffalo's carcass. The flesh on the ribs was cut into strips and left attached, then rubbed with the poison-laced meat. When John "Kootenai" Brown was wolfing in the mid-1870s, he used four ⅛-ounce bottles of strychnine on a grown bull, two bottles on a two-year-old, and one bottle on a calf.[4]

When the poisoning was complete, a red flag was put in place to flutter over the carcass until the meat was thoroughly frozen, thus keeping the wolves away. The hunters didn't want them to feed on the carcass while it was warm, as only a dozen or two of them could eat all the poisoned meat and the "harvest" would be small. Rather, they waited until the body was thoroughly frozen before remov-ing the flag, knowing that as little as a quarter pound of meat would be enough to kill a wolf.

Entitled "A Wolfer's Roost," this view by L. A. Huffman in the late 1870s shows a cabin in the Missouri badlands that was considered to be much tidier than most. (Glenbow Archives, NA-207-69)

Next day when they returned to the site, they often found at least twenty dead wolves, and during the next several weeks, or until the carcass was gone, over a hundred animals might be found lying scattered around on the prairie. In bitterly cold weather, it was impossible to skin the wolves, so the whole carcasses were tossed into a wagon and hauled back to camp. There they were piled like cordwood to protect them from the magpies, and skinned when the weather warmed. As long as the circuit kept providing carcasses, the wolfers stayed in the same camp and kept piling up their wolf skins. They might be in one camp for four or five months, making trips to Benton or a trading post only when they needed more supplies or when their take of skins became too large.

If the weather was good, the wolves could be skinned on the spot. Donald Graham, a Canadian, experienced this in 1873 while staying at Healy & Hamilton's post on the Elbow River. Word was received that some wolfers north of the Bow had been driven out by Indians, and the cook, known as the "Big-headed Dutchman," said there were some forty or fifty wolves that the men had left unskinned.

"He did not like to risk going after them alone," recalled Graham, "but if anyone went with him he would go. After some conversation, I agreed to go along with him on the understanding that we were to work separately and that we should both skin wolves as long as there were any in sight."[5]

Graham was warned that the Dutchman was an unsavoury character, and he found this to be true. They crossed the Bow and reached the kill site at dusk, where about fifty wolves had already been skinned. Next morning, they searched farther afield and found unskinned carcasses scattered within a mile of the poisoned buffalo. Both set to work on the understanding that each man could claim only the wolf he was skinning and that each would keep his own catch of skins.

About noon, Graham came over a hill and found the cook busily engaged in dragging the few remaining carcasses into a pile for himself. Realizing that his companion was breaking their deal, he rode down to the pile and was dragging a carcass free when the Dutchman saw him and came running towards him, claiming the wolves were his. "That's played out, Dutchman," replied Graham, "I found this bunch."[6] At this, the wolfer drew his revolver, but as he did so, Graham picked up the rifle that lay beside him, and they stood in a standoff. Finally, the cook lowered his revolver and said there were four more wolves just over the next hill that Graham could have. The visitor agreed and the two men spent the rest of the day skinning the wolves and keeping their distance from each other. That evening, the Dutchman was more friendly. As Graham noted:

> He thawed out after a bit, and then began telling me how angry he was when he saw my rifle cocked and pointed at him, apparently not giving a thought to the fact that he had drawn his

---

revolver first. He said that it was all that he could do to keep from shooting me in the back when I passed him. He swore positively that if it had been either a half-breed or an Indian he would have shot without hesitation.[7]

The going price for good prime wolf pelts in the early 1870s was sometimes as high as $2.50 which, considering that buffalo robes were getting only $5.00, meant that large profits could be made over the winter. Usually the wolfers had their own camping outfit, but if the buffalo herds were grazing close to a whisky fort such as Whoop-Up or Spitzee Post, the trappers might board there. Or if they sold their catch, they might hang around the fort for several days drinking up their profits. As a result, the relationship between wolfers and traders was very close.

Al Wilkins, whose father had a trading post on the Marias River in the mid-1870s, remembered the wolfers who worked near their place.

> Wolfing was a real business in those days, when wolves could be seen in droves of 200 to 300, following buffalo herds. It was the custom, if a party wanted to go hunting or wolfing for the winter, for them to go to one of the three general stores at Fort Benton to be outfitted. Any of the stores would supply them with bacon, flour, sugar, tea, tobacco, strychnine, and ammunition. Off they would go, usually in a little old wagon, with some saddle horses, an Indian lodge made of tanned buffalo hides to live in, and a frying pan and a few stew pans and kettles to cook in.[8]

In the view of U.S. special agent Fellows D. Pease, wolfing was to be encouraged as the wolves would be a detriment to ranching once the buffalo herds were gone. However, he was adamant that wolfing and whisky trading should be kept separate, and wolfers should be discouraged from working out of trading posts. He stated:

> Men go into the Buffalo Range with a Winter Outfit, Provisions, Arms, Strychnine, &c., generally about three men to each party, and having light wagon, Ponies, &c. The Wolfing Season corresponds to the Indian Robe-making Season, and the parties commonly meet on the range, and stay near each other during this period. The "Catching" is pursued to best advantage in very cold weather, which freezes the bait, causing the wolves to linger and die close at hand, and also preserves their carcasses from spoiling before they are "Skinned up."[9]

By 1874, the wolf skin trade nearly equalled the buffalo robe trade in value, and wolves were being killed "by tens of thousands."[10] Some trading posts were getting as many as four thousand skins in a season, and both Power and Baker were shipping large quantities either by river or overland to the railway.

Although John Healy was not a wolf hunter, he was aware of the profits to be made by buying wolf skins. "Wolfing was a regular profession," he said. "For instance, you poisoned a lot with the bait you put and then you ride out in the morning and see 15 or 20 of them dead and 15 to 20 of them all around crazy; those are the wolves that are dangerous."[11]

He found this out for himself one day while travelling between Whoop-Up and Sun River. He saw a beautiful white wolf in a pack and decided to rope it and take its skin. He dropped the loop over its head but the animal quickly turned and snapped the rope in half with its razor-sharp teeth. The trader dashed after the wolf again and made two more tries, but each time it sliced through the rope. By then the rope was too short to make a new loop, so Healy decided to run the wolf down and kill it under the hooves of his horse.

He hit the animal straight on and knocked it head over heels but it jumped to its feet and continued to run. As Healy approached it the second time, the wolf suddenly spun around and leapt at the trader.

> He struck me right here on the leg and I pulled away and struck him with the whip right across the nose … I had fine calf skin leggings on and he tore that calf skin as though it were brown paper … Then he suddenly turned away. I was bleeding awfully bad; he had struck into a small artery. I then tied up my leg and commenced following him.[12]

Healy pursued the wolf onto the prairie for some 2 or 3 miles until the animal finally stopped in exhaustion. Thinking that all fight had gone out of it, he approached it on foot with a short rope, but the wolf dashed towards him, forcing him to retreat to his horse. Giving up any idea of taking a clean wolf skin, Healy drew his revolver and shot the wolf in the neck, but it still kept moving so he shot it again in the head. As it fell to the ground, Healy jumped off his horse but was amazed when the wolf tried to attack him again, so he struck it with a club and crushed its skull. He got his wolf, but he also carried a scar on his leg for the rest of his life.

Although wolfers in Whoop-Up country experienced difficulties with weather and isolation, the Indians who did not like them and did not want them in their territory posed the biggest danger. The main reason for this resentment was that Indian dogs—"the Sentinels of an Indian Camp"—were often inadvertently killed when they fed on a poisoned carcass.[13] In some instances Indians themselves fed on the poisoned meat and died. The Blackfoot also believed that the wolfers drove away the buffalo, which was of real concern to them in the winter when it was sometimes impossible for the Indians to move camp. Another concern was that, in the spring, the strychnine in the carcasses could poison the grass.[14] As a result, as trader Peter Koch stated, "If possible, the place selected must be one where the Indians do not hunt much."[15]

The Blackfoot believed that the wolfers were invading their hunting grounds and taking away valuable wolf skins without compensating them. Accordingly, if they came across dead wolves on the prairie, they had no hesitation in skinning them for themselves. This sometimes led to dangerous confrontations, such as in the winter of 1872–73, when W. B. "Whiskey" Smith, "Poker" Brown, Dan Lavalley, and John LaMott left Spitzee Post and went wolfing north of the Bow River. They set out their bait, and while making daily rounds, found the remains of 103 poisoned wolves that had already been skinned. It was obvious that Indians had done the deed and had then headed north. According to the story:

> The four whites decided they would stand for no such treatment and after returning to camp and equipping themselves for travel, took the trail of the Indians. They followed it for more than 300 miles into the valley of the Red Deer (then known as Elk river). Here they came up with a camp of 70 lodges of Assiniboines, which could be no other than the Indians who had stolen their wolf skins, for the trail had been direct and rapid. The Indians were comparatively well armed. They had hidden the stolen pelts beneath their bed robes and then with their sawed off flintlock guns concealed under their blankets, they sat upon the beds. The white men, however, made war talk and bluffed the Indians. They pulled 700 wolf skins from hiding places, loaded them onto their sleds and hit the trail back.[16]

This account seems to indicate that while the Assiniboines took 103 skins, the wolfers reclaimed them and robbed the Indians of another 600, providing yet another reason for the Indians to look upon the wolfers as interlopers and thieves.

The relationship between wolfers and Indians was clearly demonstrated in the spring of 1872 when Thomas Hardwick, with a group of sixteen white wolfers and nine Métis, went wolfing and trading along the southern edge of the Sweetgrass Hills. Early in April about twenty Assiniboines approached their fort to trade but were warned away by Métis interpreters. When they continued to approach, Hardwick opened fire on them and caused them to withdraw. About two hours later they returned, double in number, and marching in procession, the two in front carrying a flag or banner as was usual with a trading party. When they got within 200 yards of the fort, they again were told to leave, and when they ignored the warning the wolfers opened fire. According to Isaac Dawson:

> After the first volley was discharged, they scattered on their back trails as before; but after crossing a small cooley [sic], they rallied and returned our fire, but being closely pursued fled again, and proving themselves too fleet of foot for their pursuers, they soon placed themselves in safety.[17]

When the wolfers checked the killing ground, they found four dead Assiniboines, one of whom was promptly scalped by Hardwick. Later, Indian agent A. J. Simmons spoke to the survivors who told him they had been fired upon without provocation. Hearing that they "were going up to the camp of the half-breeds and white men peaceably and without demonstration," Simmons did not hesitate to condemn the killings as ruthless murders. "These lawless desperadoes persist in going into the Indian country," he said. "They kill and destroy their game and poison the carcasses for wolf-baits, at which the Indians are greatly incensed, as they regard with superstitious horror the poisoning of buffalo carcasses."[18] Yet no action was taken to punish Hardwick and his fellow murderers.

Hardwick was known to be a violent man with a checkered career. Born in Missouri, he enlisted in the Confederate army and after the war went west to prospect for gold. In 1870, he joined a Crow war party in attacking a Sioux camp, and at Fort Holly he helped fend off an attack by Sioux and Assiniboine Indians. During the winter of 1870, he became involved in a dispute with two Crows, killing one and wounding the other. He was wounded himself and spent the winter at Fort Browning, working for the Indian department. In 1871 he turned to wolfing and trading, but seemed to spend much of his time fighting with Indians. During the winter, for example, his wolfing party had a fight with some Peigans, killing four of them.[19]

The shooting incident near the Sweetgrass Hills was dubbed the "Sweetgrass Hills Massacre," but it was mild compared with what was to follow a year later. Hardwick spent the winter of 1872–73 on the British side of the line, wolfing near the Bow River and doing some trading with the Indians in the area. In the spring, he and his crew packed their season's take into light wagons and headed south for Fort Benton. When they reached the Teton River on 17 May, less than a day's travel from the village, they were raided by a Peigan war party who ran off nineteen of their horses.[20] For the next three days, the angry wolfers carted their skins into Benton and, after unsuccessfully trying to convince the authorities to take some action, they formed a posse of twelve men who were determined to recover their missing stock. This was not a new experience for some of the wolfers. In the previous year, a war party of Sioux had taken horses from Hardwick's party but the wolfers had pursued them for 150 miles and recovered their stock. In this instance, the wolfers vowed "they would recover their property even if they had to go to the Saskatchewan for it. Each man was armed with a Henry rifle and two Smith & Wesson large revolvers and was well mounted. In addition, five pack animals were taken along with the men."[21]

Tom Hardwick and John H. Evans were in charge of the wolfers; others in the party included Trevanion Hale, Elijah Devereaux, Edward Grace, James Hughes, Charles Smith, S. Vincent, and S. A. Harper. The trail was old when they picked it up about 8 miles north of the Teton, but they followed it for three days without difficulty. During the next night, there was a heavy rainfall, and after a full day of tracking, the wolfers had to admit that all signs of the trail had been wiped out. Then, with the Cypress Hills dominating the skyline to the north, they decided to enter British territory and visit one of the whisky forts in the area.

In the summer of 1871, traders from Benton had invaded the Cypress Hills where they sold liquor to a mixed patronage of Blackfoot, Assiniboine, Sioux, and Cree hunters. Because their forts served tribes that, for the most part, were enemies of each other, there was as much violence around them as there was at Whoop-Up. Late in 1871, for example, Sioux Indians attacked a party of ten traders in the Cypress Hills and two of them, Benjamin Short and someone named Bastien, were seriously wounded.[22] Irate Indians also fired on the forts, especially after they believed they had been cheated.[23] And, just days before the wolfers arrived, there had been a fight between Blackfoot and Assiniboine Indians about 2 or 3 miles from the forts.[24]

Over the winter of 1872–73, at least thirteen traders operated in the Cypress Hills, some of them Métis from Red River but most from Montana. Among the Montanans were Moses Solomon, who had moved from his former post near Standoff; Charles Rowe, owner of the Overland Hotel in Fort Benton; and Abel Farwell, one-time chief trader for Durfee & Peck.[25] The traders had imported some seventy-five barrels of whisky in the early winter and traded it for thirteen hundred robes. As a result, many Assiniboines became impoverished and went to the Indian agency at Fort Peck in a starving condition.[26] By the time the wolfers arrived, most of the Montana traders had closed their forts for the season, with only Farwell and Solomon remaining open.

As the wolfers did not know the exact locations of the whisky forts, Hardwick and Evans went ahead to scout and to see if there were any Indians nearby that might have their stolen horses. They found both Farwell's and Solomon's forts, close together near a small creek. "We approached the posts very cautiously," said Evans, "and discovered about forty lodges of Indians, but as they had only eleven head of horses in the camp, we concluded they were not the thieves, so went in and camped within a short distance."[27]

Next morning, 1 June, the rest of the wolfers arrived; some congregated at Farwell's Post while others went to Solomon's for whisky and drank heavily all day. They learned that Solomon had not been getting along well with the Assiniboines and that the Indians had fired shots at his trading post. Farwell, on the other hand, seemed to be quite friendly with them. The Indians were Northern Assiniboines from the Wood Mountain area, under a chief named Little Soldier, and were considered to be part of the Milk River Agency at Fort Peck.[28] Farwell had been with Durfee & Peck since 1865 and had supervised the construction of Fort Peck, so he likely knew the band very well.

A short time before the wolfers arrived, a war party of seventeen Indians had come to Farwell's Post and had stayed for two nights. Although the traders had kept their eye on them, on the second night some of the warriors broke open the corral gate and were leading three horses away when an Assiniboine from Little Soldier's camp saw them. He managed to recover one of the horses before the men fled; the horse belonged to a Canadian employee named George Hammond.

During the day while the wolfers were drinking, Hammond told them that his horse was missing again and blamed Little Soldier's band. But Farwell said, "No, these Indians brought the horse back and gave it to you, and if they had wanted it they would have kept it."[29] At that point, a Métis freighter said that two of his horses also were missing. Hammond went inside the fort and came out carrying his gun. "Let's go and clean out the camp," he told the wolfers, and one of them replied, "Yes, let's go."[30]

In order to defuse the tense situation, Farwell offered to let Hammond have any two horses from his own herd and he in turn would take two of Little Soldier's horses to hold until the missing animal was returned. When Farwell went to the Assiniboine camp, he found many of the Indians had been drinking heavily, including the chief. They were excited, knowing that something was going on at Farwell's and Solomon's forts, and had been advised by a local Métis that they were about to be attacked. When Farwell approached them, they were dancing, singing, and yelling, and many were obviously drunk. The trader told the chief what he had arranged.

"Yes," said Little Soldier, "I am the only man who has got two horses." The others in the camp were poor and some were using dogs as pack animals. Little Soldier asked his men if anyone knew about Hammond's missing horse, and one of them commented, "Yes, the horse is on the hill back of your fort with two other horses."[31]

Meanwhile, the wolfers became more drunk and angry as the day wore on, incited by Hammond and some of the other whisky-trade employees who were anxious to "teach the Assiniboines a lesson." Finally, Hardwick decided to "clean them out" and led the wolfers and a few of the traders towards the Indian camp, crossing the creek and stopping at a coulee that separated them from the lodges.

When Hardwick's men saw that Abel Farwell was still with the Indians, they shouted, "Come out or you'll get killed as we're going to open fire on the camp."[32] As Farwell later testified:

> I then knew that they meant that I must come out or I would get killed by them; then I said to the Indians, "They are going to fire on the camp, and you had better scatter." I said I would go and stop it if I could, but I was not at all sure that I would succeed. They did not want me to leave them; they thought the party would not open fire on the camp as long as I was with them.[33]

Farwell walked to the nearby coulee where the wolfers and the traders were waiting. Hardwick immediately complained that the Indians were scattering and Farwell had prevented him from getting a good shot at them while they were still in a crowd. Farwell tried to explain that Hammond's horse wasn't missing after all and that it was being brought down from the hill as they spoke. He offered to get an interpreter from his trading post so that the wolfers could hear what had transpired directly from the Indians. When John Evans urged Hardwick to agree, Hardwick said he would give Farwell five minutes. However, just then they noticed that the Assiniboines were taking cover and interpreted their actions as hostile. As Evans later said, "We saw at once they had made up their minds to fight us, and so right there the affair commenced."[34] George Hammond was the first to open fire; that seemed to be the signal, and soon the small camp was being riddled with bullets.

According to Evans, the wolfers and traders "kept up a pretty lively fire for some time on the Indians. The party then split up, the main body staying in the ravine, while two or three of the party took to the hills on each side of the creek, where they got a fair view of the Indians, and soon compelled them to evacuate their position."[35] Others were shooting at the camp from the roof of Solomon's post.

When the firing ceased, Hardwick and a number of men rode across the creek to kill any Indians they could find. One of the victims was Little Soldier, who by this time was in a drunken stupor in his lodge. His wife, Woman Who Eats Grizzly Bear, recalled what happened next.

> I looked through a hole in the lodge [and] I saw some white men coming towards the lodges. After they reached the lodges, they began to pull up the pins of the lodges; they came to my lodge last … I was sitting alongside my husband; he said come out, you will have your life; he told me three times to come out. I turned back and got my husband around the neck.

My husband then woke up. I thought they would kill him, and I wanted to be killed with him. They tore up the pins of my lodge and threw the lodge over us. One of the white men caught me by the hand, while I had the other hand around my husband; he tried to pull me up. I saw my old mother coming, she grabbed the hand of my husband, my old mother, and I got up and led my husband out. The white man said, come along to the Fort and you will have your life. The first thing I saw was my husband's father lying dead, he being killed. We passed about five steps. My husband threw up his arms and broke away and was shot dead by another white man.[36]

Little Soldier's mother-in-law, Apasteeninchaco, saw the killing. "I heard my son-in-law, Little Soldier, say … here is my father already dead. Turning to them he said, white men, you will know what you have done today, you never knew a 'woody mountain Assiniboine' Indian to harm a white man."[37] According to Farwell, Little Soldier was killed by wolfer S. Vincent, after which the chief's head was cut off and mounted on a pole. The Man Who Took the Coat (who later became chief of the band) said that

when we reached the timber [we] tried to defend ourselves … Most of the Indians went round to the bush on the top of the hill. I and some others remained where we were; from where I was I saw some of the Americans come to where the "Old Man" [Little Soldier] was and strike him on the head with an hatchet, leaving the hatchet there in his head.

He identified three of the dead as Little Soldier, Fast Runner, and Dog's Backbone. "The rest were women and children," he said.[38]

At one point the wolfers on the hill were repelled momentarily when the Assiniboines counterattacked. When wolfers who were looting the camp saw the reversal, they rushed to their comrades' aid, but as they crossed the river they did not see a wounded Assiniboine lying in the brush. He pointed his gun at wolfer Ed Grace and shot him fatally in the chest. The Assiniboine was dispatched moments later by the other wolfers.

This ended the active fighting, but the wolfers and traders weren't finished. They went into the remains of the Assiniboine camp, killing anyone they found alive. "We counted thirteen dead Indians around the lodges," said Evans, "and since then have heard from parties who were there afterwards that twenty-six were found dead in that vicinity. There must also have been great numbers wounded."[39]

Five women and a small child were taken prisoner by Antonio "Tony" Amei, a man known as The Spaniard. One woman and her child escaped, but the others weren't so lucky. Little Soldier's widow was claimed by one of the wolfers, who took her to Amei's cabin adjoining Solomon's fort and raped her several times. Three old women were put in another room; the youngest was taken away where she "had many men with her" again and again during the night.[40] In the morning, Abel Farwell's wife, a Crow Indian named Mary, bravely went to Amei's cabin and successfully demanded the release of the prisoners. All the women were convinced that if they hadn't been rescued, they would have been murdered. In fact, one wolfer told Little Soldier's widow that she "would not live till morning."[41]

The next day, the wolfers and traders prepared to leave. They were afraid that the Indians might organize an attack, but they had nothing to fear. An Assiniboine named Cutter, who had been shot three times in the back, recalled:

> After dark I hid my family, I went to my lodge, I got some sinew and cut up my lodge to make a bag … I then returned to my family, not only myself but the whole forty lodges started off, carrying everything on our back, all our dogs having run off. We started in the night for the end of the mountain to the halfbreeds. They treated us kindly, giving us dogs, kettles, etc.[42]

The site of the Cypress Hills Massacre is preserved as an historic site. This photo shows a reconstruction of Solomon's Post. (Glenbow Archives, NA-2446-13).

The wanton destruction of the Indian camp continued the following day. As wolfer John Evans stated:

> We are not disturbed that night, and so next morning went over to camp, made piles of their lodges and other trash, and set them on fire, after which we made a coffin, put the corpse [of Ed Grace] into it, and buried it inside one of the Forts. The traders having all left, we burned the Fort down, so that the Indians would be unable to find the grave and dig up the remains.[43]

At this point, the wolfing party split, some continuing to search for their missing horses—the original purpose of the expedition—travelling some two hundred miles to the Blackfoot camps in the Fort Whoop-Up area before conceding defeat. The others returned directly to Fort Benton with the traders.[44] There they were treated like homecoming heroes and saluted as a band of "Kit Carsons" who had been attacked by warlike Assiniboines and had successfully defended themselves.[45] Yet not all Americans praised their actions. A. J. Simmons, Indian agent for the Milk River Agency, reported to his superiors that the wolfers had "attacked a camp of forty lodges of peaceful Assinaboines [*sic*] attached to this agency, who were almost entirely defenceless and killed sixteen of their number, men, women and children and mutilated their bodies in a most outrageous and disgusting manner."[46] He had spoken to two witnesses to the event and was convinced that there "was no provocation for this cowardly assault and brutal murder."[47]

Because this tragedy, which became known as the Cypress Hills Massacre, occurred on British soil, there was nothing Agent Simmons or other American authorities could do about it. And as long as the Canadian government ignored its responsibilities, the killers would remain at large. And so the incident ended—at least for the time being.

By late summer, Thomas Hardwick and his crew were back on the British side of the line for another season of trading and poisoning wolves, as though nothing had happened. Besides Hardwick, the group included Tony Lachappelle, Charles Duval, Harry "Kamoose" Taylor, Joe McMullen, a mixed-blood boy named Dixie, and three women. On the way north, they were attacked on the Little Bow River by a party they identified as Sioux, but who were probably Assiniboines, and in the melee one Indian was killed.[48] The wolfers proceeded on to the lower waters of the Bow River where they set up camp for the winter. At that time an estimated seventy-five wolfers were busy at work between the Bow and Red Deer Rivers.[49]

In September, Hardwick's outfit was again attacked by Assiniboines. The wolfers were asleep in camp when the Indians took a position in a nearby cutbank and opened fire on their tents, reminiscent of the way the wolfers had attacked Little Soldier's camp in the Cypress Hills. Joe McMullen, clad only in a flannel shirt, tried to get to one of the wagons for a rifle and ammunition, while the others simply fled the scene. As a result, McMullen became the target of the attackers and was struck eight times before he managed to crawl into the brush and hide. All the others, including the slightly wounded wives of Duval and McMullen, disappeared into the darkness. Taking whatever they could salvage and believing McMullen to be dead, the escapees set off for Whoop-Up.

From his hiding place, the wounded man saw the Assiniboines plunder the camp; then, while the Indians were celebrating their triumph, he managed to swim across the Bow River and escape. Although weak from his wounds and loss of blood, he began to make his painful way south. According to a press report at the time: "For twelve weary days [he] walked, crawled and dragged himself towards Healy & Hamilton's trading post, living upon bark and berries and naked to the skin, having used his shirt to bandage his wounds and to wind around his lacerated and bleeding feet, continued his painful and agonizing journey."[50] When near Grassy Lake, he found an abandoned wolfer's cabin and stumbled in there to die.

As fate would have it, there was a Blood camp in the area and one of the leaders, One Spot, was searching for missing horses when he noticed two huge rattlesnakes near the cabin door. He shot one and followed the other inside where he saw the wounded man lying in a bunk. "The Indian was very frightened," said the storyteller, "but McMullen called feebly to him and made himself known. The Indian then made a travois and carried him to the camp, thirteen miles distant, and messengers were sent to Whoop Up to notify the white men there."[51]

A rescue party made up of D. W. Davis, James McDevitt, Joe Day, Sandy Cunningham, Thomas Hardwick, and several others went to the wounded man. He was a most pitiful object, his clothing mostly gone except for the remains of his shirt, his body scratched and bruised, and his face so covered with grime that they could hardly recognize him. "An examination reveals the fact that he had been shot twice through the arm, twice in the body near the shoulder, twice in the side, once under the shoulder blade, and one other shot in the leg. He was carefully taken to Whoop Up and tenderly cared for, and eventually recovered."[52]

While he was recuperating, the traders and wolfers at Whoop-Up took up a collection and raised five hundred dollars for him which, as the *Helena Herald* commented, "goes to show that the milk of human kindness flows at Whoop-Up, as well as in more civilized communities."[53]

Incidents such as this did not deter Montanans from making their forays into Blackfoot country in their quest for robes. However, the catches dropped off drastically by the middle part of the decade. Late in 1873, for example, Tom

Power said that "wolfers are meeting with but little success,"[54] and in the spring of 1874, a trader at Fort Kipp stated that the wolf returns would be much lower that season.[55] As predicted by Special Agent Pease, the surviving prairie wolves did become a menace to the ranching industry once the buffalo herds were gone, and governments found it necessary to place bounties on them to destroy the remaining packs. As for the wolfers, they followed the paths of their prey into obscurity. Yet, in 1886, a Bentonite praised them and commented, "We have among us men who bear evidences of great suffering, and I trust that the pilgrim will at least be charitable and give them the praise which is due them, but which has been grudgingly bestowed."[56]

Although the whisky trade in the British possessions would continue unabated for another few years, the Cypress Hills Massacre started a chain of events that would bring about its eventual demise.

9. *The Canadian Response*

On 22 October 1870, just four months after the western prairies had been transferred from Great Britain to the new Dominion of Canada, the Territorial government passed a proclamation outlawing the sale of liquor within its boundaries, an area formerly known as Rupert's Land. The regulations provided for a fine of up to £100 for the importation or possession of any "rum, whiskey or other spiritous liquor whatever."[1] This legislation was not directed against Healy & Hamilton or any of the other traders on the Belly River, for the government apparently was not yet aware of their existence. Rather, it was an attempt to curb the trafficking in liquor from the new Province of Manitoba, where the possession of alcohol was legal. Free traders from there were taking intoxicants to the various Hudson's Bay Company (HBC) forts along the North Saskatchewan River and wreaking havoc among the Indians and Métis in those areas.

Two days after the proclamation was enacted, Lieutenant William F. Butler of the 69th Regiment was dispatched to the West to notify traders and missionaries about the prohibition. He was also to advise on the desirability of sending troops to the North Saskatchewan in order to maintain law and order at the HBC settlements. In a gruelling 119 days, the officer covered some twenty-seven hundred miles, travelling as far west as Rocky Mountain House. He had planned to go south from there to check on reports of American whisky traders on Canadian soil, but his inability to find a guide forced him to retrace his route back to Winnipeg via the North Saskatchewan.

Butler reported:

> As matters at present rest, the region of the Saskatchewan is without law, order, or security for life or property; robbery and murder for years have gone unpunished; Indian massacres are unchecked even in the close vicinity of the Hudson's Bay Company's posts, and all civil and legal institutions are entirely unknown.[2]

He was concerned about the flow of liquor into the region from Winnipeg and posted the prohibition proclamation at the various trading posts along his route.

At Fort Edmonton, Butler became aware of American incursions into the southern prairies. He expressed the concern that if the gold prospectors who were invading Blackfoot hunting grounds found anything of value, they would soon be followed by merchants and others from Montana. He then stated:

> Indians visiting the Rocky Mountain House during the fall of 1870 have spoken of the existence of a trading post of Americans from Fort Benton, upon the Belly River, sixty miles within the British boundary-line. They have asserted that two American traders, well-known on the Missouri, named Culverston and Healy, have established themselves at this post for the purpose of trading alcohol, whiskey, and arms and ammunition of the most improved description, with the Blackfeet Indians; and that an active trade is being carried on in all these articles, which, it is said, are constantly smuggled across the boundary-line by people from Fort Benton.[3]

This information, contained in Butler's report to the lieutenant-governor, Adams G. Archibald, dated 10 March 1871, was the first official word that the Canadian government had received about the existence of the whisky traders.

Butler suggested that a magistrate be appointed in Fort Edmonton, who would make regular tours of the district to hold court. He also recommended that military stations be established near Forts Edmonton and Carlton, as well as

> the organization of a well-equipped force of from 100 to 150 men, one-third to be mounted, specially recruited and engaged for service in the Saskatchewan; enlisting for two or three years' service, and at the expiration of that period to become military settlers, receiving grants of land, but still remaining as a reserve force should their services be required.[4]

The report was received in Winnipeg and transmitted to Ottawa, but no immediate action was taken. During this time, the lieutenant-governor began to collect and transmit reports about the whisky problem to his superiors in the nation's capital in support of the recommendation for police support.

Less than a month after Butler submitted his report, leading Cree chiefs Sweetgrass, Kehiwin, Little Hunter, and Bobtail met with HBC chief factor William J. Christie at Fort Edmonton to express their concerns about the whisky trade. They stated, in part, "We want you to stop the Americans from coming to Trade on our Lands and giving Fire Water, Ammunition & Arms to our Enemies, the Blackfeet."[5] The lieutenant-governor sent them a polite reply, but with no commitment to suppress the illicit trade. About the same time, missionary George McDougall wrote of "the poor Blackfeet, who for months, and that on Dominion soil, have been pillaged and depopulated by American alcohol traders."[6] He demanded that the federal government establish a military post on the Bow River to put down the illicit traffic.

Late in 1871, Jean L'Heureux, a white man who lived with the Blackfoot, wrote to Chief Factor Christie with more information about the American traders. He spoke of a "good many Fenians at Belly River last winter, and a lot of any amount of low traders from the States."[7] He said he expected to be near their trading posts during the winter, and if they planned any incursion into the Edmonton area, he would inform the traders at Rocky Mountain House. Later in the year he provided more detailed figures, indicating the importation of some 12,000 gallons of liquor and the collecting of twenty-four thousand robes by the Belly River traders.[8]

In the face of all this information, Lieutenant-Governor Archibald wrote to Prime Minister John A. Macdonald in January 1872, expressing concern about the whisky traders "who have already established Posts within our line, in the country between Fort Benton & Edmonton."[9] Using William Christie as his source, he concluded, "You must move so soon as the Spring opens, upon being ready with a force of mounted Troops for the North West."[10] However, instead of taking any action, either on Butler's report or Archibald's recommendation, the prime minister decided to seek further confirmation of the problem. Accordingly, Colonel Peter Robertson-Ross, commanding officer of the Militia of Canada, was ordered to make a reconnaissance of the West and to offer recommendations regarding the need for law and order.

He left Ottawa in July 1872 and, for the next four months, travelled through the West, reaching Fort Edmonton, then continuing on to Rocky Mountain House. Unlike Butler, who had been stymied from going farther south, Robertson-Ross found a guide who took him along the foothills to the Crowsnest Pass, then across the mountains to the West Coast. However, this route did not place him in contact with any of the illicit trading posts.

When he first reached Winnipeg, Robertson-Ross met with Frank Moberly, a Canadian Pacific Railway surveyor, who told him there were three American posts on the Belly River, each with about thirty men and equipped with large guns. The occupants were described as outlaws and "the worst class of people from Montana."[11] Moberly said the principal fort, presumably Whoop-Up, was at the junction of the Belly and Bow Rivers, an incorrect location that Robertson-Ross included in his report and that gave no end of confusion to the North-West Mounted Police two years later. Moberly added:

> These people trade in Whisky, ammunition & take Robes in
> return. Henry repeaters, 16 shooters, I have seen with the

Blackfeet & Blood Indians ... The Indians have been shooting at each other. They get drunk and fight. John Rann [Wren] is a white man being at one of these Forts, U.S. citizen, killed a half breed last summer, shot during a drunken quarrel.[12]

When the militia officer arrived in Edmonton, he was told by Chief Factor Richard Hardisty that the residents needed military protection. "There is no security for life or property here," he was told, "murder is committed with impunity, etc., etc., also whisky selling to Indians contrary to law by Free Traders from the States."[13] He also learned that six Montana traders had come all the way to Fort Edmonton to sell whisky to the Indians and Métis, and when they were remonstrated, they said there was no law to stop them from doing whatever they wished. From Edmonton, Robertson-Ross proceeded on to Rocky Mountain House where he learned more about the whisky trade. He was told that during the previous year, twenty-seven South Peigans, thirteen North Peigans, forty-six Bloods, and three Siksikas had died as a direct result of the trade. Robertson-Ross noted:

They have a post which they have named "Fort Hamilton" and are and have for some time past been trading whisky, fire arms and goods to the Indians for fur, horses, etc. The Yankee agents who are carrying on this illicit traffic are in the employment it appears of Healy Hamilton & Co., American Merchants residing at Fort Benton, State of Montana, and of the firm I. G. Baker & Co., residing at the same place.[14]

By the time he got back to Ottawa, Robertson-Ross could do little more than confirm all that Butler had seen, but he recommended more direct action, taking the police right into Blackfoot territory rather than remaining near Edmonton and other HBC posts. In Robertson-Ross's view, there was no law in the West; liquor was being sold openly around Fort Edmonton, and the Blackfoot tribes were being decimated by the American whisky trade. His report, written on 17 March 1873, and presented to the House of Commons, recommended "the establishment of a Custom House on the Belly River near the Porcupine Hills with a military guard of about 150 soldiers."[15] A second recommendation was the formation of "one regiment of mounted riflemen, 550 strong, divided into companies of 50, as sufficient to support the government in establishing law and order, preserving the peace of the North-West Territories ..."[16] He believed that these steps would stop the whisky trade, eliminate horse stealing, and open the area for settlement.

Prime Minister Macdonald reacted by introducing an act, on 23 May 1873, to establish law and order in the West. However, the details weren't spelled out and Macdonald's idea at that time was to have a police force stationed in Winnipeg that would simply protect those areas where there was agricultural settlement.[17]

Alexander Morris, who had succeeded Archibald as lieutenant-governor, tried to convince the prime minister to take a more comprehensive approach to the problem. He forwarded all reports he received that had anything to do with the unrest in the interior, even wild rumours such as trader Archibald McDonald telling of the supposed poisoning of Sitting Bull by American traders in the Cypress Hills.[18] Other accounts were more substantial, such as one from Edward McKay, a Métis, complaining that "American traders from Benton and the Missouri have established five posts in British Territory at Cypress Hills and took out between six and ten thousand buffalo robes."[19]

Later in 1873, HBC factor William Traill wrote that the Belly River traders were made up of desperate men from Montana, Omaha, and the lower Missouri, many being fugitives from the law. Among them he named John Bond, John Henley, Richard Berry, Jesse Thompson, George Pool, and George Johnson. "As may be expected from such a class of men," he said, "they lead a desperate life, murder being of common occurrence among themselves. They all have Indian Wives and at the present time have regularly employed Indian scouts and are all well armed and a thoroughly organized party."[20] Traill added that if a military force was sent against them, they would probably fight. A copy of this report, together with a request for 150 men, was dispatched to the secretary of State in Ottawa who, in turn, took it to the Privy Council. But much to Lieutenant-Governor Morris's chagrin, he was told "that the Government after a full consideration of all the facts, has come to the conclusion that the state of affairs in the North West is not so grave a character as to warrant them in incurring so heavy an expense as the measure you suggest would involve."[21]

It took the Cypress Hills Massacre to finally get the government moving. Although it occurred on 1 June official notice of it was not received by the Canadian government until early August, in a dispatch from United States officials to Sir Edward Thornton, the British minister. About the same time as the information was wending its way through Washington, London, and Ottawa, Edward McKay was giving the news to Lieutenant-Governor Morris. McKay told him of the loss of the wolfers' horses and of Hardwick and his men following the Indians' trail to the Cypress Hills. He continued:

> There were some of their countrymen selling liquor to the Assiniboines; they camped their [sic] all that night, the Indians being made drunk by the Traders, were noisy & troublesome. They, the horse pursuers, being enraged at the loss of there [sic] horses & encouraged by the traders to help them, fell on the

unprepared Indians & killed twenty-two Men, women & children, besides wounding a great many others, also burning all their effects & killing there [*sic*] animals. Naked & starved the remainder travelled for four days, when they fell in with a camp of Crees who pitying there [*sic*] bad condition, subscribed & supplied them with all there [*sic*] necessarys.[22]

This news came hard on the heels of Macdonald's announcement that he was not yet ready to move on the police question. Morris now insisted that the government take immediate steps to dispatch a police force to the West. "In my judgement," he said, "it will be impossible to govern what is, in fact, almost the half of a Continent, without a considerable force, and the events detailed in my despatch of this date, with regard to the murder of Indians on our soil by American traders, confirm this view."[23]

Over the next few weeks, pressures for action increased as more information about the massacre trickled in. Narcisse Lacerte, a Métis hunter, reported visiting the battle site. "I saw with mine own eyes the dead bodies of five Indians killed," he said, "and of a sixth who died in my presence. The dead whom I saw were two old men, one young man, one woman and one little child."[24] On the basis of Lacerte's deposition, the prime minister ordered that warrants be issued for the arrest of Thomas Hardwick and the other accused parties and notified the United States government that they planned to extradite the men. An arresting party under Gilbert McMicken was actually sent out from Winnipeg near the end of the year, bound for Montana, but the u.s. army informed them that Hardwick was back on Canadian soil, wolf hunting on the Bow River.

McMicken observed that it would be impossible for him to follow the wolfers north into Canadian territory or even to approach them from Fort Edmonton because of the lateness of the season. He added:

There could be no doubt that the American wolfers, or traders, were then within British Territory and would be so for the winter. That they [the traders and wolfers] were a desperate set of men, all numbered from 150 to 200 upwards, that their operations take them some 100 miles or more within the British Lines. That within our territory, they have posts established and fortified numbering as variously stated from five to eight or more.[25]

As a result of this report, the Canadian government decided to postpone the extraditions and arrests until a later date.

However, under the weight of the appeals from Morris and an indication from Great Britain that the formation of the police was a diplomatic necessity,

Prime Minister Macdonald finally announced the formation of the North-West Mounted Police (NWMP) and that the first contingent of police would be sent to the Red River before the end of 1873. Yet, another year was to pass before any action was taken to actually suppress the Belly River traders.

Meanwhile, Methodist missionaries and the HBC continued to rail against the illicit trade. In later years, a number of whisky traders claimed that the HBC had been their worst enemy, telling lies about them and misrepresenting them to the Canadian government. John Healy, for example, complained that the HBC reported "five hundred desperadoes and cutthroats under John Healy had invaded Canada and were demoralizing the Indians."[26] He denied their claims that he was selling repeating rifles to the Blackfoot, stating (untruthfully) they only sold single shot muzzle-loaders, and adding that the HBC complaints were "a tissue of lies."[27] Charles Schafft, who was at Whoop-Up when the NWMP arrived, stated:

> Whoop Up was pictured as an almost invincible stronghold, defended by hundreds of American renegades, and bristling with needle guns and cannon. This report, coming from religious sources, backed by interesting testimony of the Hudson Bay Company, gained credence, and the Canadian Government organized the Northwest Mounted Police for the purpose of driving out the American "freebooters."[28]

And according to James Willard Schultz, "The Hudson's Bay Company ... had been urging the Dominion Government to come to its aid and suppress the American traders,"[29] because "the various tribes of the Blackfeet no longer traded at their posts, and they were losing a large amount of furs and buffalo robes, to which their charter entitled them."[30]

There can be no question that the HBC was adversely affected by the American trade and that it lost a significant amount of business. It was not too interested in buffalo robes, which were bulky and difficult to ship on its expensive water routes, but it needed horses for its inland transportation system and dried meat to supply its isolated trading posts farther north.

At Rocky Mountain House, the main post for the Blackfoot, the HBC trader made it clear that his business was being drastically reduced by the whisky traders. In 1872, he commented that "no Indians have been in worth talking about all Summer,"[31] and in 1873, "no word of the Blackfeet coming. We did have a few but what they bring is the leaving of Belly River whiskey."[32] At Fort Edmonton, the last Blackfoot came to trade in 1872; after that, they never returned. In just two or three years, the entire Blackfoot trade had been diverted to the Americans, and there was no way the HBC could compete as long as it was unable to use alcohol in its business.

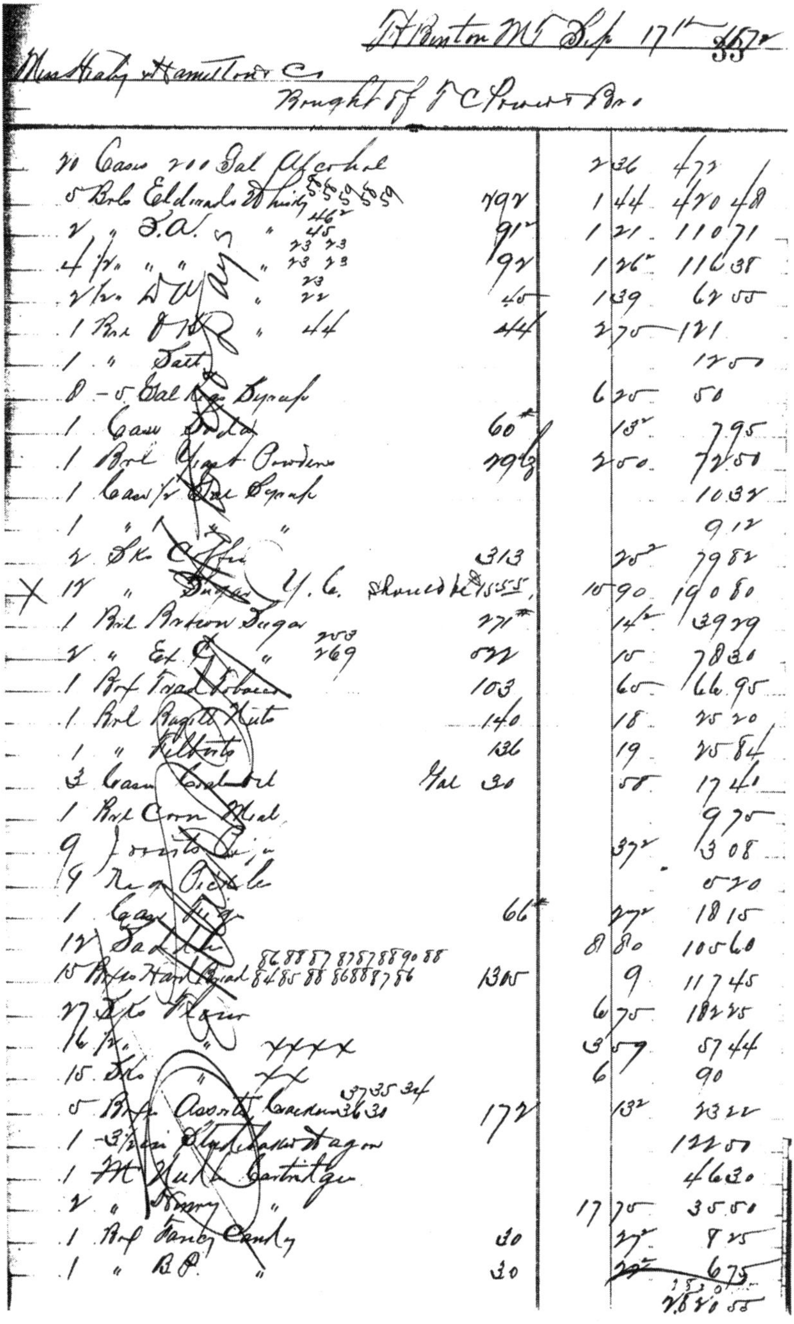

Account book of T. C. Power & Bro. showing sales to Healy & Hamilton of 200 gallons of alcohol and more than 500 gallons of whisky in the fall of 1872. (Power Papers, MC 55, vol. 214, Montana Historical Society)

However, the HBC seemed to have had no more success than Lieutenant-Governor Morris in getting John A. Macdonald to take action. In 1873, the company's chief commissioner, Donald A. Smith, explained:

> The Saskatchewan Country at this moment certainly appears to be in a thoroughly lawless and deplorable condition, entirely without protection notwithstanding that it is invaded by bands of men across the line bringing with them intoxicating drinks and in their dealings with the natives so acting as to make it a matter for surprise that even worse evils than those now existing have not sprung from such state of things.
>
> Representations to this effect I have again and again made to the Dominion Government; indeed in every quarter from which relief was likely to be had, but so far unfortunately without any action have been taken to provide the much-needed protection.[33]

As a result of the presence of American traders and its lack of success in getting the Canadian government to act, the HBC abandoned Rocky Mountain House in 1874, and for the first time in forty years, tried to take some of its trade south to the Bow River. By this time, the imminent arrival of the NWMP had dried up some of the whisky traffic, but American traders could still compete

View of Fort Whoop-Up with Blood Indians in the foreground. Although some believe the flag is American, it is most likely a trading banner. This photograph was taken in 1878, four years after the arrival of the NWMP. (Hook View Company)

because they could stock a larger supply of trade goods and often sell them cheaper than the HBC could. American goods could be shipped inexpensively on steamboats coming up the Missouri River to Fort Benton, while the British goods had to traverse a long and expensive water route from the shores of Hudson Bay or from the depot in Winnipeg.

Attempts by missionaries to suppress the liquor traffic in the West appeared to be no more successful than those by the HBC, yet they too were blamed by the whisky traders for telling "lies" about them. One denizen of Fort Whoop-Up stated:

> An old preacher travelling through the country, had met a lot of the boys just returning from a successful trading expedition, taking a slight recreation and feeling generally happy. He being evidently unused to the rough hospitality and expressions of frontier life, sent a lengthy report to the Canadian press, painting a most fearful picture of outlawry and crimes committed upon the British Indians.[34]

He was referring to the Reverend George McDougall, who was travelling to Fort Benton in the summer of 1873 and seeing the whisky forts for the first time. His party included his missionary son, John, superintendent Dr. Lachlin Taylor, teacher A. J. Snyder, and two Indian guides. A good indication of what they saw was provided in the memoirs of Reverend John. When they crossed the Oldman River near the present site of Fort Macleod, they came upon the ominous signs of a recent fight, with several dead horses lying about. From there the party went downstream, arriving at Fort Kipp at sunset. John McDougall wrote: "Here we met the first white men we had seen since leaving Edmonton, and, with one exception, they were a wild-looking lot, all but this one being more or less under the stimulus of alcohol, and all heavily armed."[35]

While the others in the missionary party made camp, John McDougall obtained directions and information from the only sober man in the fort. They were fed by a Spaniard who was especially kind to them, and that evening Dr. Taylor held a church service, which was well received, some of the men having tears in their eyes. The next day the party proceeded on to Fort Whoop-Up, accompanied by some of the traders at Fort Kipp. During their ride, Reverend John was disturbed at how casually the traders referred to the killing of Indians, considering it "a meritorious act."[36]

At Whoop-Up, they met John Weatherwax, "Dutch Fred" Wachter, and carpenter William Gladstone, and while they were having lunch with them near the river, they were suddenly surrounded by a wild, whooping, swearing troop of horsemen. They had just arrived from the northeast after a fight with some

Indians and had a wounded man among them. They demanded that Dr. Taylor treat him, and when the younger McDougall tried to explain that the clergyman was a doctor of divinity and not a doctor of medicine, they refused to listen and became quite belligerent. Finally, Gladstone, with the assistance of chief trader D. W. Davis, convinced the drunken men to go on to the fort. The missionary party then packed up and quickly headed south for Fort Benton.

Upon his return home to Fort Edmonton, George McDougall shared his first-hand knowledge with a number of clergymen, politicians, and HBC officers. His first contact was with Robert Hamilton, chief inspector for the HBC, who passed on the missionary's information to Government House in Winnipeg. "When in Edmonton," he wrote, "I had the pleasure of meeting with the Rev. G. McDougall, a most energetic and intelligent Missionary of the Wesleyan Church, who had just returned from a trip to Benton. He represented these Posts as being perfect sinks of iniquity."[37] McDougall wrote to the Reverend George Young telling him that he saw six American forts on Canadian soil, three being as large as HBC posts and occupied by some two hundred men who revealed their "desperate wickedness."[38] He also wrote a detailed letter to Donald A. Smith, commissioner of the HBC, stating:

> Last September and October I crossed the plains from Edmonton to the Missouri & visited the different forts located by the Americans on our rivers. I also carefully observed the condition of the natives and the impression received was that an unmitigated wrong is being inflicted on a wretched helpless people, and that on Dominion soil. Last spring upwards of 50,000 robes and other pelts to large amount were carried over to Benton. These, almost without exception, were purchased, not with the ordinary liquors used in trade, but with a drugged alcohol which has poisoned scores, if not hundreds of the Blackfeet, and producing any amount of misery that cannot be written.[39]

In the end, the pressures exerted by Lieutenant Governor Morris, the missionaries, the HBC, and, ultimately, the British ambassador finally produced results some four years after the illicit trade had started on British territory and three years after it had come to the attention of Sir John A. Macdonald and the Canadian government. During the interim, scores of Blackfoot had fallen victim to the liquor trade—their ranks seriously decimated by drunken quarrels and by the deadly effects of the whisky itself. Macdonald had the reputation of putting off important matters as long as possible; in this instance, his delays were deadly to the Blackfoot nation.

10. *Chaos and Misery*

The chaos and misery created by the whisky traffic continued into its fourth year as traders ranged far and wide in their competition for buffalo robes. By now, there were forts, or sometimes one-room shacks, dispensing liquor from just about every place where the Blackfoot wintered. Archaeologist Margaret Kennedy conservatively estimates that there were more than fifty such trading establishments on the Canadian side of the line during the early 1870s.[1] These were along the Belly, Oldman, Bow, Elbow, Sheep, and Highwood Rivers, and in the vicinity of Waterton Lakes, Porcupine Hills, Lee's Creek, Blackfoot Crossing, and the Cypress Hills. Some were used only for a season and then abandoned, the deserted buildings either burned by Indians or destroyed by the traders themselves to prevent their competitors from using them. Others, such as Whoop-Up, were occupied year-round and provided semi-permanent living quarters for some of the traders and wolfers.

Most of the establishments handled some trade goods, such as blankets, utensils, and cloth, but their profits came from liquor, either whisky or pure alcohol flavoured with caramel, tobacco, and other ingredients. Another stock in trade for the larger forts were repeating rifles and ammunition. With these weapons, the Blackfoot could kill more buffalo and bring back more robes to the traders. An additional popular item was the revolver, and by now just about every grown man carried one. The Blackfoot could use these handguns in hunting and as defensive weapons to protect themselves from enemy attacks, but also, regretably, to settle arguments that often arose at or near the whisky forts. Quick-firing guns and whisky are a bad combination, and this became tragically true for the Blackfoot.

The results of the whisky trade were catastrophic for the Blackfoot people. Oblate missionary Constantine Scollen summed up the situation succinctly when he wrote that the traders

> carried on to an extraordinary extent the illicit traffic in intoxi-
> cating liquor to the Blackfeet. The fiery water flowed as freely,
> if I may use the metaphor, as the streams running from the
> Rocky Mountains, and hundreds of the poor Indians fell
> victims to the white man's craving for money, some poisoned,

some frozen to death whilst in a state of intoxication, and many shot down by American bullets.[2]

He said that after the 1870 smallpox epidemic, many Indians tried to drown their grief in alcohol.

> They sold their robes and horses by the hundred for it, and now they began killing one another, so that in a short time they were divided into several small parties, afraid to meet … It was painful to me to see the state of poverty to which they had been reduced. Formerly they had been the most opulent Indians in the country, and now they were clothed in rags, without horses and without guns.[3]

Because much of the trade took place in the winter months, death by freezing was not uncommon, as a person could easily wander away from a drinking party or lose his way coming home from a whisky fort and lie down to die on the prairie. It was hard enough for a sober person to keep a sense of direction if a snowstorm should suddenly strike, but for someone who was intoxicated there was little chance of survival. Also, whisky often became the catalyst that turned a minor argument into a fatal encounter or a chance meeting into a senseless killing. People were murdered because they refused to share their liquor, or because they had no liquor to share. They were killed because they were chiefs, or because they were parents, or because they were strangers. They were shot, beaten to death, or sliced open with skinning knives. And if the weather or disputes didn't get them, sometimes the liquor itself accomplished this goal, as the poisonous effects of blue stone, laudanum, or other noxious additives were more than the body could stand.

Chiefs lost their authority over their bands, and if they were not drinking themselves, they found themselves acting as mediators, trying to prevent a quarrel from escalating into a bloody feud. Blackfoot tradition allowed for murders, or even accidental deaths, to be settled by a payment of horses to the bereaved family; alternatively, a person might avoid retribution by fleeing from his camp and living with another Blackfoot tribe until his family could make the appropriate amends. But even with these provisions, anger, hostility, and fear became part of the daily lives of the Blackfoot—not dreading an attack from an enemy but rather a violent and often fatal confrontation in their own camps as a result of excessive drinking.

As Blood Indian Red Tail Feathers stated, "The Indian took to liquor like a duck takes to water. And then began the wholesale slaughter of humans which were, for the greatest part, Indians."[4]

Many stories were told by the Blackfoot about the tragedies caused by alcohol. One was of Hind Bull, a chief of the Siksika tribe, who was drinking with Mule Painted Lodge at a whisky post near Blackfoot Crossing. The two men were friends and had never quarrelled before, but in their drunken state they got into a bitter argument, and Mule Painted Lodge crossed the Bow River to the south side to get his rifle. Standing on the bank, he fired a shot across the water at Hind Bull but missed him. Hind Bull then picked up his gun, returned the fire, and killed his friend.[5]

Also among the Siksika was a minor chief named Spotted Calf who had a litany of alcohol-related problems. On one occasion, he and Calf Child, another chief, went with their families to a whisky fort, where they all got drunk. During this time, Calf Child tried to molest his friend's wife, but Spotted Calf stumbled upon them and the attacker fled. In his drunken anger, Spotted Calf wandered through the camp searching for the culprit, and when he failed to find him he shot Calf Child's younger brother instead.[6]

This was not the only drunken dispute between these two leaders. On another occasion, Calf Child bought some whisky and then sat in a circle with his friends, passing it around. When Spotted Calf and another man saw them, they sat down, hoping the chief would offer them a drink. When he didn't, one of the men in the circle suggested, "Give a drink to our friends." Instead, Calf Child shot Spotted Calf in the chest. As the wounded man toppled over, he drew his own gun and shot his attacker in the arm.[7] Later, the matter was resolved by an exchange of horses.

Blood Indians inside Fort Whoop-Up in 1881. Note that the windows provided sunlight but were high enough to prevent anyone from climbing into the rooms. Photograph by George M. Dawson. (Glenbow Archives NA-302-2)

One of the most well-known stories relating to the tragedy of the whisky trade concerned a Blood band known as the Bear People, led by Young Sun and Many Shot, the sons of Hide Scraper. Their mother was Bear Woman, a shaman who once had a dream that gave her the power of the bear. She, in turn, named some of her children after bears, such as Going to the Bear, White Bear, and Spotted Bear, all of whom believed they had received the power and strength of the bear.[8] They had the reputation of being wild and turbulent, but when whisky was introduced into their lives, they completely lost control. Not only did they sell virtually everything they had for liquor, but when they had nothing more to trade, they beat up people and stole their liquor from them. Not surprisingly, many people were afraid of them and avoided them whenever possible.

In the Siksika tribe, a chief named Bull Turning Around, leader of the Slapped Faces band, killed a friend in a drunken brawl and decided to drown his sorrows in alcohol. In the fall of 1872, while camped on Crowfoot Creek, he sent one of his wives to fetch a young man to come and drink with him. The horses were brought to the chief's lodge, but just as the two men were prepared to leave, they were stopped by Feather Collar, the young man's father. He was aware of the troubles that had been occurring near the whisky fort at Blackfoot Crossing, especially since the Bear People band had arrived, and did not want his son to go.

The young man respected his father's wishes and stayed in camp, so Bull Turning Around sent his wife to find Bull Horn, a minor chief from another band, who agreed to go and drink with him. Feather Collar also tried to dissuade this man, but he would not listen. After the pair had made their purchases at the fort, they were immediately accosted by one of the Bear People, who invited them to come and drink with them. "Just come over, we've got some stuff to drink," he said. "Leave your stuff; we won't touch it."[9] When they went into the brush, the two men saw that the Bear People had their whisky in a skin bag and were drinking it like horses being watered. Bull Horn took very little, but Bull Turning Around stayed with the bag until it was empty and he was thoroughly intoxicated.

When the two Siksikas decided to leave, some of the Bear People went with them, demanding to start on their supply of liquor. They followed the men to a small coulee where Bull Horn finally agreed to share some of his whisky, but insisted that afterwards they would go their own separate ways. Young Sun, of the Bear People, took offence at this remark and got up and started to dance, singing, "I'm looking for someone I want to kill." Realizing the danger of their situation, Bull Horn lifted the almost catatonic Bull Turning Around onto his horse and led him away towards the river crossing. However, they had gone only a short distance when the chief's horse became skittish, jerked the rein out of Bull Horn's hands, and galloped back along the trail. When horse and rider got to the Bear People, Young Sun shot the chief in the head. When Bull Turning

Around fell to the ground, others in the party pounced on him, drunkenly slashing him with their broad knives.

Feather Collar had been worried ever since the chief and his companion had left their camp, and as he looked across the river, he could see the Bear People drinking in the coulee. He saw someone fall from a horse, but at that distance couldn't tell who it was. He quickly sought out his friend Scalp Walker, and they rode over to the place where the Bear People were still drinking.

"Who's that you killed?" asked Feather Collar, pointing to the body on the ground.

"We killed one of ourselves, not a Blackfoot," was the reply.[10]

Feather Collar knew they were lying, but when he walked over to the body, the face had been so slashed that at first he didn't recognize it. On closer examination, he realized it was their chief. Young Sun was just saddling his horse, but Scalp Walker yelled to him, "Don't bother putting that saddle on. I'm going to kill you."[11]

At this point, fighting broke out. Scalp Walker dashed towards the Bear People chief but instead of trying to escape, Young Sun gave the cry of a grizzly bear and ran forward, brandishing his knife. Scalp Walker, however, was armed with a gun and shot Young Sun in the chest; Feather Collar, who was right behind them, saw that Young Sun was still alive, so he shot him in the face and killed him.[12]

Bull Horn had seen the killing of Bull Turning Around and had rushed back to his own camp crying. When people asked him what had happened, he told them about the murder of the chief. This was the last straw; the people had had enough of the Bear People. Mounting their horses, several Siksika warriors swept down on the Bear People's camp, determined to exterminate them. Many Shots, the co-leader of the Bear People, was killed when he tried to ride away. His father, Hide Scraper, mounted a fast horse, only to be pursued and killed on the banks of the Bow River. Others fled into the brush, but one by one they were hunted down and slain.

Bear Woman, the mother of the chiefs, was trapped by White Eagle, a leader of the Slapped Faces band, and when she begged for mercy he said, "You should have brought up your children right, so this wouldn't have happened!" and killed her.[13]

When the Siksikas gathered at the now-deserted Bear People camp, they began to loot it of religious objects, clothing, lodges, and utensils. In the search, Three Eagles discovered the wife of Young Sun, who was hiding. "I take this woman to give to my mother," he proclaimed. But just then another man rode up and said, "Why is this woman alive? She is the wife of the leader." He then shot and killed her. Two other women were found hiding in the camp and they too were slain.[14] When the Siksika were finished looting, all that was left in the camp were the fireplaces.

Buck Running Rabbit, a Siksika elder, explained what happened next.

> Only one Bear Person got back to the Bloods. He was Spotted
> Bull. These Bear People were always making trouble for the
> Bloods and tried to make trouble also for the Blackfoot. After
> all was over, one man went to the Bloods and said, there are no
> more Bear People. He said the Slapped Face band did it and
> now there would be no more trouble.[15]

Added Wolf Leg, another Siksika elder, "All the Bloods were glad that the
Bear People were killed, for they hated these people. There were no hard feelings
between the Bloods and the Blackfoot. The Bloods were pleased."[16]

A whisky fort on Sheep River was the site of another Blackfoot tragedy. Some
Siksikas had been drinking when a visitor named Calf Robe tried to cadge a drink
from Old Person, son of the band chief Flathead Bull. Instead of treating him, Old
Person, who was known to be a mean and vicious drunk, beat the visitor unmerci-
fully with his whip. Calf Robe then staggered over to Running Rabbit and asked
the chief for help. When his friend demurred, Calf Robe accused him of being a
coward, one of the worst insults that can be levied against a Blackfoot. The chief
replied, "I don't want to hurt any of my children [i.e., his followers] but I will kill
him for I'm not afraid. Where is he?" Calf Robe replied, "He is still at the traders."[17]

The two men hid in the bushes beside the trail to the whisky fort, but they
were seen by someone who warned Old Person to take a different route home.
In his intoxicated condition, however, the young man would not listen to reason.
"I'm taking the direct road," he said, and set off singing, "We have to die when
we have to die."[18] As he approached the bushes, the two men confronted him and
dared him to strike Calf Robe again. In reply, the young man got off his horse,
took his whip, and lashed out at Calf Robe several times. At this point, Running
Rabbit stepped in and shot him, killing him instantly.

Next day, when people were relatively sober, Running Rabbit's followers
broke camp and no one attempted to stop them, nor was anything further done
to avenge the murder. The dead boy's father said, "It was his own fault. Calf Robe
didn't say anything. I've been trying to stop my son from doing this, for he was
always mean when drunk. I'm not angry."[19] Then, to keep the peace, Calf Robe
sent two horses to the dead man's family.

Another incident occurred near Spitzee Post when a group of Blood and
Siksika men were drinking. During the evening's revelry, someone fired a shot
into a lodge and wounded a man in the hand. The man's son, Lone Rock, burst
out of the lodge with his gun and went searching for the guilty party, but without success. In his drunken rage, he fired a shot into a nearby teepee and struck
Flathead Bull's wife in the leg.

Next morning, an elder took the role of peacemaker and went to Flathead Bull's lodge. He said, "Your wife was shot by Lone Rock. We still don't know who shot his father. I'm going over there to ask Lone Rock to pay you."[20] The elder then went to Lone Rock's father and told the family to pay one horse in compensation. Lone Rock agreed and turned one of his best horses over to the mediator. The horse went to Flathead Bull, not his injured wife, as he was the chief of the band. In this way, a tense situation created by whisky was resolved peacefully.

This period was remembered in the Blackfoot winter counts as the "time we Indians killed ourselves by drinking."[21]

Of the four tribes, the Bloods suffered the most disruption and chaos in their lives, as Fort Whoop-Up and the Belly River forts were in the heart of their hunting grounds. Several of their leading chiefs and scores of men and women died during this time as a result of the whisky traffic. When Donald Graham passed through the area in the spring of 1873, he noted that a group of Bloods known as the Mule family, which had once numbered twenty-eight lodges, had become involved in a feud with another band and "at the time I speak of, the Mule family had been reduced to two lodges and the survivors had taken refuge in the South Piegan camp in order to avoid complete extinction."[22]

This group, which later became known as the Many Children, were part of the Many Fat Horses band in the early 1870s; their leader was an outstanding chief named Many Spotted Horses. The Mules were a big family, under the leadership of their father, Not Afraid of the Gros Ventres. One of his daughters was married to No Chief, a half-brother of the famous plainsman Jerry Potts. No Chief was a quiet, thoughtful man, and Many Spotted Horses had shown a marked liking for him over the rowdy brothers-in-law and invited him to stay in his lodge.

One day, several of the Mules were going to the trading post, so No Chief asked his brother-in-law, Morning Chief, to get him a gallon of whisky. When the party returned, word was sent to No Chief to come and pick up his keg. Many Spotted Horses warned the young man that his brothers-in-law were jealous of him and to be on his guard.[23]

No Chief rode over to the Mules's camp, and as he tied his horse to a travois, he noticed that most of the men in the camp were drunk. When he entered Morning Chief's lodge, his brother-in-law invited him to sit down. "There is your whisky," he said, pointing at a wooden cask, then prepared a pipe for the two of them to smoke. Just then they heard the voice of another brother-in-law, Hairy Face, who was standing at the entrance to the lodge. "I see that No Chief is here again," he said. Then he staggered inside and sat beside him.

"He is here on a friendly visit," said Morning Chief. "Don't be quarrelsome."

Hairy Face began singing a loud and boisterous drinking song, and when he finished, he grabbed No Chief by the arm and tried to throw him out of the lodge. When they reached the doorway, No Chief pulled away from the drunken man and sat down again. Morning Chief did nothing; he just sat and watched.

Finally, No Chief decided to leave. He picked up his cask and had stepped outside when Hairy Face cried out, "Come out everyone! Now we have No Chief where we want him." As the crowd gathered, No Chief panicked and shot Hairy Face in the back and killed him. When the head of the family, Not Afraid of the Gros Ventres, heard the shot, he came outside and saw that his son was dead. As he chanted a wailing song, he went after No Chief who was desperately trying to reload his gun. "I'll show you how to capture this man," said the chief, grasping No Chief by the shoulders. At this, No Chief dropped his gun and grabbed his war knife. As the crowd closed in, he made a vicious thrust and sliced the chief's stomach open so cleanly from hip to hip that his intestines fell out. Not Afraid of the Gros Ventres stumbled, gave a cry, and fell to the ground, mortally wounded.

Big Snake, another son of the leader, grabbed No Chief from behind, but the desperate man swung his arm back and cut his adversary's shoulder. Big Snake jumped back in pain, and as he did so, Good Young Man, another brother, shot and killed No Chief. Big Snake, now the leader of the clan, told the others, "We will leave No Chief here. We won't bury him."

A young boy from the camp hurried over to the lodge of Many Spotted Horses to spread the news about the killings, and that No Chief's body had been left to rot in the sun. Crooked Back, the mother of No Chief, heard the news and announced that she would bring her son's body home for burial. She hitched a travois to her horse and went to the Mules's camp, wailing as she neared the body of her son. When Good Young Man saw her approaching, he stopped her and said, "What are you doing here?" She replied, "My child, I have come to look after my child. You have killed him. I want to bury him." This angered Good Young Man, and in his drunken rage he shot and killed her.

At the time of his mother's murder, Jerry Potts was working for Joe Kipp as a wrangler at Fort Kipp. When he heard of the killing he said, "This isn't right. They had no reason to kill her. I'll get revenge by killing anyone I see from that family."

Some time later, the Mules moved from their hunting grounds to a camp close to Fort Kipp where they could trade their buffalo robes for more whisky. One day, Good Young Man caught a ride with Morning Writing who was going to the fort. When they went inside to trade, someone told them about Jerry Potts's threat and said they had been crazy to come to the fort. When they heard this, Morning Writing and Good Young Man got back on the horse and were riding away when they were seen by Potts, who was driving the fort's horses to the river.

"I said I wouldn't spend my time crying," he said. "I said I would get my revenge and I will."

Potts saddled a fast horse, grabbed his gun, and followed the two men. They saw him and urged their horse to go faster but they were riding double and could not keep ahead of their pursuer. As he got close, Potts fired a shot at the men but missed. Then, as they came to a steep bank, Potts fired again, striking Good Young Man in the spine. As he watched him tumble down the bank, he was satisfied that his mother's death had been avenged.

By this time, Many Spotted Horses had grown disgusted at the effects of excessive drinking on his followers and at the rowdy actions of the Mules, so he gave up his position as leader and moved to the Lone Fighters band. Big Snake inherited the leadership of his family, which broke away from the Mules and became known as the Many Children band. However, the band members continued to cause trouble within the tribe, usually when they were drunk and looking for a fight. A short time after they separated, they became involved in a brawl with members of the All Tall People band. They were soundly beaten, but as they were running away, one of the Many Children killed an innocent old man named Porcupine Bull, a minor chief of the band. This resulted in a long and deadly feud that caused several deaths on both sides.[24]

The anger of the Blackfoot, combined with alcohol, did result in the deaths of a number of traders. Whisky trader Charley Rowe recalled a scene that he encountered near the present site of Fort Macleod while walking along the ice of a stream.

> When I got to the top of the rise, I saw the most blood-curdling thing that I ever expect to see in this life. There at the bottom of the ravine were two dead men. From appearances, they had been killed the night before. The tent was torn down, and I believe there must have been a thousand arrows lying around in the snow. My first impulse was to run for camp and prepare for a fight, but I thought better of it and went down to the bottom of the ravine to examine the bodies, and found them to be the fellows who had started ahead of us—men that I knew very well. One was a little fellow from Missouri, and the other an immense Frenchman who had come down from eastern Canada.[25]

Upon examination, Rowe saw that the Missourian had been shot between the eyes with an arrow and had died quickly. "The big fellow, though," he added, "had made a terrible fight. There must have been twenty-five Indians, I imagined, from the tracks, and they had fought down the ravine for twenty-five yards before they had killed him."[26]

Although killings occurred, there appeared to be little or no animosity shown to the whisky traders as a whole. As Wolf Moccasin commented, "The Indians liked Fort Whoop-Up. There was a lot of life there."[27] But they heartily despised certain individuals who cheated them, or were particularly abusive, or insulted them. The most hated of all the traders was undoubtedly

Jerry Potts, of Blood-Scottish parentage, worked for the whisky traders and later became a scout for the NWMP. (Glenbow Archives NA-1237-1)

William Bond, a half-black, half-Mexican whom the Bloods called *Estapomau*, or "Money." He was accused of murdering Indians, including children, raping their women, and cheating them in the trade.

One time, when Bond was working for him, Joe Kipp was having trouble with a Blood chief named Calf Shirt who kept demanding free liquor. In order to get rid of him, Kipp bet Calf Shirt that he could not beat Bond in a wrestling match. Bond had a powerful physique and had been known to kill people with his fists. To lure the chief, Kipp promised him a keg of free liquor if he could win the match. Calf Shirt agreed, but first he demanded that he be given a drink. As a storyteller stated, "Kipp had no alternative but to give in to his demands. He filled his tin cup which he had tied to a piece of string around his neck, which would be about a quart sized cup. When he finished the drink he pulled out his pipe and had a smoke. Four times he drank and smoked. He was ready to wrestle now."[28] According to one account, the whisky was laced with poison but it had no effect on the chief.

The two men faced each other and Bond made a grab for the chief, wrapping his huge arms around his waist in an attempt to throw him to the ground. But Calf Shirt proved to be more than a match for the murderous Bond. Four times Bond rushed the chief, each time pummelling him and thrusting his full weight on him, but Calf Shirt stood as firm as a post. When at last Bond backed off, Calf Shirt grabbed him, lifted him bodily in the air, and hurled him to the ground, knocking him unconscious. The Bloods were delighted that Kipp had lost his bet and was forced to give free whisky to their chief. It was one of the few times the Bloods got the best of the whisky traders.

Where Indian women were concerned, their relationships with whisky traders varied greatly from situation to situation. Some men, like Al Hamilton, had a permanent marriage to one woman that lasted long past the whisky-trading era. Others had brief sexual liaisons, while still others had "wintering wives," that is, a relationship that lasted only for the season. Many traders were quite casual about their women. Fred Kanouse, for example, told Cecil Denny "that the squaw he then had was Number 57."[29] While travelling through the area, Alex Staveley Hill noticed that Dave Akers, the last owner of Fort Whoop-Up, had a girl who was only about fourteen years old. Akers told him that she was his sixth mate; he traded each one in for a younger woman after about six months. He paid each of the fathers a horse worth about five dollars and the mothers a couple of handfuls of tea for the girls. But he was proud of the fact that he never beat his wives.[30]

According to North-West Mounted Policeman Cecil Denny,

> As nearly all these traders had married Indian women, according to the Indian custom, that is by purchase, and in many cases the women were connected with some of the leading chiefs, they

had a certain influence through these women with the Indians themselves for, strange as it may seem, the women in most cases became attached to the white men with whom they lived, and used their influence in the tribe for the benefit of their husbands, and in many instances would undertake to trade whisky in the camps for robes, bringing back their robes and taking pleasure in making a sharp bargain for their masters.[31]

A few years after the liquor traffic was shut down, a Bentonite wrote about his Blood Indian wife, as follows.

My lawful partner is a squaw, and she is not a high-toned lady, as some persons may suppose on account of direct descent from the Bloods. When I first met her she was picking huckleberries amidst the tangled briars of the forest in the vicinity of Chief Mountain. To my unsophisticated eyes she seemed a beauty, and as the father of her family offered to transfer her to me for a broken down pony, I considered it a cheap way to make an end to my lonely existence and associate myself with a life partner, whom it was my intention to get married to at the first meeting of any chance parson or other person authorized to perform the ceremony.

I felt proud of my new possession, and would gaze for hours upon her unwashed countenance with the deepest admiration ... Her ways were very aboriginal, but I expected that in the course of time they would give way to the usages of civilization, and that she would learn to wash her face regularly and keep her hands from interfering with the victuals in preparation in the camp kettle or frying pan ... [But] the conclusion has forced itself upon me that my woman will never turn out to be a princess ... I have become so used to her ways that I don't mind her shortcomings very much anymore, and I can relish a meal even if the food has been prepared and dished up in utensils which are usually washed by dogs and cats. White strangers hardly ever visit us, and we never invite any of them to our fireside. I have been what I am through choice, and social status does not bother me.[32]

He concluded by saying, "My two boys left me about six months ago to join a party of Indians on a horse stealing expedition against the Sioux. I have not heard from them since, but suppose they are all right."[33]

John LaMott showed a humorous indifference to a Blackfoot girl who came to live at Spitzee Post. "I am a white woman now," the woman said proudly. "I am going to live with the whites."[34] She wanted to learn how to cook and decided to start with dried apples. She filled a camp kettle with them, pressed them down, added water, and put them on to cook. Then she took some dried beans and handled them the same way. As LaMott watched from a hiding place, he saw the apples grow and grow, spilling over the sides of the kettle while the frantic woman tried to scoop them up and wrap them in dishrags.

"You ought to have seen her when the beans began coming out," he said. "It just kept her jumping from the bean pot to the dried apple pot, and she filled those rags full of beans and dried apples."[35]

That the woman should be the butt of LaMott's humour is not surprising, as it reflects the role in which most of the traders saw these women. They were possessions, bought and discarded as they pleased, treated well or beaten as they wished, and killed if they displeased their lord and master. As one Blood elder stated, "The men who married the Indian women used to beat them and killed many of them."[36] Another said, "The women were treated badly when they were drinking. Some married white men and then they began to drink too. It was bad. It was devastating to us the way the white man treated us at that time."[37]

It should be pointed out, however, that within the Blackfoot camps there were many women who did not drink, or did so in moderation. Often their task was to maintain some sort of order in their household when their husbands got drunk. They put their mates to bed when they were intoxicated, tied them up when they became violent, and withstood the brutal treatment they sometimes received when the men became angry and abusive. These women limited the amount they drank, moved away from their camp when activities became violent, and placed their trust in their spiritual protectors to look after them.

Many older men also showed restraint during this difficult period, accustomed as they were to the traditional twice-yearly visits to the Hudson's Bay Company posts. The worst offenders were the young and middle-aged men. They plunged into this strange new world with no concern for the future and no memory of the past. They lived for the moment when alcohol carried them into a delirium of intoxication and into a self-destructive way of life they had never known before. Their aggressions, once directed towards their enemies, now pointed inward towards their own people. They were easily offended, often reacting to an innocent comment or action with such violence that death or permanent injury was the inevitable result. They drank, they argued, they fought, and they killed.

In later years, many Blackfoot were convinced they would have been wiped off the face of the earth had the North-West Mounted Police not come and driven the whisky traders away. And they were probably right.

11. *Unsettled Times*

When the legislation to create the North-West Mounted Police (NWMP) was passed by the Canadian Parliament on 23 May 1873, it didn't take long for the information to reach Fort Benton.[1] Within days of receiving the news, Tom Power and Charles Conrad, on behalf of I. G. Baker, were in touch with Indian superintendent James Wright, telling him they wanted to get out of the whisky business. With skilful guile, they informed the official that "they are tired of the business. They find that it has injured their legitimate trade. That it impoverishes the Indians."[2] The latter comment is ludicrous given that they were the primary agents of the trade and knew exactly what effects their nefarious trade was having on the Indians north of the line.

Wright in his naïveté was elated with the proposal. "They being strong Competitors have had some fears one of the other," he said. "They now propose to abandon this business. Each says that if the other will quit, he will do so. If these men abandon this traffic we will have but little difficulty in restraining it in our own country."[3] Clearly, Wright had no idea of the real motivation behind the decision of the two companies, for he added in his report that the British government should now be encouraged to send soldiers along the border to take the final steps in suppressing the liquor traffic.

The Indian superintendent also indicated that he was in negotiations with the two companies to facilitate their abandonment of the liquor business, and implied that they may have been using the move as a bargaining chip to receive concessions from the federal government. However, almost immediately after this meeting, Superintendent Wright was notified that his office was being abolished on 30 June as a cost-cutting measure. From that time onward, Indian agents and others would have to deal directly with Washington.

This was a setback for the two whisky merchants, so Isaac Baker, who was in the company's St. Louis office, immediately appealed to the secretary of the Interior to have Wright reinstated. He praised the superintendent for opposing the whisky trade and for ordering the examination of all incoming steamboats to report those importing liquor. He said that this action alone had reduced liquor shipments by 50 per cent. "As soon as it was reported that the Superintendency was likely to be abolished," he said, "these shipments to Fort Benton commenced and is like to continue during the boating season." Baker concluded: "There is no portion of the Indian country that is so badly controlled by Whiskey Traders as Montana."[4]

The Power and Baker companies also made their views known to Deputy Marshal Charles Hard. Hard reported to Wright that "they were anxious to fight the whisky traffic [and agree] not [to] deal in the article in any manner, provided that they can be assured of the assistance that you & the Department have promised them."[5] However, the nature of the assistance was not stated, other than a promise that the government would do its utmost to wipe out the whisky trade.

When Wright learned that the superintendency would be closed, he wrote to the Indian commissioner in Washington.

> Both Mr. Hard and myself pledged the aid of the U.S. Indian Department in Montana to suppress or do all in our power toward the accomplishment of this object, the liquor traffic among the Indians in Montana. Baker & Power have gone into the matter in good faith. Now that the Superintendency is abolished there is no head to this work in Montana … In as much as the word of Supt. and Detective was pledged to Messrs. Baker and Power to see that the Contract made with them to aid in suppressing the liquor traffic was carried out, I hope that the Indian Department at Washington will take this matter in hand, and use the power of the Government to its fullest extent to wipe out this unlawful and ruinous trade among the Indians.[6]

Regardless of this setback, Power and Conrad went ahead with their plans. Interestingly, their whisky supplies were sold to Scott Wetzel (who was now in full partnership with John Weatherwax) and that firm proceeded to open a wholesale liquor business.[7] Accordingly, one might question the sincerity of Power and Conrad in wanting to suppress the whisky traffic after selling their liquor supplies to the very man who was sure to carry on the trade. In addition, Wetzel, Power, and Baker concluded a business deal that they called the "Belley [sic] River Agreement." While not spelled out, it seemed to have been a far-reaching document that was nothing less than a means of dividing up any money accrued from dealings in the Whoop-Up country. Using their own formula, Power and Baker would outfit Wetzel & Weatherwax, and perhaps other firms as well, and divide the profits. Power's business manager at Fort Benton, M. A. Flanagan, commented in the fall that "Scott Wetzel is buying a small assortment of goods here & at Bakers – Robes & Goods to be divided according to Belley River agreement."[8] And some time later, Power wrote to his trader on the Belly River saying, "We settled up the winter's business with Baker & Co. by their keeping all they made & we the same, we to pay your wages so you see they have nothing to do with your Post."[9]

Some of Tom Power's liquor stock also went to an old friend, Ben Stickney, in Helena, where Power kept his finger in that part of the business as well. For example, he told Stickney:

> [Asa] Samples [at Spitzee Post] will want some Liquor for him which you can let him have out of freight. I told him we would sell him 5 Bbls. Double Anchor at 1.75 per Gallon or if he wants Eldorado which is 20 per cent above proof, give him that at same price … If he wants any Alcohol sell it for $3.25 per Gal but that must be for cash …
>
> Jo [sic] Kipp [at Fort Kipp] may want some Alcohol and says he has the cash to pay for it. Try and see him – told him he should get it for $3.25 per Gal if he wants some time on it, all right, his paying interest, but would prefer the cash.[10]

Even more to the point was Power's correspondence with Ben Stickney in September, saying that he was sending him an assortment of liquors. "There was lots of it wanted by people from the country," he said. "Try and sell them if they have the cash, and keep mum when Charles Hard asks you any thing about what whisky you are selling."[11]

Over the summer, Power continued to receive supplies of liquor and to ship it to the consignees. On 24 August, he entered in his discharge book that he had shipped to Joe Kipp 6 barrels of OK whisky containing 41 gallons each, 12 barrels of Shawhan whisky of 42 gallons each, 14 cases of Plantation Bitters, 40 cases of Hostetters Bitters, 4 barrels of rum, 1 barrel of OD whisky, and 8 cases of pure alcohol.[12] On the same day, he shipped to Asa Sample 9 barrels of Eldorado whisky containing 45 gallons each, 10 barrels of Shawhan whisky of 44 gallons each, 9 large and 6 small barrels of unidentified liquor, 10 barrels of DA whisky, 5 cases of Hostetters Bitters, 3 cases of Home Bitters, and 106 cases of pure alcohol.[13] All of this—some 2,400 gallons of whisky, plus more than 1,000 gallons of pure alcohol—was bound for Whoop-Up country. Yet this was only the tip of the iceberg, for Deputy Marshal Hard estimated at that time that there were two hundred barrels of whisky and at least 1,200 gallons of alcohol in Fort Benton, "stored and waiting chance to ship into & through to British America."[14]

The news that the NWMP had been formed did not immediately become common knowledge in Montana—besides Power and Conrad—so most of the traders planned for their usual trafficking in whisky for the 1873–74 season.

The first public word about the Mounted Police came in September 1873 when the *Rocky Mountain Gazette* reported that "British troops had entered the Whoop-up country, and that trouble with American trappers there was 'imminent.'"[15] In fact, the NWMP had arrived in Manitoba, more than 1,000 miles east of Whoop-Up, and would not reach that place for another year. Accordingly, the story was promptly discounted, the newspaper expressing the opinion that John Power, Tom's brother, had "spun that yarn about the British red coats invading Whoop-up."[16]

John Healy wasn't so sure. Of all the traders, the firm of Healy Hamilton & Co. had the biggest investment in Canadian territory and the most to lose if their fort was closed down. Healy's first reaction was to get out of the business, so he immediately placed an ad in a Helena newspaper, with the headline "Trading Post for Sale." In it, he offered to sell Fort Whoop-Up, which he said was situated between the St. Mary and Belly Rivers, 180 miles north of Sun River Crossing. He stated:

> Said Post is finely built of Hewn Timber, is 120 x 150 feet square, has 270 feet of buildings with Stockade and Bastions: Has Blacksmith shop, Carpenter shop, three large Warerooms, Store, Stable, Coal House, Hay Corral, a well within the Fort and all the necessary buildings for the accommodation of a Trading Post.[17]

He suggested that interested parties contact him at Sun River during the next two weeks and that he would provide a "satisfactory reason for selling."[18] The advertisement appeared only once and apparently there were no takers. By this time, Healy had probably learned that the NWMP were not actually in Whoop-Up country and there seemed to be no reason to panic. Less than a month after the advertisement appeared, D. W. Davis, Healy & Hamilton's trader at Whoop-Up, arrogantly said, "Well, I can tell you, there will be no Mounted Police in this country this year. You can bet on that."[19]

This meant that for most traders, life went on as before, with whisky continuing to be sold to the hapless Blackfoot, who were becoming more impoverished and pitiful every day. Life for them had deteriorated into a benumbing and chaotic routine of killing buffalo, selling the hides, buying whisky, and killing each other or dying from the effects of the whisky in their prairie lodges.

By 1873, Whoop-Up had become known as "one of the toughest camps now existing in the Rocky Mountains" and even some Montanans who had once turned a blind eye to the liquor traffic now seemed less tolerant of the vicious trade. Commented the Republican *Helena Weekly Herald*:

At this place congregate some of the worst characters from every source, many of whom engage in the traffic of whisky to Indians, and rows which result in death are of frequent occurrence. Innocent parties, of course, are as frequently killed as are those who deal out the lightning to the red men at fabulous profits.[20]

Violence among the traders also was commonplace. Pablo Starr, a well-known mixed-blood, was killed in the Belly River area.[21] John Fairweather, a prominent prospector, noted that, in June 1873, a friend of his in Helena had received the following letter from Fort Whoop-Up:

Dear Bob. I am enjoying good health. The winter's trade was quite brisk, and for want of more exciting scenes I am now engaged in the peaceful occupation of raising a garden. My partner, Bill Akorn, got to putting on airs and I shot him and he is dead. My potatoes are looking well. Yours truly, Sandy.[22]

Trading Post for Sale

The undersigned offers for sale their Trading Post (Fort Hamilton) situated between

St. Mary's and Belly Rivers,

180 Miles North of Sun River Crossing,

Said Post is finely built of Hewn Timber, is 120x150 feet square, has 270 feet of buildings with

STOCKADE AND BASTIONS!

Has Blacksmith shop, Carpenter shop, three large Warerooms, Store, Stable, Coal House, Hay Corral, a well within the Fort and all the necessary buildings for the accommodation of a

TRADING POST

Parties wishing to engage in the Indian Trade will find this a rare opportunity, as the Post has been in successful operation for four years and the location is the best in the Buffalo Ranges A satisfactory reason for selling will be given.

For particulars call on or address the undersigned for two weeks at Sun River, M. T.

sep10daw1w   HEALY. HAMILTON & CO.

When Healy and Hamilton learned that the NWMP had been organized in Ottawa, they briefly offered Fort Whoop-Up for sale. This advertisement appeared in the Rocky Mountain Gazette *on 10 September 1873. It found no buyers.*

The principals involved likely were Sandy Cunningham, a trader at Whoop-Up, and Jacob Korn, a Fort Benton saloon keeper who was among the many Montanans to gravitate to the northern whisky fort.[23]

George Houk, a Fort Benton resident, claimed that during this time a party of black traders experienced problems when they tried to enter the Blackfoot market. Most of them had been roustabouts on the Mississippi River when they decided to go north to try their hand at trading. Outfitted at Fort Benton, they followed the trail north into the British possessions, camping across the river from Fort Whoop-Up. Houk said that they had an edge on the white traders as "the Indians were too superstitious to kill them,"[24] but also claimed they did not do well because of their unfamiliarity with the cold climate. As a result, a few of them froze to death. According to Houk, "Some of the old timers say that the whites crossed the river one dark night and massacred the whole outfit," but Houk claimed they had disbanded on their own. "At any rate," he concluded, "their coming was the means of naming another spot, the place being called 'Nigger Bottom.'"[25]

Only passing references to these black traders were made by others of that era. T. C. Power's account books record at least four blacks who dealt with the firm, including Jackson Kelly, James Vandenburg, D. E. Bond, and John Hughes, the latter two being listed as dead by 1871.[26] Wolf Moccasin, a Blood Indian, said that "the liquor supply from the nigger gangs (who travelled the country) steadily grew, until one could even find the dead lying around uncovered."[27] And in a deposition to the Canadian government, a man named Johnston commented that the whisky traders "comprise people of all classes and kinds, even to Negroes, about four hundred of them in all."[28]

Whoop-Up was also a refuge for those in trouble with the law. During the summer of 1873, Pat Lynch, alias Paddy Sky, murdered a man named Dennis McCormick in the mining camps and fled across the Rockies "making for Whoop-Up."[29] In spite of a one hundred dollar reward he was not apprehended. Similarly, when Pat Coughlin and Michael Welsh were arrested for whisky trading, they fled to the British possessions as soon as they got out on bail.[30] One of the traders at Whoop-Up, O. P. Rush, was really N. L. Mitchell, believed to be a fugitive from justice, and another trader, Fred Kanouse, remained a fugitive in Canada long after the whisky trade had ended.

Although the Montana superintendency had been closed, Deputy Marshal Hard believed he had a mandate to carry on with the task of suppressing the trade. In July he seized the steamboat *DeSmet* after he discovered it had several hundred gallons of whisky on board destined for Fort Benton. He also learned that a steamboat employee had been selling whisky off the boat along the way to individual traders and Indians. Hard notified Merritt C. Page, United States government attorney in Helena, to lay formal charges that could result in the forfeiture of the boat, but Page refused. He claimed the evidence was too weak and ordered the steamboat be released. A short time later, however, Page received instructions from Washington to proceed with the case, but by that time the *DeSmet* had already unloaded its cargo of whisky at Fort Benton and left the Territory.[31]

The failure of field officers to apprehend the *DeSmet*, which was also suspected of being used to smuggle repeating rifles and ammunition for traders Durfee & Peck, angered bureaucrats in Washington, even more so when they learned that the whisky was now stored in warehouses at Fort Benton, which legally was on the Blackfeet Reservation. This was clearly in violation of the Intercourse Law of 1834 but, of course, it had been going on for years and had been ignored by everyone.

Reacting as though the information was new to them, officials in Washington ordered in September 1873 that the Intercourse Law be enforced and that any liquor at Fort Benton be seized. However, Power, Conrad, and Wetzel had clearly been tipped off beforehand, for when the raid was made, their warehouses were empty. The Indian agent reported that "a large quantity of whiskey had a short time before they received orders to make seizure, been shipped to Helena, about one hundred miles from the reservation."[32] All the marshals found were three saloons with small amounts of liquor in stock.

As the winter season of 1873–74 approached, both Power and Conrad began to lay plans for the arrival of the NWMP, which they knew would happen in the relatively near future. Both companies had decided to continue to finance the Indian trade and supply everything except whisky. This item could come from Scott Wetzel or Ben Stickney, with the ultimate profits in robes still accruing to the Benton merchants.

The I. G. Baker firm was already directly involved in the northern trade through its own trading posts, but T. C. Power had been just a supplier. With the competitive spirit that had marked the relationship between the two companies, Power now decided to become directly involved as an honest trader who could greet the NWMP when they came west and do business with them. Tom Power had no intention of being upstaged by his rival.

In the fall of 1873, T. C. Power bought Fort Kipp from Joe Kipp and Charlie Thomas.[33] Power appointed his Fort Benton store manager, S. F. Williams, to take charge and sent him north with a large supply of goods. He was both to trade with the Blackfoot and be a supplier to smaller firms; however, Williams quickly discovered that in the Indian trade he could not compete against those selling liquor. During the winter, Tom Power commented that Williams would not be "doing much till spring, as up till that time whisky gets all the trade in that country ... There will be more money made at Whoopup than anywhere else."[34]

Williams had relatively little experience in trading, but being so isolated, he had to make his own decisions. In early January 1874, Power chided:

I fear you are too high priced on your Mdse for the boys. You will have to have an eye out and if you think you are going to carry any goods over, sell cheaper, at the same time sell for a fair profit. You ought to be able to sell out in a jobbing way to such men as Kipp and Thomas, Waxey, Dave Acres and such men. Sell to them on a/c to be paid in here in the Spring if they would rather.[35]

Power told Williams to pay $4.00 for good split robes, $5.00 for good whole robes, $2.50 for good calf robes, and $2.00 for wolf hides. Prices were lower for coyote, badger, beaver, deer, antelope, and elk. "All kinds of fine furs are a way way down in price," he added. "You will pay proportional very low prices for poor robes."[36] Williams also was instructed to cooperate with Charles Conrad, of I. G. Baker & Co., and give him anything he wanted. "I have requested Mr. Baker to write you his news about the trade," he said. "Advise with Chas. Conrad the best to do."[37]

Meanwhile, Conrad had also added a new whisky-free post to the I. G. Baker inventory. In the fall he was reported to be "building a post for winter trade on Bow river, and expect to trade there during the winter."[38] This fort was located on the Elbow River, west of the present city of Calgary, in competition with Healy & Hamilton's outpost being run again that winter by D. W. Davis. Conrad placed William Berry in charge of the new fort; he was a brother of Dick Berry, who worked for I. G. Baker at their Spitzee Post. According to journalist Leroy Kelly, the I. G. Baker crew started to build near Fred Kanouse's old post, but had not even laid down a log when they were attacked and driven away by a band of Bloods. Accordingly, they moved several miles up the Elbow to the present Springbank area, where they built their fort. However, their problems with the Bloods persisted and, during the winter, a warrior named Old Woman's Child ambushed Berry, shot and killed him, and took his scalp.[39] Mounted Policeman Cecil Denny was likely referring to William Berry in 1875 when he commented:

We ... found the remains of a white man who had been killed and buried by his trader friends some seven miles up the Elbow, at which place a trading post had stood some two years before with a party of whisky traders living in it. They had been attacked by Blackfeet their horses run off and one of their number killed and several wounded. Mr. Davis who was trading whisky a few miles above, had loaned them horses and they had all gone south. The Indians sacked the stores and burnt them to the ground. They buried their comrade, but we found that wolves had dug him up and we reburied what remained of him.[40]

As a result of this setback, Charles Conrad moved his post to the mouth of Sheep Creek and traded there all winter. Constantine Scollen, writing from his Oblate mission on the Elbow River, commented that "Conrad who is trading about 40 miles from this place will leave in the Spring with no less than about 8,000 robes; he trades no whiskey." He then added, "Between this and Belly River there are above 20 trading posts, yet everyone gets his share. The destruction of buffalo is fearful."[41] Among the traders in this area were Fred Kanouse, "Dutch Fred" Wachter, John Weatherwax, Asa Sample, and Herman Brinkman; other forts extended all the way to the Hand Hills.

Yet Healy & Hamilton's Fort Whoop-Up remained the granddaddy of them all. It was open for twelve months of the year, trading whisky and other goods directly to the Blackfoot, selling wholesale to other traders, and buying robes from wolfers and traders, either for the firm or on behalf of Tom Power.

Besides the existing posts, there were at least two new whisky forts built on the Oldman River, close to the present town of Fort Macleod, for the 1873–74 season. Joseph Girard and Joe Miller arranged for John LaMott to construct a fort, but before arrangements had been concluded, Moses Solomon heard about it and wanted to be included in the deal.

"I will send Bill Hart out there to help the boys build two houses," he said, "and I will trade in one and you can trade in the other, and it will be our protection."[42] Bill Hart, also known as Hardy Bill, was described by missionary John McDougall as a violent man—a wild, haggard, bleary-eyed, swollen-faced drunk who had threatened to cut off the head of the man who had stolen his horses and to kick it around the fort like a football.[43] LaMott, Hart, and their crew arrived at the site, "down the lower end of where Ft. Macleod is now," and before they started to work, a band of Bloods arrived and camped nearby.[44]

"They were called the Mule Family," said LaMott, "and they were supposed to be the worst bunch of Indians that were out, and so we unloaded the load right in the snow and we covered up the best we could our bed and stuff, so as to cache it."[45]

They cut a few trees, but because they had trouble dragging them to their chosen site, they decided to build the fort right around their hidden cache. When the Bloods began to bother them, LaMott told them that the sooner the fort was built, the sooner the whisky and trade goods would be delivered to them. He did not let them know that the liquor and supplies were already there. As a result, the Bloods withdrew and the men were able to build the houses and get them chinked before the weather got too cold.

Once they started trading, LaMott found that his boss, Joe Miller, was mean and vicious when dealing with the Indians. LaMott kept warning him to be more friendly, but the man wouldn't listen. When they began to run out of goods and liquor, Miller said, "I'll go in and get an outfit and another supply." Two men from the neighbouring fort were also going to Whoop-Up for more goods, so LaMott said, "Now, when you get in there you can hire those men to come back with you, because, Joe, the first opportunity [the Bloods] get to kill you they are going to kill you and it won't cost more than $10.00 for them to stay over one night with you."[46]

But Miller was a cheapskate and wouldn't pay for the men to accompany him back. William Gladstone picks up the story from there.

> This man was hauling some stuff … one day when he met some Blood Indians and they killed him and stole his stuff. An Indian boy come to Belly River and told us about it. I was there and about 10 of us started to get the dead man. We found him laying on the prairies. We took the body to the fort at Belly River and put him in a hole. We went into the shack and had a few drinks of bug juice and got talking about what we should do. There was no use staying there for the Indians would not come any more to trade. A Dutchman in the gang said we had better slide out, and it has been called Slide Out ever since.[47]

The fort in question was not the one where LaMott was working, but a new one located at the base of the buttes on the Belly River. According to Gladstone, this previously unnamed post consisted of some shacks built by "a party of men … on the Belly river to trade in the year 1873."[48] Because Miller had been killed close to the fort, the men decided to abandon it. The two forts on the Oldman River, however, continued their operations all winter.

Another new fort was built in the fall of 1873 by Kipp & Thomas—a second Fort Kipp. As soon as they sold out to Tom Power, they constructed a new post in the same vicinity and dubbed their new establishment Fort Kipp. This tended to cause some confusion, because Power often called his place Fort Kipp (and sometimes Belly River Post).

This second Fort Kipp gained notoriety and a place in Blackfoot folklore when Joe Kipp and Blood war chief Calf Shirt locked horns. This was the same chief who had tried to kill the Jesuit priest, Father Imoda, in Montana and who had defeated the Mexican-black trader William Bond in a dramatic wrestling match at the first Fort Kipp. About 1 February 1874, Calf Shirt came to Fort Kipp demanding whisky.[49]

"I have nothing," said Calf Shirt when he was asked to pay, "but I am going to have some liquor, just the same, for I am the chief; yes, the chief of this country. I'll just kill you, young man, and take what I want."[50]

Kipp knew from experience how dangerous the chief could be, especially when he was drinking, so he decided to defend himself. But just as he reached for his gun, which was hidden in a pile of blankets, the Blood chief whipped a revolver out from under his robe and pointed it at the trader. Kipp jumped to one side just as the gun exploded and the ball struck harmlessly against the wall. Calf Shirt then turned to leave the trading room, but before he could go, Kipp opened fire.

"I shot at him as he went out," said Kipp, "and think my bullet struck into his left shoulder."[51]

Meanwhile, Charlie Thomas was playing poker in the kitchen-dining room with Dick Berry, Sol Abbott, James "Diamond R" Brown, Henry Powell, and Jeff Devereaux. When they heard the shots, they dashed outside and saw Calf Shirt, gun in hand, walking across the yard towards the gate. They immediately opened fire, causing the chief to stagger but he kept on going. Outside, he walked for about 100 yards, then fell headlong into a hole that had been dug when the men were taking out sod for the fort's roof. When Kipp got to the body, he found it was peppered with sixteen bullet holes.

The traders carried the corpse to the nearby Belly River and shoved it through a hole in the ice used for watering the stock. This seemed like the easiest way to get rid of it. The body drifted under the ice to a nearby bend in the river, where it snagged on some driftwood in an area of open water near a spring. Kipp tried to dislodge it with a long pole but was unsuccessful, so the body was still in place next day when Calf Shirt's wives came to find him. Dragging the body onto the ice, they set to work to try to revive him.

Calf Shirt was said to possess the spiritual powers of the grizzly bear. His ferociousness was well known, for he had killed one of his wives and four of his own people while drunk or angry. "He frequently told his wives that he had powerful medicine," said storyteller James Schultz, "that Sun greatly favored him. If he should happen to be killed, he had instructed them, they must sing certain songs, offer certain prayers over his body for three days, and he would return to life."[52]

As his wives began the rituals, a number of curious people gathered around the body. Among them were some Siksikas under their great chief Crowfoot, who had just traded for some whisky at Fort Kipp. When there was no immediate response to the prayers and incantations over the frozen body, a medicine man from Crowfoot's group offered to help. He stood over the prostrate form singing his own holy songs, but the body remained curled up in a fetal position. When the rituals did not work, the medicine man put some whisky into a cup and poured it into the mouth of the slain chief; slowly but steadily, one of Calf Shirt's legs unfolded as if he was a man awakening from a long sleep.

The medicine man looked pleased, but a murmur of fear rippled through the crowd. The Bloods remembered that Calf Shirt had promised to return to life as a grizzly bear, even more ferocious than he had been in his former life. Crowfoot was clearly frightened by the turn of events and quickly fled the scene with a number of his followers. Meanwhile, the medicine man was just resuming his ritual when one of the Bloods stopped him.

"But I can give him another drink of whiskey and bring him back to life," protested the medicine man.

"We don't want him back with us," answered the Blood. "We will be happier if he is dead."[53]

Only his wives mourned his passing, but Calf Shirt's name had forever become a part of Blackfoot mythology because of his near revival. And the incident is remembered with humour as the time that Crowfoot became frightened.

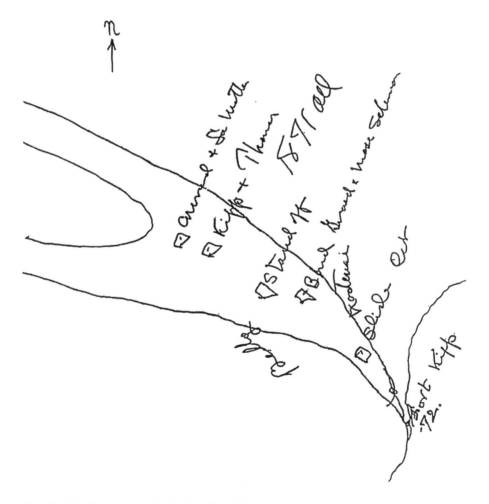

Map of whisky forts drawn by John LaMott. The Oldman River is on the right, with the Belly River at the bottom, and the Waterton (Kootenai) River at the top. The four forts on the left are on or near Standoff Bottom. (Schultz Papers, Montana State University Library)

Several miles west of the Belly River forts were a number of other whisky posts, located near Waterton Lakes and on Kennedy Creek. After Fred Kanouse recovered from wounds incurred on the Elbow River, he built a post at the north end of Waterton Lakes "half way up from the Big Lake, just where the trail started."[54] There, in partnership with George Houk, he intercepted the Kootenay Indians as they crossed back and forth over the Rockies. John Evans also wintered by the lake for one season, while John Kennedy had a shack on the creek that now bears his name.[55] When Julius Morley prospected through that region in the summer of 1873, he made no mention of whisky traders or their forts,[56] but George M. Dawson, a dominion land surveyor who went through the area in the summer of 1874 with a survey crew, met two or three traders who had been there over the winter. One was Joe Aranna, also known as Castillian Joe or Spanish Joe; his post was on the St. Mary River within the shadow of Chief Mountain. When Dawson met him, he had more than a hundred horses he had traded from the Indians, but he was worried because his shanty was south of the line and he was afraid of being arrested by American troops who were accompanying the international boundary surveyors. Dawson said that Aranna and his partners "intend moving up N of the line tomorrow or next day & burning their shanties. They have never traded two years on the same spot, always burning their shanties on leaving for fear of opposition."[57]

According to Aranna, he and his men had traded horses for whisky in the summer, then sold the horses back to the Indians for buffalo robes in the winter. He claimed they had traded fourteen thousand robes at their shanties during the 1873–74 season. "Evidently a set of desperadoes & having no regard whatever for life," wrote Dawson in his diary. "Told me that 8 Indians had been killed & 5 wounded 'round their shanties' during the last 18 days. Not long ago some Indians made a plan to shoot him but were discovered & three of them shot on the spot."[58]

When Aranna told Dawson and his crew about the immense profits to be made in the whisky trade, he gained two converts. Neil Campbell and a man named Armstrong, who were teamsters on the boundary survey crew, took their discharges and headed north, ultimately to go into the whisky business for themselves on Sheep Creek. They, like the denizens of Fort Benton and Sun River, were prepared to trade the lives and well-being of the Blackfoot for the rich harvest of buffalo robes that awaited them on the northern frontier.

While the Baker and Power companies were trying to cover their tracks and rid themselves of the reputation of being whisky dealers, the violence in Whoop-Up country continued unabated—murder was common, whisky sales remained unchecked, and the traders were completely uncontrolled. Neither the threat of the Mounties' arrival nor enforcement of the 1834 Intercourse Law prevented the traders from reaping their rich harvests from the besieged Blackfoot camps.

12. *Vagaries of the Law*

When the United States commissioner of Indian Affairs decided to enforce federal laws in 1873, including the Intercourse Law of 1834, the local marshals and Indian agents thought they might at last have a chance to suppress the whisky trade. However, this was before the influence pedlars, land-hungry settlers, and Territorial courts got involved.

The biggest difficulty experienced by law enforcement agencies centred on the status of the Blackfeet Reservation. In 1873, Washington confirmed that its southern boundary was on the Sun and Missouri Rivers, not on the Teton River as many people believed. Washington dictated that the Intercourse Law was to be enforced, and that anyone introducing intoxicating liquor to the reservation be arrested. However, the Territorial courts were not nearly so accommodating on the subject. Much of the problem related to federal versus Territorial perceptions of the law. While the federal government may have forbidden the sale of intoxicants on reservations, the Territorial government issued permits for anyone to sell their wares in the Territory, and some interpreted this licence to supercede the federal law, even though Washington said otherwise. And when land patents were being issued by the Territorial government, not only did it agree to provide these to persons residing on the Blackfeet Reservation north of Sun River, but surveyors were sent to lay out the desired parcels on the Indian lands. Thus, the Healy brothers and other settlers held land patents on reservation lands.

This became the subject of controversy after the Healys were raided. According to Indian department detective Andrew Dusold:

> On the 26th day of October 1873, having discovered that 80 gallons of whiskey had been secretly introduced and smuggled across Sun River to the north side of it, I visited the premises of J. J. & Thos. F. Healy, seized and destroyed 80 gallons of whiskey and seized a lot of property consisting of two wagons 30 horses 15 head of cattle and other property. I also arrested

Thos. F. Healy who was subsequently bound over by the U.S. Commissioner and has since been indicted by the Grand Jury.[1]

However, when the case came before Chief Justice Decius S. Wade, he threw it out and ordered that the Healys' property be returned. "The Court held the Blackfoot treaty set apart all the country north of Helena as a reservation for the Blackfoot Indians and neighboring tribes," stated the *Helena Weekly Herald*, "but that it did not necessarily follow that United States patents for lands were wholly void, and that the licenses granted to the claimants for the introduction of liquors, forbid their confiscation."[2] In spite of directives from Washington, the chief justice obviously showed a preference both for Territorial patents on Indian lands and Territorial licences to possess and sell liquor.

The people at Sun River and Benton were furious about the Healy raid, and their anger was shared by local Democrats. "Our citizens are anxious to know by what authority an organized county of Montana is turned over to Indian agents and Deputy United States Marshals," raged the *Rocky Mountain Gazette*, "and the property of citizens destroyed, and guards of soldiers placed around their premises."[3] The response of Montanans was to begin lobbying, not to suppress the whisky trade but to move the boundary of the reservation northward, so that the traffic could continue without interference from federal authorities.

They found a willing ally in Martin Maginnis, Democratic delegate to Congress and close friend of John Healy. Maginnis used the seizure as an example of federal oppression and agreed with the chief justice "that the Executive Order so far as it interfered with these rights of private property was illegal and void."[4] He demanded that the southern boundary of the reservation be moved from the Sun River–Missouri River line northward to the Marias River. He also added that "the suppression of the whisky traffic within its limits has been defeated by the decision of the courts."[5]

Maginnis claimed that moving the border northward would actually help in halting the whisky trade, as it would form a barrier between settlers and the reservation that could easily be patrolled. This desire to reduce the size of the Blackfeet Reservation cut across political lines, with both Charles Conrad and Tom Power clearly supporting the move. Wrote Conrad to Maginnis, "We think this is as it should be, and appreciate your efforts in getting that line established. If you should conclude to run for Congress again, we think this one act will secure you nineteen-twentieths of the vote of Chouteau county."[6] Wrote Tom Power to Maginnis:

> I telegraphed you yesterday to do all you can to get Reservation removed to Teton or Marias river. We are all in for it. Last spring I did not care as I thought it [confirmation of the Sun

River–Missouri River boundary] would stop the Liquor trade but it only assists it and gave irresponsible parties and smugglers a good chance and more pay for their trouble. It will be a big feather in your cap if you can assist in the removal.[7]

As a result of the political pressures applied, the federal government passed an act on 15 April 1874, reducing the size of the reservation. The Blackfoot, who had not been informed about this action, were incensed and petitioned the superintendent of Indian Affairs. Their petition stated in part:

The object in taking this country from us, is to satisfy the cupidity of not exceeding twenty men, none of whom live here but who want to turn their herds in upon rich pastures. This country between the Teton and Marias rivers is very dear to us. Here we pasture our horses in winter, and hunt buffalo for meat to feed our families. Neither our wishes, or our rights have been consulted in this new and unjust scheme to take our best country from us. Great Father! this robbery will cause our hearts to bleed and our hopes to fly away.[8]

Freight yard at Fort Benton showing bull trains being loaded near the docks in 1878. All supplies and whisky destined for northern posts were loaded at yards like this one. (Hook View Company)

But the government ignored their pleas, and contrary to Maginnis's rosy predictions, the immediate effects of the act on suppressing the whisky trade were disastrous. First, the marshal and his deputies were notified that they no longer had any jurisdiction in the towns of Fort Benton or Sun River on Indian matters, nor could they arrest whisky traders south of the Marias. This meant that they could not place either of the towns under surveillance and nab whisky traders as they headed north to Whoop-Up country. And, to make matters worse, a number of traders built shacks on the south bank of the Marias where they did not require Indian department licences, and dispensed whisky when the law wasn't around.

The situation was bad, but it got worse. Late in October 1873, the irrepressible John "Liver-Eating" Johnson was again arrested, this time while in possession of whisky on the Blackfeet Reservation. He was charged with introducing spiritous liquors into Indian country, and when he pleaded not guilty, he was tried by a jury before Chief Justice Decius S. Wade. After hearing the evidence, the jury came back with a verdict of not guilty, reasoning that Johnson was on his way to Fort Whoop-Up and was more than halfway across the reservation when arrested. Therefore, according to his lawyer, he was "taking whisky out of Indian Territory ... instead of taking it into Indian Territory."[9]

A further emasculation of law enforcement began on Christmas Eve 1873, when the marshal nabbed Joseph Carr on the Blackfeet Reservation in possession of 10 gallons of liquor. The whisky was destroyed, two horses and chattels were seized, and Carr was charged with unlawfully introducing whisky into Indian country. The case was heard in district court in the spring of 1874 by Judge Hiram N. Knowles, who, according to the United States prosecutor, "is considered by the entire bar of Montana ... as quite incompetent for the position he holds."[10]

During the trial, Carr's lawyer claimed that "at the time of said seizure, he was on his way through the Territory of Montana to Whoop-up in the British possessions; and that he was not seeking to dispose of, or introduce said whiskey into any Indian country within the jurisdiction of the United States."[11] After the evidence was heard, Judge Knowles instructed the jury as follows:

> If the jury believe from the evidence that the defendant was simply passing through the country mentioned in the Indictment with spiritous liquor with a view and for the purpose of taking said liquor beyond the limits of the United States and not for the purpose of introducing or using the same in any Indian Country within the jurisdiction of the United States, then you should find the defendant not guilty.[12]

The jury went along with these instructions and brought in a verdict of not guilty. When questioned later about his instructions, Judge Knowles stated:

> All that region of Country embraced within the boundaries specified in what is known as the Blackfoot Treaty made by Stephens [sic] was Indian Country for the purpose of intercourse with the Indians. But that the Whites had a right to pass through this Country, that this was guaranteed by treaty. And in passing through the same had a right to transport all the necessaries and luxuries of life.[13]

On this point, United States attorney Merritt Page strongly disagreed. He said that Article 7 of the 1855 treaty with the Blackfoot Nation "confers no rights upon individual citizens, as such, either to live in or pass through the Territory described, for they are not parties to the treaty. It only confers the general right upon the United States Government, which the United States may, in turn, confer upon individual citizens."[14]

Judge Knowles also had stated that "the term 'introduce' as used in the law prohibiting spiritous liquors to be introduced into an Indian Country ment [sic] the bringing of liquors into an Indian Country as its ultimate destination, the place where it was to be used." Here again Attorney Page disagreed. "If by the merest quibble," he said, "it is held that liquor traders can carry liquor *through* an Indian Country without *introducing* it *into* the same, then it is only necessary for them to set up such a claim on trial, and the law becomes a dead letter. The United States cannot show the *intention* of the party charged except by his acts." [italics in original][15]

Knowles's ruling meant that any trader could enter the Blackfeet Reservation with as much whisky as he could carry and claim he was going across the border to the British possessions, and no marshal or soldier could stop him. In effect, it opened wide the floodgates for whisky to flow unimpeded into Whoop-Up country. However, there was a development that ultimately made the decision irrelevant. Page appealed the ruling to the u.s. Supreme Court, claiming there had been an error in law, that the verdict was against the law and that Knowles's instruction to the jury had been erroneous. The Supreme Court ultimately upheld the not guilty verdict, but its judgement was not rendered until January 1875. By that time, the North-West Mounted Police were in full control of the Canadian West and the result no longer mattered. Had the decision come two or three years earlier, the situation could have been even more catastrophic for the Blackfoot than it already was.

Merritt Page was both frustrated and disgusted by the turn of events, believing that the courts were making decisions not based upon law but upon the perceived rights of local white citizens. After the Johnson and Carr cases were thrown out, he wrote to the commissioner of Indian Affairs in Washington, reviewing the entire shoddy situation. He argued that the judges time and again erred in permitting people to pass through the reservation at will, as this was clearly not allowed under the 1855 treaty. He also said that the granting of patents to individuals on Indian lands was illegal, and that revenue licences did not automatically permit persons to sell liquor on the Blackfeet Reservation. He concluded by saying, "Either the licenses and patents should be revoked or the Treaty annulled."[16] Of course, neither happened, and the law enforcement officers struggled along with uncooperative and obdurate judges, an unsympathetic local public, a federal government unwilling to ensure that its own laws were enforced, and a liquor traffic that was "a thoroughly organized system."[17]

Some cases involving whisky traders were resolved only because they were open and shut or were not appealed to a higher court. For example, in May 1873, Deputy Marshal Hard seized 160 gallons of whisky on the Blackfeet Reservation and made two arrests. The whisky traders fled to Whoop-Up while out on bail, but the whisky was destroyed and a dozen horses, three wagons, and other chattels were confiscated. Similarly, W. L. Murray was arrested but jumped his five hundred dollar bond and crossed the line to avoid jail time.[18]

Also, early in 1874, Indian department detective Andrew Dusold learned that a whisky trader had entered the Peigan camps and that his merchandise had created two days of havoc and misery. On the first night, a man shot and killed his wife in a violent quarrel only a mile and a half from the Indian agency. The next night a drunken fight occurred in which a man named Heavy Runner was shot and killed, two others were seriously wounded, and three more received minor bullet wounds. The detective caught the whisky trader, Louis Molitaire, and committed him for trial. Two members of the tribe, Medicine Weasel and Big Swan, gave testimony, and the Métis trafficker was convicted, given a one-year jail sentence, and levied a one hundred dollar fine.[19] As the Indian agent commented, "The Indian Tribes under charge of this Agency are now peacefully disposed, except when liquors are illicitly introduced among them by unprincipled white men, then disorder and violence and fighting to the death among themselves, as well as with white men, are almost sure to result."[20]

While the authorities were having trouble enforcing the laws in Montana Territory, there was no law north of the forty-ninth parallel. It was a dog-eat-dog existence, where no great value was placed on a human life, particularly on the life of an Indian. Disputes and murders among the traders themselves were relatively commonplace, and nothing was done either to prevent these acts or to punish the wrongdoers.

Americans had experienced this kind of predicament before on the frontier and sometimes reacted by establishing their own forms of government, or at least by implementing their own ideas of justice. This was true of the vigilante committees that sprang up in the gold mining camps of California in the 1850s, and then spread to Montana in the 1860s. Thomas Dimsdale, referring to the vigilantes of Montana, wrote that "the necessity for some effective organization of a judicial and protective character is more keenly felt than it is in other places, where the less exciting pursuits of agriculture and commerce mainly attract the attention and occupy the time of the first inhabitants."[21]

Such was the situation in the British possessions where there was neither law nor justice. In the winter of 1873–74, a number of wolfers and traders in the Highwood–Bow River area saw the need for some type of organization to protect them from the ongoing hostility of the Blackfoot and Assiniboine Indians. In particular, they were concerned about the increased firepower of these tribes as they acquired repeating rifles to replace their old Hudson's Bay muzzle-loaders. The wolfers and traders held a number of meetings at Spitzee Post and decided to form a quasi-government with its own police force. Because it was essentially a mounted force and many of its members were Civil War veterans, they identified their group as a cavalry unit, and named it after their meeting place. As a result, the Spitzee Cavalry was formed.

Dave Akers, not an admirer of the group, stated: "This Spitzi [sic] cavalry was a band of about a hundred wolfers who organized themselves into a band under that name. There was no police nor no law in this country then, and these fellers undertook to run it to suit themselves. They passed laws to give themselves all the best of it."[22] John Healy was more understanding, commenting:

> They thought it necessary to band together for protection and to keep order among themselves. For the Indians had become shiftless, were not hunting as they had, and some of the wild ones had killed some white men and stolen their outfits. There were some traders among them too. I knew all of them. Some of them were friends of mine. There were good men among them, the best there were in Montana, but there were some hard men also among them. They were in desperate shape.[23]

Following a democratic process, the Spitzee Cavalry elected John Evans as their captain and Harry "Kamoose" Taylor as secretary. Among its identified members were Asa and Daniel Sample, Bedrock Jim, George Hammond, Mike Walsh, and Shorty McLaughlin. Some of these men, including Evans and Hammond, had been involved in the Cypress Hills Massacre earlier in 1873. The only one of this group that Healy completely distrusted was Kamoose Taylor.[24] Born in England, Taylor had studied for the ministry before leaving to join the California gold rush. He was accused of murdering a man in Washington

Territory and fled to the British possessions, where he began wolfing in 1872 and later became a trader. According to Healy, "Taylor was what was called a 'prairie lawyer,' and it was he that instigated them." He added that Taylor was under the control of "sinister forces."[25]

During the winter, the Spitzee Cavalry drew up a "formidable" document for the signatures of all traders in the Blackfoot territory in which they promised not to sell repeating rifles or fixed ammunition. Said Akers:

> What they wanted to do was to keep arms and cartridges away from the Injuns. The Injuns was their natral enemies, coz they used to rob their traps and bait whenever they found it. A wolfer would put out pizen an' the Injuns 'ud come along an' pick up all the dead wolves they could find. The Injuns was pooty well armed, an' allus gittin' cartridges an' ammunition from us, and the wolfers was a leetle afeared to tackle 'em, so they passed a law that we wasn't to sell 'em any arms or ammunition.[26]

As delegates from the Spitzee Cavalry toured the area, they were able to obtain the signatures of many of the traders. Some did not handle guns anyway, while others were intimidated by the wolfers who threatened to burn them out if they refused. Prominent among the holdouts were Healy and Hamilton at Fort Whoop-Up, Dave Akers, who was trading for Tom Power, S. F. Williams at Fort Kipp, and Henry Kennerly on Badger Creek in Montana. Kennerly's response to the delegation is said to have been: "I shall keep on selling ammunition, so just turn yourselves loose when you get ready. There are not many of us here, but we'll try to make things interesting for you while you're doing the burning."[27] However, the wolfers left without taking any action.

When the Spitzee Cavalry visited Dave Akers, he invited them into his trading room but told them to leave their guns on the counter. Akers, however, did not surrender his own six-shooter, which he carried in his waistband. Once inside, the Spitzee Cavalrymen told Akers that he must stop selling cartridges to the Blackfoot or they would confiscate his whole outfit. The trader thought for a moment and said:

> Gentlemen, I have heard what you have to say, an' while I don't recognize your authority, coz there is no law in this country and every man is doin' pretty much as he likes, I don't mind sayin', as a personal friend to you, that you'd better reconsider this thing. It's dead wrong from fust to last; you've got no more right to dictate to me what I shall do than I have to you. We're all looking for the best of it, an' I tell you I ain't goin' to give up

what I have got here without making a kick over it, and whatever kick I make, I'll make it right here, d'you understand?[28]

The wolfers responded by threatening violence; Akers cut them short, saying
that nobody would do anything if he killed them all on the spot but if they killed
him, the other traders would make them answer for it. "Now, if you want to go
on and carry out the sentence of your court, which nobody recognizes but yourselves, you can begin but recollect I'll be right here all the time."[29]

The wolfers talked it over, then told Akers that they would do nothing this
time but if he traded ammunition to the Blackfoot in the future, they would be
back. After they left, Akers resumed selling ammunition to the Indians but the
Spitzee Cavalry never returned.

Although rebuffed by two traders, the wolfers did not give up. When they
heard that S. F. Williams, who was running Fort Kipp for Tom Power, had sold
two rifles to "Long John" Fogerty, they decided to make an example of him.
Whether this was because Williams was relatively inexperienced or whether there
were other ulterior motives is not known. Williams explained to his boss (who
was in Chicago) what happened next.

> You will see readily from the heading of my epistle that I am in
> [Fort Benton] from the North, was 17 days on the road and
> suffered considerable, arriving here on the 30th. The nature of
> my case North, is as follows, On the 15th of February I was
> pounced upon by a Mob of 12 mounted wolfers—which we
> term *Spitzee Cavalry*, who held an informal court, condemned
> me for selling 2 Carbines to a white man—Sentence: seized all
> my arms & ammunition, empanelled a fine of $1300 on me to
> be paid *immediately*, for which they seized 289 of my best
> Robes, and forbid my trading with Indians for one year.
>
> I tried to hire an Express to send a message to you at once,
> but could not get one without paying an exorbitant price. I
> then tried to hire a man to take charge of the Post, but failed to
> find any, except Jo Kipp, whom I had no faith in, as he was one
> of the *instigators* of my *prosecution*. I then sent for J. J. Healy to
> whom I arranged to make a *bona fide sale* of my entire outfit at
> cost laid down there. I am to have all of his Robes & furs there
> at going rates, the Invoice of goods to be cancelled first, then
> the expense of running Post; the balance of Profits or Losses to
> be equally divided. I am to take back what merchandise on
> hand at cost prices. This is the same as I would of done had the
> goods been mine.

If not satisfactory, I cannot help it. I am ready to quit & go home when you so choose. I am sick & tired of that kind of work … My prospects were flattering, ere the Mob made a raid on me … I think I may go back North [at the] first good opportunity and attend to settling up myself, as John [Power] says it will be impossible for him to go. [italics in original][30]

The raid also was reported in the Montana press. The *Helena Daily Independent* stated that thirteen wolfers had gone to the T. C. Power post and held court where they found the company guilty of selling firearms. They assessed a fine of one hundred dollars worth of furs to each member of the "investigating committee," and when Williams refused to comply, they seized the furs. "Mr. Williams, the agent, left the country," said the newspaper, "turned the business over to another man and struck out for Ft. Benton, a little disgusted, we presume with 'Wolfer's justice at Whoop Up!'"[31]

The *Helena Daily Herald* had a similar article, adding:

The reason given for this lawless act was, that the agent in charge of the store had been selling breach-loading rifles and fixed ammunition to the Indians. We are credibly informed that the only foundation for this charge was, that a Henry rifle and ammunition had been sold to a white man (and a "wolfer" at that), and that this wolfer had himself "swapped" them off to an Indian for robes. The post is now prepared to defend itself against another similar visitation—which has been threatened.[32]

John Healy believed there was much more to the story than a mere flexing of muscles by the Spitzee Cavalry. Rather, he was convinced that Charles Conrad, of I. G. Baker & Co., was behind the whole incident. There can be no question that Conrad was trading that winter in the Highwood–Bow River country where the agitation started, and that the two most prominent supporters of the Spitzee Cavalry were the Sample brothers, both employees of the Baker company. Conrad was probably the "sinister force" behind Kamoose Taylor that Healy mentioned. Healy also quotes an unnamed trader who said "that the Baker concern … proposed the matter, certainly had been the first to sign."[33]

If this is true, it may have been a result of the federal government placing a complete ban on the sale of repeating rifles and ammunition to Indians in Montana. In addition, there was a scandal surrounding the firm of Durfee & Peck, which had been discovered smuggling arms into Montana Territory. Both the Power and Baker companies knew that the whisky-trading days were near an end and that their future business could very well be centred upon contracts with the United States Indian and war departments, and with the Canadian troops when they arrived. If Conrad could discredit Tom Power, it could improve the Baker company's chances of getting the United States and Canadian governments' business.

It is significant that the businesses targeted by the Spitzee Cavalry all belonged to or were controlled by Tom Power. These included Kennerly's post on Badger Creek, Williams's post at Fort Kipp, and Dave Akers's post—Akers was outfitted by Power, who considered him to be his employee.[34] The wolfers also targeted Healy and Hamilton who were agents for, and consistently did business with, Tom Power. As Healy said, "That would be one way of putting their competitor, the Power concern, out of business!"[35]

When Williams sent his frantic message to John Healy for help, the Whoop-Up trader went to Fort Kipp to find out what had happened. After Williams explained the situation and asked what he should do, Healy advised him to ignore the Spitzee Cavalry and go on selling his goods, including the guns and ammunition.

"But they will confiscate my goods and burn the post," he exclaimed.[36]

When it was obvious that Williams was afraid to go up against the wolfers, Healy suggested that he sell out to him.

"Sell you the goods?"

"Yes, sell the goods to me. I will sell the Injuns anything they want."[37]

Healy offered to pay 20 per cent down on the provision that Williams take back all unsold goods in the spring. The inventory was examined and valued at twenty thousand dollars, after which the agreement was made and the papers signed. Healy commented:

> Williams was pretty badly frightened. He was afraid of the Spitzees. He asked if he could go up to Fort Whoop-up and stay around until the trouble was over. I told him he had no right to leave his place. He was responsible to the men who owned the goods and it was a cowardly thing to leave his post. I told him he could either stay or get to Fort Benton as quick as he could start. I would have no such man around. So he elected to wait until some party was going out, for the Injuns were pretty troublesome and he was in danger of being waylaid by a war party.[38]

Just before Williams left, Healy told him to write a note to the Spitzee Cavalry, telling them that he had sold out. Then Healy penned the following letter to the same group.

I have this day bought the stock of Williams, and am going to sell to the Indians anything they want to buy. I will have traders out on the prairie. You may meet some of them. Please don't interfere with any of them, as they are under my orders, and if you have anything to say, come to me. I am the one who is responsible. Yours truly, John J. Healy.[39]

Later on, Healy learned that the two letters had created an uproar among the traders and wolfers in the Spitzee Post area. Williams's letter arrived first and was greeted with disbelief. However, when Healy's missive came the following day, they knew it was true: John Healy had taken charge of Fort Kipp and would continue selling rifles and ammunition. When the Spitzee Cavalry decided to confront the trader, Asa and Dan Samples withdrew from the group, claiming the action would only lead to bloodshed. However, under the urging of Kamoose Taylor a committee of eighteen men was chosen to go to Fort Kipp and place Healy on trial.

Healy, having heard of their planned visit, sent all his men away from Fort Kipp, with the exception of Long John Fogerty, cook John Tallemache, and horse wrangler Jack Reese. Reese was to be on guard, and if the wolfers attacked the fort, was to ride to Whoop-Up for help. The main trading room was where Healy would make his stand. It was a large room, with a long, high counter across one side and a platform behind it where a man could stand. A trapdoor on the floor led to the cellar and could be used as an escape route, if needed. Healy told Reese that if he had to bring back a rescue party, they should look for him in the cellar.

Healy had a small brass howitzer brought over from Whoop-Up, loaded with 6 pounds of powder, and filled it with almost two hundred lead balls. At one end of the trading room, he cut a hole in the log wall and hung a blanket over it. Behind it, he set up the howitzer so that a shot would rake the entire room. He also cut the ends off a double-barrelled shotgun and loaded it with some small pieces of lead cut from bullets. This gun, together with a couple of revolvers and a Winchester rifle, was placed out of sight on a shelf behind the counter. When all was in readiness, recalled Healy, "I was feeling just as good as I ever did in my life."[40]

A short time later, Tony Lachappelle, who had a trading post a few miles upstream, rode to Fort Kipp to let Healy know that the Spitzee Cavalry were on the Belly River, trying to recruit more men for their confrontation. However, they were having little luck, for traders along the river were saying the affair was none of their business. "They won't raise a hand," they told Lachappelle. "They've got to settle it themselves."[41]

Some time later, Healy saw the cavalrymen approaching, some in wagons but most on horseback. He called to Reese to open the gates wide and let them in, and as they entered the compound, he saw they were all heavily armed. Instead of confronting them, Healy said, "Good day, gentlemen! You had better put up your horses so they can get something to eat and I'll fix up some supper for you!"[42] Suspicious and wary, the wolfers entered the dining room where a meal was ready and waiting for them. Afterwards, they followed Healy into the trading room for their meeting.

When they were all assembled, Kamoose Taylor announced that he was the spokesman for the group. Reese obligingly brought chairs, placing them in a semicircle, and set a table against the wall for Taylor to use. The placement was such that the "secretary" and men were directly in the howitzer's line of fire. As Healy recalled, "I had the cannon pointed so I could blow them all to hell."[43]

"Mr. Healy," began Taylor, "there is a serious charge preferred against you of selling guns and ammunition to the Injuns and we have come down to see about it."[44] He then read a long paper about Healy trading repeating rifles and ammunition to Indians contrary to the orders of the Spitzee Cavalry and acting against the wishes of all the white men in Whoop-Up country. Healy was then asked to plead guilty or not guilty. Said Healy later:

> Until that moment, I had not the first thought of what I was going to answer until he said "Guilty or not guilty?" and I turned and said, "Guilty and you be damned." Then I turned loose. "What right have *you* to come down here to try *me*? Who are you? What are you? a renegade from justice! You! you! you're a mad dog got among a pack of decent hounds and poisoned them! There were good men until you got among them!" [italics in original][45]

After hearing this violent outburst, Bedrock Jim snarled at him, "I suppose that I am one of the hounds!"

"Who are you?" responded Healy. "Who do you represent?"

"I represent Mr. Conrad," he replied.[46]

Right at that point, Healy was convinced that the Spitzee Cavalry, or at least Kamoose Taylor and others, were there at the instigation of I. G. Baker & Co. and that Charles Conrad was determined to drive T. C. Power & Bro. out of the country.

As Bedrock Jim stalked towards him, Healy drew the shotgun from under the shelf and pointed it at him, threatening to blow a hole in him if he came any closer. He then chided the men for going along with Taylor and his scheme to discredit the Power firm.

"These goods belong to Tom Power," he said. "A good many of you owe him for your outfits. He was good to you and gave you credit. And now you'd turn around and repay his kindness by destroying and confiscating his goods!"[47] Healy carried on for about fifteen minutes, saying that the Baker company was no longer selling guns in Whoop-Up country but since its traders were taking orders from the Indians who could then pick up the guns at Fort Benton, it was no different than selling them at the forts.

After a long silence, a wolfer named Mike Walsh stood up and said, "Gentlemen, I move that we all go down to the river and wash some of the wool out of our eyes."[48]

During the discussions, Long John Fogerty had stood silently behind the curtain, next to the cannon. Healy said that if his arguments failed, and the wolfers planned to kill him and burn down the fort, he would signal Fogerty by saying, "Gentlemen, since you will not listen to reason, you must take the consequences." When he heard those words, Fogerty was to pull a string attached to a fuse and the cannon would fire.

When the discussions were over, Healy asked the wolfers to step into the storeroom, and there he showed them the loaded cannon.

"Johnny, old man," said Taylor, "if we had refused to drop the matter, would that old cannon have mowed us down, or was that a bluff you were running in on us?"

"Ask Long John," he replied.

"I was just waitin' to hear him say the word," said John, "and then I was to touch her off."[49]

As a shocked and contrite group of wolfers turned to leave, Healy reminded them that they had taken thirteen hundred dollars worth of Power's robes. He produced a sheet of paper and they all signed to have them released from the stores of another trader, probably Conrad. "They sent the robes back," said Healy, "and that was the last I ever heard of the Spitzee Cavalry."[50]

The activities of the Spitzee Cavalry illustrate the lawlessness that prevailed in Whoop-Up country. This, combined with the ineffective enforcement of American laws—in large part due to partisan and incompetent judges—allowed the whisky traders to continue their destructive activities with little fear of prosecution.

13. *Beginning of the End*

Although the North-West Mounted Police (NWMP) failed to arrive in Whoop-Up country in 1873, everyone knew they would get there eventually. Not surprisingly, different people reacted to their impending arrival in different ways: some whisky traders were determined to carry on as before, others planned to become legitimate traders, and still others chose to stay south of the border.

From the Saskatchewan country, a few ambitious Canadians decided to enter the region from the north and be well established by the time the police arrived. During the intervening period, they were prepared to go head-to-head with the Americans. The first of these were Methodist missionary John McDougall and his trader brother David. The Reverend John, having laboured for years among the Stoney Indians who inhabited the region along the foothills to the Bow River, selected a mission site late in 1873 that was near the mountains but beyond the usual realm of the whisky traders and Blackfoot. During the winter the two men, their wives, and their children lived at the little mission they named Morleyville. "South of us and within one day's journey from our fort," said the Reverend John, "several whiskey mills were vigorously at work, demoralizing and decimating the plains tribes."[1] He was told that forty-two Blackfoot were killed in drunken arguments at these posts over the winter.

Although both brothers were staunch anti-drinking Methodists, their American detractors accused David of competing with them by dealing in whisky. From Fort Whoop-Up, a trader wrote: "I will state that the Mission … has been established in order that their converts may be kept on British soil and drink good liquor instead of American adulterated whisky, so that in the chase they may be brave and capture many robes."[2] Another Montanan went even further, quoting from a supposed sermon by McDougall:

> My brothers, whenever you get tired of listening to me, just pass into the trading room, where my brother will attend to your wants. If you do not trade here today, you will have bad medicine. Just step in, and when you have had enough (meaning whiskey), come again to me and hear the words of the Great

Spirit. He then whispered to the brother: Let it run ten cups for a head and tail robe.[3]

The accusations, of course, were untrue.

Some distance east of the McDougalls, on the upper waters of Elbow River, the Roman Catholics also established a mission in the fall of 1873. Named Our Lady of Peace, it was operated by Father Constantine Scollen, an anti-British Fenian who also detested the American whisky trade. The following spring, he was joined by Sam Livingston, a gold miner who earlier had settled in the Edmonton area and was now raising a large family. Having once prospected with John Healy, Joe Kipp, and Charlie Thomas, he had no concerns about trading in opposition to the Montanans. With his wife and four children along, he built a two-room shack beside the Elbow River, one room for the family and the other for trading. Like David McDougall, he carried no liquor. That fall, Livingston commented:

> In these parts there is plenty of [whisky] at every trading post …
> In a distance of forty miles from here, down Bow River, there are
> four posts where the Indians say they buy whiskey, and they have
> brought some to this place, and were drunk all one night … I
> have just received news of the death of some of them in the
> storm … through being drunk. Notwithstanding they are still
> heading for the whiskey shops with their furs. Some of them are
> destitute of horses, blankets, and guns—all gone for whiskey.[4]

Then, after an absence of forty years from the Bow River country, the Hudson's Bay Company also decided to move south. Encouraged by the success of David McDougall, the company sent John Bunn in the fall of 1874 to open a trading post near the mission of Morleyville. Upon his arrival, Bunn stated: "A few Blackfeet have been in who report that most of them have gone to Belly river to trade but that a good many intend coming in here … I sent out tobacco to them to tell them to keep away for ten days and then come in if they liked."[5]

In the Belly River country, Al Hamilton opted to get out of the whisky business. By the beginning of 1874 he was no longer involved with Fort Whoop-Up, John Healy, or the T. C. Power interests. Instead, he returned to the family fold when he accepted the position of licenced trader for his uncle's firm, I. G. Baker & Co., and took charge of the trading post at the Blackfoot Agency.[6] To replace him, Healy arranged to hire Dave Akers, who had been running his own post over the winter of 1873–74.

If the traders had any doubts about the coming of the NWMP, these were dispelled in April 1874 when the *Helena Daily Herald* announced: "We understand that the British Government has become convinced of the necessity therefor, and has ordered the construction of a military post at Whoop-Up, situated at the base of the Rocky Mountains, just above the northern border of Montana. The post is to be completed the present season." The report added that "the presence of the British troops will have a healthy effect upon the residents and frequenters of that hitherto lawless section, where might has so long proclaimed itself right."[7]

To prepare for this new order, Tom Power settled up with John Healy for running Fort Kipp and then resumed the operation himself. This time he sent John Kerler, an experienced trader, to take over the business. Kerler, a Canadian, had entered the Montana Territory in 1871 with a large hunting party of Métis from Red River and had promptly been arrested for selling whisky.[8] Since then, he had been trading both in Montana and Whoop-Up country.

Kerler reached Fort Kipp early in June and began settling all the accounts left behind when S. F. Williams fled the scene in the wake of the Spitzee Cavalry. Seeing that the area was in a state of unrest because of the NWMP's imminent arrival, Tom Power instructed Kerler not to open any new accounts and to "sell no goods without cash or equivalent, except to responsible parties such as Weatherwax, Fred Wachter, and such men."[9] For those who already had accounts he said, "Don't allow those boys to run much of an acct. as they owe us plenty from last year.[10] He also arranged for Joe Kipp to cut and stack 10 tons of hay for the horses and oxen. He added:

> From appearances there will be English troops in your country
> next season, or rather this season, when they come. Show your
> invoices if necessary and tell them we stand ready to pay any
> duties the law demands. If you have any strychnine take it off
> the invoices … Do not allow any whisky or contraband goods
> in your post. If officers of Police or boundary survey call on
> you, treat them well.[11]

A number of other traders also decided that the buffalo robe business was simply too good to give up. They returned to Whoop-Up country for the winter of 1874–75, most trading in whisky but prepared to cache it at the first signs of the NWMP. Wetzel & Weatherwax, now the main liquor wholesaler, had a post on the Oldman River where it supplied some of the smaller traders with goods, both wet and dry. According to Isaac Baker, "Rumors of the coming Expedition did not stop the Whiskey Traders. Large quantities of liquor were sent out."[12]

Fred Kanouse, after a season near Waterton Lakes, moved to the Oldman River for the 1874–75 season, building a post about 2 miles upstream from where the police would later establish Fort Macleod. One of his first customers was Old Woman's Child, the Blood warrior who had killed and scalped William Berry some time earlier. According to journalist Leroy Kelly, the Indian was apparently a bullying blustering desperado, for the other members of his tribe feared him heartily and longed for his death, though they feared to take upon themselves the work of destruction. But one night when he slept they screwed up sufficient courage—probably of the Dutch sort—to hack and stab him with the knife which Old Woman's Child had used on Berry.[13]

On 24 September 1874, Kanouse's fort was visited by a mixed party of Kootenay and Pend d'Oreille Indians from the west side of the Rockies. They camped on the south side of the river, while across the stream was a camp of Peigans, Bloods, and Siksikas. While the Blackfoot tribes were friendly with the Kootenays, they were at war with the Pend d'Oreilles and were angry at seeing them in their hunting grounds. Kanouse's wife, who was a Blood, told her husband of the possible consequences of trading with the enemy tribe; when he refused to serve them, the Pend d'Oreilles withdrew and began to attack the fort. The Kootenays, who had been visiting with the Peigans at the time, went to join their comrades, while a number of Blackfoot rushed to the aid of those in the fort—Kanouse, his wife, and three other white men.

The scattering of Blackfoot quickly found themselves outnumbered and fled from the onslaught of the Pend d'Oreille rifles. Most saved themselves by jumping over a cutbank, but a Siksika warrior named Axe kept fighting until his revolver jammed. He was then killed along with two women from the tribe.[14]

Kanouse had held his fire while he watched the fight take place, but when a bullet struck his wife in the chest, he and his men opened fire and killed three of the enemy, causing them to withdraw. Kanouse, afraid they would be back to try to destroy the fort, sent one of his traders to Fort Whoop-Up for help as soon as the coast was clear. However, according to a man who was at Whoop-Up at the time,

A Blood woman carrying a load of firewood on a travois outside the walls of Fort Whoop-Up in 1881. (Geological Survey of Canada, 400)

Four men started for the seat of war. They arrived at the scene of action after all the fighting was over. It so happened that one of the men, while trying to explain to the new comers how the fuss commenced, accidentally discharged his rifle into an open dish of powder standing beside an open 25 pound can full of the same material. The result was a most tremendous explosion; two houses were totally demolished in a flash, and yet, strange to say, not one of the six men in the house were seriously injured; one was blown through the roof and escaped with a sprained ankle and a little scorching; others were buried under the ruins, yet all the injuries in the crowd were a few sprains and the loss of some hair by singeing.[15]

The fort was rebuilt and was soon back in business.

As a result of the fight, the Blackfoot and Kootenays were again at war, and the western tribes retreated across the mountains. It fell to the NWMP the following summer to arrange a peace treaty between the tribes "on a spot of ground, not long since stained with the blood of some of their young men."[16]

The plethora of traders that returned once more to Whoop-Up country meant that when the fall and winter season was ready to begin, it was again flooded with whisky. There were at least eight posts along the Oldman River, two or three on the Belly, and others to the north at Pine Coulee, Sheep Creek, Highwood River, and Bow River. Other smaller shacks may also have dotted the countryside.

But not all whisky traders went north that autumn, no doubt reacting to the news about the Mounted Police and not wishing to risk the loss of their outfits. The earlier announcement about the NWMP was confirmed in a report from Fort Benton in early September 1874:

> It is understood that the Mounted Police of Her Majesty, the Queen of England, are about establishing a Custom House, or introducing and enforcing the British laws in the Whoop Up country. They design making Fort Benton the general point of intercourse, as it is the most convenient place adjacent to their country from which to receive their supplies.[17]

With the impending arrival of the law north of the border, a number of traders decided to go back to their old stomping grounds—the Blackfeet Reservation in Montana. For the past four years, the reservation had been relatively free of trafficking, as most of the whisky was flowing into Whoop-Up country. True, there had been several alcohol-related incidents where chiefs or other prominent Peigans had been killed, but these were few and far between when compared to the chaos occurring north of the line. Deputy Marshal Charles Hard admitted as much late in 1873 when he commented that "he may prevent the traffic this side of the line entirely, but so long as it is a legitimate trade in the British Possessions it is impossible to prevent the Indians being supplied."[18] Near the end of the year, he commented, "In regard to the traffic of whisky & ammunition on this side of the British line it has been very small and only one seizure made consisting of ten Gallons of alcohol."[19]

The flood of whisky back into the Blackfeet Reservation was triggered not only by the anticipated appearance of the NWMP across the line, but also by the reduction in the size of the reservation on 15 April 1873, which made it more difficult to catch traders coming out of Fort Benton or Sun River. Because of the buffer zone north of the towns, traders could choose to follow one of several routes onto the reservation and could easily escape detection.

Unlicenced traders could also now build shanties on the south side of the Marias, just off the reservation, and operate as long as they had a Territorial licence. They could stock a small supply of whisky and claim it was for their own use. Before the winter of 1874–75, there were at least five such shacks along the river, the largest being operated by Sol Abbott, who had moved down from Whoop-Up country.

Trouble wasn't long in coming. In September 1874, whisky traders got into a Peigan camp just north of the Marias and in the ensuing bacchanalia, a chief named Lodge Pole and his wife tried to stop a man from shooting another. In his drunken rage, the man turned on the pair and opened fire, killing the woman instantly. Weasel Horn, another leader, tried to prevent further mayhem, but he too was shot and killed. Finally, other members of the tribe overpowered the culprit but not before he had shot and seriously injured another man.[20] Less than two weeks later, these Peigans were camped at the Willow Rounds, near Badger Creek, when they were again beset by traffickers in whisky. This time, Cut Hand, one of their leading chiefs, was shot in the head and killed by a fellow member of the tribe. Cut Hand had threatened Fort Whoop-Up during its construction and also extended a hand of friendship and reconciliation to the United States military after the tragic Baker Massacre of 1870.[21] Immediately prior to his murder, Cut Hand had been assisting white settlers in recovering some of their stolen horses.

Within the same week as the Cut Hand killing, two whisky traders named Annerson and Sacramento sold a gill of whisky to some Peigans north of the Sun River. Before the traders had a chance to leave, an argument arose in which Annerson shot and killed one of the tribesmen and Sacramento wounded another in the mouth.[22] Annerson fled to Whoop-Up, but Sacramento, a Mexican, was captured by Indian department detective Andrew Dusold and charged with introducing whisky onto the reservation. Depositions were taken from two Indian witnesses, Strangle Wolf and Mary Kite, and based upon their testimony, the whisky trader was convicted and sentenced to a term in the Deer Lodge penitentiary.[23]

But perhaps the most sensational case involving whisky traders returning to the Blackfeet Reservation occurred at the beginning of October, when a rumour was circulated that two white men had been killed by Peigans. An investigation by Detective Dusold determined that the report was true and that the dead men were William Mitchell and Joseph Wei, the latter being the famous "mayor of Whoop-Up" and the person who reportedly gave the fort its colourful name. Dusold stated that Wei, travelling alone, had gone to Kennedy's old post on Badger Creek and told the Peigans there that he was on his way to Whoop-Up. The Peigans were suspicious, so they watched him and saw him travel a wide circuit and end up back on Badger Creek at the mouth of Medicine Lodge Creek, about 5 miles below the old fort. There Wei was joined by William Mitchell, who was leading a pack horse loaded with 7 gallons of whisky. The next day the two men approached Boy Chief's camp, but a young man met them and told them they could not come any closer. He showed them a paper in which the Indian agent authorized Boy Chief to seize and destroy any liquor he found on the reservation and to bring the traders to the agency.

Wei and Mitchell immediately retreated and pitched their camp a short distance up Medicine Lodge Creek; seven men from Boy Chief's camp who wanted to get liquor, regardless of their chief's wishes, followed them there. They advised the traders to move to where they wouldn't be observed, so the two men travelled downstream until they were within about 5 miles of I. G. Baker's trading post. Here they hid in the brush and opened for business. During the trading and subsequent drinking, trouble soon arose. Reported Detective Dusold:

> The Indians say that a quarrell [sic] then commenced & during the quarrell Joe Wey [sic] struck Iron Crow on the Head with his Revolver and broke it. (I examined Wey's Revolver and found nothing broken about it. It was in good order & not loaded.) Another Indian called One that Took the Bear's Part cried out to kill the White Man. One Finger Up said he would kill no white man, that he came to get something to drink, whereupon Iron Crow shot & killed Joe Wey; the others then joined in the Butchery & killed Mitchell.[24]

A leader named Big Stone reported the killing to the traders at Baker's post the following day. This information was sent to the Indian agency, and a short time later, James Rutherford and another man from the agency went to search for the scene of the crime. According to Dusold:

They travelled all day until towards evening, hunting for the place & by accident found it. A dog was there, belonged to Joe Wey. He had been shot through one ear & remained there guarding his dead Master until found by the party. Both men were stript [sic] naked, their skulls had been beaten in by Clubs which were found near the Bodies clotted with Blood.[25]

Rutherford determined that Wei had been shot in the head and chest while Mitchell had received a fatal wound to the forehead. From the murder scene, Rutherford and his companion proceeded on to the camps of Big Stone and Boy Chief, where they were given a pinto horse, a mule, two coats, a hat, revolver, and rifle, all taken from the dead whisky traders. There also was money, papers, saddles, robes, and horses; these were not recovered immediately but were later delivered to the agency. The chiefs, however, refused to turn over any of the men responsible for the killings. Commented Dusold:

There is a strong feeling existing among Joe Wey's friends to take the law into their own hands, proceed to the Indian Camp & take revenge in case nothing be done by u.s. Authority. Such an act might lead to a General War. Good Indians would suffer & the guilty ones escape.[26]

The main agitators who wanted to wreak revenge on the Peigans were the vestiges of the old Spitzee Cavalry under the leadership of George Hammond; they wanted to attack and destroy the Peigan camp. However, as John Healy recalled, the wolfers were dead broke so they came over to Whoop-Up asking for ammunition.

"I know what you want that ammunition for," Healy said to them. "You want to go over there and wipe out that village, and you won't do it. I won't let you have any ammunition."

"Two white men have been killed," they said, "and we are going to settle up."

"Is that so?" Healy replied. "Now I tell you what I'll do. Put yourselves under my command and I'll lead you down there and we'll search for the men who did the murder and if we find them we will hang them. If we don't, well and good!"[27]

However, the wolfers were not willing to agree to those terms and said they were going to the Peigan camps on their own.

"Then you don't want to get the murderer," Healy said. "You want to murder and loot the village and take their goods and horses and run them off."[28]

The Spitzee Cavalry, possibly stung by the truth of his remarks and unable to get the ammunition they needed, abandoned any idea of seeking revenge or booty.

As for Indian agent R. F. May, he was not concerned about the killings. He described Wei as "a notorious dealer in whiskey, and was dreaded by all the older and orderly Piegans." In his report to Washington he added, "The death of these two men is no serious loss to society, and will have a good effect towards preventing other whiskey traders from engaging in the death insuring business."[29] As far as the records show, the killers were never apprehended nor punished.

And so, by the time the NWMP were preparing to enter Whoop-Up country, the principal players in the whisky traffic were settling into their roles. Many traders were back at their old haunts, dispensing their deadly brews as in previous years; others—American and Canadian—were in business without handling liquor; T. C. Power and I. G. Baker had become "dry" merchants; and the firm of Wetzel & Weatherwax was now the main whisky distributor to the Whoop-Up trade. And south of the border, refugees from the British possessions were poised and ready to flood the Blackfeet Reservation with the same cheap whisky that had decimated the tribes in the north.

14. The Queen's Mounted Police

A fter the creation of the North-West Mounted Police (NWMP) in 1873, the first contingent of 150 men was hurriedly recruited in eastern Canada and reached Red River in the new Province of Manitoba just before the onset of the winter. Next spring, recruitment in the Maritimes and eastern Canada raised another 217 officers and men to bring the force up to a full complement. This second contingent arrived at Red River in June 1874, and the police immediately set out for the West. Ultimately, one segment was destined for the Territorial capital at Livingstone, another for Fort Edmonton, and a third for Fort Whoop-Up, to put it out of business.

Before leaving Manitoba, the NWMP heard dire stories about the whisky traders. The general belief was that there were about five hundred desperados in heavily defended forts who were prepared to do battle with the red-coated police. For example, the *New York Times* stated that

> a thieves' colony, formidable in numbers, had been established in Dominion territory, close to the Rocky Mountains ... it appeared that this colony was made up entirely of persons who had murdered and robbed to such an extent in the United States that they were compelled, in order to escape "Judge Lynch," to seek safety in flight. Repeated reinforcements from over the border soon swelled the male population to five hundred.[1]

En route west, a Métis told NWMP commissioner George A. French that there were "500 Americans working all summer at their forts at the Forks, making underground galleries, &c."[2] Not knowing whether to believe him or not, the commissioner concluded that "it was considered quite likely that they would offer resistance."[3]

During the previous four years, the Royal Engineers had joined with their American counterparts to survey the forty-ninth parallel between Canada and the United States, and had established storage depots at various places along the line. The government decided that those NWMP bound for Whoop-Up would travel due west near the border and make use of these supplies. The force set out in early July and spent the next three months on the trail in a gruelling ordeal that became known as The Great March. Their horses weakened and died, rations ran out, water was scarce, and by the time they got to Old Wives Lake, they were hopelessly lost. The maps of the earlier Palliser exploring expedition proved to be inaccurate, and Colonel Robertson-Ross's description of the location of Fort Whoop-Up, from his 1872 reconnaissance of the West for the Canadian government, was incorrect.

The farther west they got, the more difficulty they had finding reliable guides, but at last they hired a Métis named Guy Moreau. However, they were so afraid he was an American spy, they didn't trust a word he said, which was too bad because his information turned out to be quite reliable. Two years later, Mounted Policeman S. J. Clarke at Fort Walsh described him as "one of the best known guides in this country."[4]

When the force reached the confluence of the Bow and Belly (later Oldman) Rivers, Fort Whoop-Up was not where it was supposed to be. Commissioner French commented with disgust, "The fort!!! at the Forks of the Bow and Belly rivers turns out to be three log huts without roofs in which some fellows occasionally stopped when trapping or rather poisoning wolves."[5] By this time the Mounties had met a few Métis and Indians and from them learned that the whisky traders were aware of their coming and were abandoning their forts. The anticipated battle would not happen. "I understand the whiskey traders are not here now," said French, "but are about Benton, and propose remaining there till the Force returns. A post at or near the Boundary Line will spoil their little game."[6] French was referring to one of the many rumours floating around Montana that the NWMP would close down Whoop-Up and then go back to permanent quarters in Manitoba.

Realizing that their maps were wrong, feed for their horses and oxen non-existent, and the lives of the men in jeopardy, Commissioner French decided to ignore the directive that he build his fort at the confluence of the Bow and Belly. NWMP surgeon Richard B. Nevitt described the area as "a lonely desert place, one island with a few trees on it, high banks and not a soul near it, no grass, no road."[7] The commissioner chose instead to turn southwest towards the Sweetgrass Hills, which he could see in the distance. The tree-covered slopes were in contrast to the barren, dry plains over which the police had travelled. Once the troop had settled in place along the Milk River, Commissioner French made tentative plans to stay there for the winter; then, with Assistant Commissioner James F. Macleod, surgeon Richard Nevitt, and six men, he set out on 22 September for Fort Benton "to communicate with Government and obtain supplies."[8]

Once across the border, the police made good time and reached Fort Benton in less than three days. Here were the headquarters of both I. G. Baker & Co. and T. C. Power & Bro., but there was no question as to where the Mounties would go. Because Fort Benton would have to be the provisioning point for the NWMP, the Canadian government had made inquiries about a possible supplier. One of those contacted was Robert W. Donnell, a New York businessman, who told the Ottawa officials that "there was not a finer man in the United States than I. G. Baker."[9] So regardless of all the preliminary posturing and jockeying for position by Power and Baker, the latter company won the contest hands down—a classic case of not what you know but who you know. It was ironic that Tom Power should have dominated the whisky-trading era through his aggressiveness, business acumen, and political influence, yet lose out to his opposition on a much more lucrative (and legitimate) business deal as that offered by the NWMP.

Commissioner French and his party went directly to Baker's store where they received a warm welcome. Surgeon Nevitt, a former American southerner, wrote to his lady friend:

> Did I tell you how well we are treated at Benton? Mr. Baker of
> the firm Baker & Conrad insisted on our stopping at his place
> as long as we were in Benton and he fed us most royally, treat-
> ing us in the most hospitable manner. I said to Major Macleod
> that these could not be Yankees and as we afterwards found out,
> Mr. Baker was from Missouri and the Conrads, old Confederate
> soldiers from Virginia. So my prejudice did not carry me too far
> wrong in that case.[10]

The arrival of the NWMP was duly noted in the Montana press, with the prediction that across the border "the illicit whisky traffic will be speedily stopped."[11] Also, with an eye to the business opportunities offered by the Canadian force, the Helena press expected that much of their goods would be purchased on the local market and be a boon to their economy. And, true enough, a few days later it reported, "Mr. I. G. Baker, of the extensive mercantile trading and forwarding house of I. G. Baker & Co., Benton, has been several days in the city purchasing groceries, hardware, clothing and other goods to fill out a complement of 40,000 pounds of supplies and stores for the Queen's Mounted Police."[12]

Charles Conrad became I. G. Baker's agent to deal with the Mounties. One of his first actions was to recommend the hiring of Jerry Potts, a mixed-blood plainsman who could serve as their guide. The second was to suggest that they not stay at Milk River, which lacked adequate timber, but to proceed north to the centre of the whisky trade on the Belly and Oldman Rivers. When French and his party returned north from Benton a few days later, Charles Conrad was with them and announced that his company would construct a trading store close to their future headquarters.

While the officers were away, the police at Milk River saw their first whisky trader, an unnamed man travelling south along the Whoop-Up–Benton Trail with an ox train loaded with buffalo robes. They suspected that these had been traded for whisky, but a search of the wagons turned up no intoxicants so they had to let him go.

Once they were back at Milk River, Commissioner French and part of the troop returned to Manitoba and the remainder went north under Assistant Commissioner Macleod. With Potts as their guide, Macleod's contingent had no trouble finding Fort Whoop-Up, which they reached on 9 October. And there is no doubt that the traders knew they were on their way. A freighter named Charles Schafft was at Fort Whoop-Up at the time and recalled:

> Reports of the coming of the Police reached us now very frequently; those who had contraband in stock cached it; everything was quiet and trade nearly at a stand still, because no one knew to what extent the red-coats would interfere in business matters. At length a reliable messenger on running gear, came in and brought the intelligence that the force would be here in a few days.[13]

By this time John Healy was conveniently down at Sun River, and there were only six or seven men at the fort, as well as a number of Native wives and their children. The day after the police arrived at Whoop-Up, Schafft wrote:

> The Manitoba Mounted Police, a force of 150 men under command of Major McLeod [*sic*], encamped on Belly River a short distance below here last night. In the evening the Major, some other officers, and a squad of men paid us an official visit. They acted with courtesy toward every one, but all appeared "dry" which after a 4 months' march on arid plains is perhaps not to be wondered at. They asked for whisky, but when we regretted our inability to give them a drop, they evidently took it as a joke, for several details under command of proper officers were soon engaged in trying to find the "critter." They searched up stairs and down stairs, peeped into all kinds of holes and crevices, but their search was of no avail and they left for other fields.[14]

From Whoop-Up, the Mounties followed a whisky trail west to the old trading post at Slide Out, where nothing remained but ashes. From there they made the short trip across the prairies, and on 13 October, reached an island on the Oldman River that was to become their headquarters. If the NWMP wanted to find American traders who only a few weeks before had been dealing in whisky, they didn't need to look very far. A trooper commented that this was where "most of the trading posts of this country are situated … we decided on a place about twenty-five miles above Whoop-Up, and within five miles of three other small trading posts."[15] These were the posts of John Weatherwax, about 4 miles away; Fred Kanouse, within walking distance downstream; and another one a short distance away, operated by a man named Michael Foley. One of the Mounties was not impressed with the men engaged in the whisky trade, noting:

> They are coarse, unpolished and uneducated; they are insulting in their conversation and disgusting to our sight. [Among them were] a bankrupt mercantile firm who dare not face their honest creditors at home, a murderer who has fled his country for his country's good, a horse thief from the Boundary survey who dare not return, and an apostate preacher who is exiled from civilized society.[16]

As soon as Macleod and his men arrived, tents were pitched and the work to construct a fort began. Within days, the balmy autumn weather was replaced by blizzards and bitterly cold temperatures that left the men shivering in their tents. They were malnourished, clothed in ragged uniforms, and exhausted from their

One of the first actions of the NWMP when they arrived on the Oldman River was to seize contraband whisky. This painting by R. B. Nevitt shows the troops pouring the liquor into the river in October 1874, while a number of Blackfoot look on. (Glenbow Art Department, Nevitt Collection)

trek. The horses that survived the journey were so weak that they were practically useless for patrol duty. In this unenviable condition, the Mounted Police faced the task of suppressing the whisky trade, establishing a friendship with the Blackfoot, and making a comfortable home for themselves for the winter.

Getting the Indians onside proved to be easy. Though unaware of it, the police had been tracked ever since they entered Blackfoot country. The Blackfoot were both curious and apprehensive for, in spite of reassurances from missionaries who visited their camps, they still looked upon the red-coated police as strangers. But after meetings with Colonel Macleod, who assured them that the police came in peace, that they would drive out the whisky traders, and that they would apply the Queen's law equally to Indian or white, the chiefs were both satisfied and pleased. As one chief said to a Mountie, "Before our [the NWMP] arrival all the Indians had to creep along for fear of the traders; now they walked erect and were not afraid." The Mountie added that the Indians were "delighted to see us, and are loud in their denunciation of the whiskey traders, who they say have cheated them of their robes and horses."[17]

As for the whisky traders, they had a "wait and see" attitude. Knowing how ineffective the judicial system was in Montana, they had no reason to believe it would be any different in the Queen's domain. They even started a rumour among the Indians that the Mounties were there only temporarily, and when they left, the whisky business would be back in full force. However, the Americans had not counted on a legal system that was both unusual and ran counter to anything they had ever seen. Because there was no civilian court system in the area, the senior officers of the NWMP were designated as magistrates. And because there were no civilian jails, convicted persons served their time in NWMP lockups. This meant that a whisky trader could be arrested by a NWMP constable, taken before a NWMP officer who was serving as a magistrate, convicted, and sentenced to the guardhouse where his jailer also was a Mountie. Under a system like that, few of the guilty could expect to go free.[18]

Colonel Macleod was a fair man who did not misuse this omnipotent authority, but he was also a practical man who knew that his troops were poorly clad. One of his plans was to seize enough robes at the time of a whisky trader's arrest to cover a fine in the event that he was convicted. These robes would be used for making clothing for his troops. And according to his commissioner, it was legal. "I see no other way in this country to secure the fine," Macleod wrote to his superior, "except by seizing property enough at the time the seizure is made, and not to wait for a distress warrant, after the fine is imposed."[19]

Within days of their arrival, a Siksika minor chief named Three Bulls came to the camp to report a trading post about 50 miles north of them at Pine Coulee where the men were selling whisky. Three Bulls said he had traded two horses for 2 gallons of the brew. Three Bulls was a half-brother of the great chief Crowfoot, so the information was likely sanctioned by the chief to see what the Mounties would do.

Knowing that he was surrounded by American traders, Colonel Macleod told Jerry Potts to quietly gather all the information he could and to meet Three Bulls on the trail the following evening. Macleod then instructed Superintendent Leif Crozier to take ten men and find enough horses that could survive the trip. "I gave Mr. Crozier written instructions to guide him," said Macleod, "amongst others, to seize all robes and furs of any kind which he suspected had been traded for liquor, and in addition a sufficient amount of goods and chattels, to satisfy the fine which in each case might be imposed."[20]

Crozier and his men were only partway to Pine Coulee when they met the whisky traders on the trail. Led by Harry "Kamoose" Taylor, former secretary of the Spitzee Cavalry, the trading party also included interpreter William Bond, the Mexican-black whom the Blackfoot so detested, and three others. When their two wagons were searched, the police found cases of alcohol and 116 buffalo robes, which were seized, together with the wagons, sixteen horses, five rifles, and two revolvers. The men were arrested and all taken back to headquarters. Crozier was lucky the trip was short, for one of the horses died as a result of the journey and the others barely made it because of their weakened condition.

As this was his first real case, Colonel Macleod decided to have a full panel of senior officers on hand. They heard the evidence, examined the contraband, and in short order found all five men guilty. Taylor and Bond, the two principals, were fined two hundred dollars each, while the three others, described as "hired men," were levied fifty-dollar fines. In addition, all robes and chattels became the property of the Queen. The next day, John Weatherwax appeared at the police camp and paid all the fines, except those of Bond, who was left to languish in jail. Macleod said this was because Bond was facing an additional charge of selling whisky to Three Bulls, and the delay gave the police time to check the rumour that the man was "accused of murdering a number of Indians and is suspected of murdering a family in Chatham, Ontario, some time ago."[21]

Because of the intervention of Weatherwax, Taylor and his cronies were freed but, as the surgeon Richard Nevitt commented about Bond, "he has had to remain in the guard tent ever since and probably will for some time."[22] However, about two weeks later, Bond was being taken to the latrine at night when he suddenly bolted for freedom. His guard fired a shot at the disappearing figure but a search the next day failed to turn up any sign of him. Next spring, however, the police found his frozen body on the plains about 30 miles south of the fort with a bullet hole in his back.[23]

The seizure of robes was a godsend for Macleod and his men. Fifty of the best ones were issued to the men to be made into coats or to be used as blankets in their freezing tents. The remainder were made into caps and mitts. This made Kamoose Taylor furious. Whenever he saw a Mountie in a buffalo coat, he would remark, "Look at that damned blankety-blank wearing one of my buffalo robes he stole from me!"[24]

Flushed with the success of their first raid, the Mounties settled into the easier routine of acting as Customs agents. They visited each of the trading posts in the area, took inventory of their stock, and assessed import duties. "Already thousands of dollars worth of goods have been taxed," reported a Mountie.[25] While visiting Fort Kipp, Colonel Macleod appropriated the hay that Joe Kipp had cut during the fall and made arrangements with John Kerler for a NWMP detachment to board at his trading post.

When Tom Power heard about the boarders, he wasn't happy. "Understand you have 10 men of the M Police quartered without," he told Kerler. "Please write Maj. McCloud [sic] our wishes about this. We can't suffer to have them in the Fort & lose our winter's trade. Would not agree to keep those 10 men for $1,000.00 during the winter."[26] Power obviously based his edict on the way the Blackfoot would have reacted to American soldiers, but Kerler knew that having the Mounties with him was an asset because of their friendly relations with the Indians. As a result, he chose to ignore the order and ultimately the NWMP purchased the post and renamed it Fort Winder, after one of their senior officers.

Power also had other instructions and advice to his man at Fort Kipp. He said that trade goods were in short supply and should not be sold to other traders but used only for buying robes. Wetzel & Weatherwax had no special deal to buy goods at Fort Kipp but if they took any, they had to pay the going prices, even if they complained they were exorbitant. "I must say we are surprised that you have allowed so many Blankets to get out of your hands," Power chided. "You must have missed some of our letters of instructions and forgot what John [Power] told you, which was not to let the goods go unless you got the Robes … for without goods we can't get the Robes."

He added:

> Notice you have sold Kanouse quite a quantity of goods but state you have [his] Robes to pay for them in store. So far so good, but hereafter we want the parties getting the goods to sell the Robes & settle as they go along … We want all the Robes we can get, up to 6 or 7 thousand, and to get them we must hold our goods to get & trade for Robes … Pay Indians big prices for good Robes which will encourage them to make good Robes …

He concluded by saying:

> We have hired & will send Mr. Dave Acres [*sic*] out to aid you.
> Mr. Acres has some experience and wish you to confer with him
> so as to get the trade & don't let your goods go unless for the
> Robes. Hope you have fixed no prices with Mr. Weatherwax for
> it would be to [*sic*] good a joke for him to get away with our
> cream when goods are certain to be so scarce.[27]

One result of the NWMP being in Whoop-Up country that took the Power
people completely by surprise was the shortage of trade goods. Each year the firm
ordered supplies from New York, Chicago, St. Louis, and other points, based on
how much was needed to service the Indian trade. However, now that whisky
was no longer available to the Canadian Blackfoot, the Indians had extra money
to spend on clothing, hardware, and other objects. This demand for goods soon
left the Fort Benton warehouses bare, even at the beginning of the trading
season. In early December, Tom Power reviewed the situation.

> The Whoopup trade is all turned round now. Whisky being
> shut down it will take staples which costs money. As it
> happened so late, [it] leaves the staples in [short supply]
> comparatively speaking. W & W [Wetzel & Weatherwax] are
> short but yet do not know if Ace Samples & Co. have fair
> supply. Baker & Co. has a good supply, together with ours,
> comprises the outfit.[28]

He told Kerler that flour was selling for ten dollars a bag in Benton and
should bring fifteen dollars at Fort Kipp. When that supply ran out, there would
be none to replace it. "Sugars are scarce," he said, "and will be high before the
Spring stocks arrive. Be careful with your sugar as you will need it for Indian
trade."[29] Horses also were in great demand as the Blackfoot restocked their herds.
When NWMP officer James Walsh visited Helena at the beginning of the new
year, he noted:

> Heretofore the traders have regularly "swapped" cheap whisky
> for robes and horses, while this winter the tables are turned and
> the Indians are resupplying themselves with horses and keep
> themselves supplied with ammunition and necessary articles of
> grub and clothing from the licensed traders by exchanging
> robes therefor.[30]

The arrest and conviction of Kamoose Taylor and the others had the desired effect on the whisky trade, at least in the Belly River region: cached liquor remained hidden, and most of the one-time whisky traders spent the winter handling legitimate stock. According to a visitor to the area, there was no whisky to be found at the trading posts of "Wetzel & Co., Baker & Bro., Sample Bros., Lee, Brown, Kanouse, and a few others ... on the river."[31] Joe Kipp and Charlie Thomas were in the process of bringing a supply of whisky to their fort when they learned that the NWMP had arrived. "They forthwith abandoned Fort Kipp and returned to Montana," commented a journalist.[32]

Colonel Macleod, however, was not being entirely forthright when he told his superior, "I am happy to be able to report the complete stoppage of the whiskey trade throughout the whole of this section of the country."[33] Rumours were filtering down from the north that whisky was still being sold at several posts in the Bow River region, although initially there was no evidence for the police to proceed. Suspicion pointed to John Weatherwax as the supplier; the fact that he had paid the fines for Taylor and his crew indicated that the whisky sellers were either working for him or being supplied by him.

A break came in late November when two Indians went to the Reverend John McDougall at Morleyville and told him they had obtained whisky from traders on Sheep Creek. The missionary took them to see John Bunn, who was not only the Hudson's Bay Company trader but a justice of the peace as well. He took depositions from both of them and forwarded these to the police. When Colonel Macleod received them, he stated:

> I was unable to send out at once, first because I had no horses and secondly on account of the very severe weather during which it would have been extremely dangerous to send a party 75 miles across the prairie with very few places where any shelter could be

This bull train out of Fort Benton is typical of those that served the northern posts. Such trains travelled only a few miles per day. (Glenbow Archives, NA-98-11)

procured in the event of a storm. So I made up my mind to wait my opportunity without saying anything about my information in the expectation that the parties implicated might be caught about here on their way with their robes into Benton.[34]

Further inquiries indicated two main posts were trafficking in whisky. One, located on the west side of the Bow River, was run by Dick Berry and said to be owned by Wetzel & Weatherwax. Accordingly, a watch was placed upon Weatherwax's post near Fort Macleod. At the end of January 1875, the police learned that two wagonloads of robes had just come down from the north and were now at his post. "I at once made up my mind to act on the information received from Mr. Mcdougall [sic]," said Macleod, "so I issued a Summons against Weatherwax and sent Inspector Winder with a party of men to seize the robes."[35]

The robes and furs were taken and Weatherwax arrested, but the Mounties were disappointed that Berry was not in the party. The catch consisted of 452 buffalo robes, 1 bear skin, 4 otter skins, and 2 coyote skins, which were placed in Conrad's warehouse. On 1 February, Weatherwax appeared before Colonel Macleod in his role as magistrate. The officer stated:

> I was able to prove by his teamsters that they had brought the robes from the Post on Bow River where I had information that liquor was being trafficked with the Indians and that they had both had liquor there, one of them from a man who went into the brush nearby and brought it to him in the Kraal and the other while cards were being played in the Fort ... I considered that with this, together with the information I had, was sufficient to ground the case at any rate as regard the detention of the robes.[36]

Macleod hoped that Indians coming to the fort would be able to give further information, but because of the bitterly cold weather, he saw only those camped nearby, who had not been north. Finally, an Indian turned up who said that he had been camped at the confluence of the Bow and Highwood Rivers since fall and "has continually seen whiskey traded at both the posts with the Indians—that 3 cups were given for a robe & 8 for a horse."[37] Macleod also found witnesses who had heard Weatherwax referring to the northern post as being his.

Still not satisfied that there was enough evidence to link Weatherwax directly with the illicit sale of whisky, Macleod decided to send an expedition north, regardless of the weather, to arrest Dick Berry and the others who had been named in an indictment. Having no horses capable of making the journey, he hired animals from local traders and on 2 February, sent Inspector Leif Crozier north with ten policemen, Jerry Potts as guide, fifteen days' rations, and a wagon.

One member of the party, Sergeant William Antrobus, kept a diary, which indicated that their trip was an ordeal right from the start. It was so cold the first night that "even Jerry Potts, although he remained rolled up in his blanket, did not sleep at all."[38] The next day they ploughed through deep snow and experienced such frigid temperatures that, at one point, they almost turned back. During the day they met Henry "Butche" Kinkle, and although they knew he worked for the traders, there were no grounds to arrest him. The Mounties also knew that Kinkle would try to warn his cohorts in the north, but there was nothing they could do about it.

On the second night they reached the Leavings of Willow Creek, where they passed another miserable night. "About midnight," said Antrobus, "a storm arose such as is seen only on the prairies. The wind blew a hurricane, blowing down our teepee, and forcing us to seek the only shelter at hand, the clumps of small willows."[39] They hoped to reach the abandoned whisky fort at Pine Coulee the following day, but the snow was so deep that the horses could barely drag the wagon through the drifts. They finally stopped on the open prairie and spent another miserable night. Commented Antrobus, who was on guard duty, "Very cold; all but four men, my party, are lying down in the tent, but none have slept, although they have our blankets as well as their own."[40]

Hearing of trader Edward L. Smith at Neil Campbell's whisky fort at the mouth of Sheep Creek in February 1875. L–R: Father Constantine Scollen; Blood Chief Strangling Wolf; two unknown persons; Edward Smith; and two Mounties. Drawn by R. B. Nevitt from a sketch by Superintendent Leif Crozier. (Glenbow Art Dept. NE.59.40.22)

By struggling all the next day through the snow, the party was able to reach the friendly confines of the Pine Coulee post. "The fort is about three miles from where we came into the gully," said Antrobus, "and is built in the mouth of a beautiful canyon. Our fort (at Fort Macleod), or rather our buildings, cannot compare with this one, ours being built of cottonwood, this of fine large pine and the roof as close as if made of boards."[41] Here they found a man named L. F. Williams "in Weatherwax's employ" guarding a wagonload of robes while his partners looked for their horses that had drifted in the storm. A second man, Edward Tingle, showed up later in the day.

Another storm raged across the prairies that night, but the men were warmly ensconced in Kamoose Taylor and William Bond's fort. Inspector Crozier had seized the wagonload of robes and set two constables to work to make warm moccasins for the men, while another two made a sleigh to replace the useless wagon. Then, still less than 60 miles from Fort Macleod, they set out again. In spite of cold piercing winds they made good time, thanks to their new sleigh, and reached the banks of the Highwood River by evening. As they settled into camp, they met another of Weatherwax's men, a trader named George Clarke, who after being questioned set out for the north, likely to warn the others.

Next day the Mounties cached their sleigh, most of their provisions, and their gear, in order to make a quick final run down the Highwood River to the illicit forts. But the trip was anything but quick for the snow was so deep that the men had to lead their horses for the first 10 miles. At mid-morning they saw a sleigh on the other side of the valley, so Crozier and seven men immediately pursued it. They struggled down one steep slope, across the valley floor, and up the other side, almost using up their horses in the process. They found the tracks of the sleigh and after a run of about 3 miles they caught up with it. The driver was a Cree half-breed who spoke no English, and as Jerry Potts was trying to communicate with him, another trader hove into sight. He proved to be Edward L. Smith, one of the men for whom a warrant had been issued. He told Crozier that he had just been down to the fort at the confluence of the Highwood and Bow that was run by Dick Berry and his partner, Shears, but there was nothing there. Having been tipped off by either Butche Kinkle or George Clarke, the traders had cleared out and the Indians had burned the fort to the ground.

With one fort out of the way, Crozier split off five men and sent them ahead to the second known whisky-trading post near the mouth of Sheep Creek. This one was operated by Neil Campbell (who had been on the boundary survey near Waterton Lakes with George M. Dawson) and his partner, Allan. The five men occupied the fort and waited until Crozier and the others, including Smith, arrived. Crozier then "took some evidence from Smith concerning Berry and Weatherwax,"[42] after which Smith was formally arrested and charged with supplying liquor to Indians.

The Mounties stayed at Campbell and Allan's fort for a few days, winds and blizzards almost constantly buffeting the place. During this time, they were visited by Oblate missionary Constantine Scollen, by a trading party of Blackfoot, who fled when they saw the police, and by a delegation led by the Siksika head chief Old Sun. The Siksikas were taken into the fort and were treated to bread, syrup, and tea from the police's scanty stores. Old Sun said he didn't know what to expect when he came to meet the police. "They are very much afraid of us," said Sergeant Antrobus, "thinking us great men, for they are afraid of the traders and know the traders are afraid of us, so that in their eyes we are no common men."[43]

While Crozier and his men were at the fort, two more sleighs arrived, loaded with robes; these were seized and the three men with them were placed under arrest. A preliminary hearing was then held on the Smith case, as a witness named Strangling Wolf was too ill to travel to Fort Macleod. His testimony was taken and Smith was bound over for trial.

The Mounties and their prisoners left Campbell and Allan's fort in fine weather, but they were hardly on the trail when it started to snow and blow. While Antrobus and some of his men were stopped to rearrange the packs on their horses, they were struck by yet another raging blizzard. By the time they were ready to move, the storm had wiped out the trail of the main party and visibility was reduced to 50 yards. "Some of the boys became greatly alarmed at the thought of becoming lost," said Antrobus, "and one of them wanted us to try to get back at once to Campbell's about eight miles. I refused, saying that Jerry would return for us when the captain found we did not come up with him in reasonable time."[44] They stayed where they were for what seemed like hours until at last Jerry Potts appeared and guided them to their camp on the upper waters of the Highwood River. "This Jerry Potts is justly called the best guide in the country," said Antrobus, "for I do not believe there is another man who could have guided us through that storm as he did."[45] The following days were clear and calm, and the police and their prisoners made it safely back to Fort Macleod.

The trials were held over the next few days. Edward L. Smith was fined three hundred dollars and given a six-month prison term. However, because he gave evidence in the Weatherwax case, incarceration was suspended if he promised to leave the country and not come back for a year. He accepted.

But Weatherwax was the prize catch, and the Mounties had no intention of letting him go, even if the evidence against him was sketchy and circumstantial. Macleod firmly believed that Dick Berry was in the employ of Weatherwax, that he had been trading whisky provided by Weatherwax, and that the seized robes were obtained through whisky sales and were destined for Wetzel & Weatherwax's warehouse. Weatherwax, on the other hand, claimed that he had outfitted Berry with trade goods, but not whisky, and that the man was an independent trader. Both versions could have an element of truth. It is quite possible that Berry was on his own, for this was a common way for suppliers and traders to operate. Tom Power had set the pace when he loaned money to traders that enabled them to buy his goods; later, they brought their robes to him to pay off their debts. If Weatherwax was operating in this same fashion, then technically Berry was not his employee but merely his customer. On the other hand, there can be little doubt that Weatherwax supplied him with whisky, for the firm of Wetzel & Weatherwax was now the primary whisky merchant of Fort Benton.

In the end, Weatherwax was convicted of "indirectly trading whiskey to the Indians" and was sentenced to a fine of three hundred dollars and six months imprisonment.[46] This was, observed one Mountie, "a finishing stroke to the whiskey trade in this country."[47] Another commented, "Weatherwax was very properly and justly condemned and found guilty of selling whiskey to Dick Berry, and ... old J. D., the chief of all the smugglers and desperadoes of the great Northwest, was locked up in jail."[48]

And so with one decisive action—the legality of which might be questioned—the entire whisky trade in Canadian territory was brought to its knees without a shot being fired. The rumours of heavily defended forts and violent desperados ready for battle proved nothing more than idle gossip. The whisky traders were shown for what they were: opportunists looking for a quick buck at somebody else's expense. They were exploiters, not fighters; bullies, not heroes. If there was no law, they were willing to live with the murder, victimization, and decimation of the Blackfoot, but as the NWMP proved, if there was law, they quietly chose to respect it or leave the country.

Needless to say, Weatherwax was furious about the ruling, threatening to take the matter all the way to officials in Washington, D.C., and to appeal to the Supreme Court of Canada "and it is surmised there will be considerable litigation over it, as he is a wealthy fellow."[49] In the meantime, he had to serve six months in the NWMP guardhouse in Fort Macleod.

Montanans were up in arms over the arrest and poured scathing invectives upon the heads of the NWMP. The *Benton Record* exclaimed in an editorial, "We did not expect that the conduct of the Queen's Regulators would be according to law; in fact we knew from experience that wherever the English flag floats, might is right." It added that when the Mounties failed to catch Dick Berry, "sooner than suffer a complete failure and ignoring law, justice and all feeling of humanity, they seized a large number of robes belonging to Wetzel & Weatherwax ..."[50] In the same vein, a *Helena Daily Herald* correspondent complained that "the rights of an American citizen are trampled under foot, without the application of law or justice, in her Majesty's dominions."[51] In reviewing the case, the writer said that the Wetzel & Weatherwax firm was accused of furnishing the goods and

Berry of selling them, but neither Wetzel nor Weatherwax were cited for actually indulging in the illegal traffic "nor was any proof to that effect obtained or offered."[52] He then noted that "the prosecution disregarded the proof that Wetzel & Co. were not partners with Berry; that they sold Berry his supplies (not whiskey); that they bought his robes and skins; that they are in no way responsible for the acts of Berry." He concluded by saying that Weatherwax was "a victim of brute force, made so under the disguise of legal proceedings that amounted to a foregone conclusion from the outset."[53]

Weatherwax contacted Martin Maginnis, the whisky-traders' friend in the House of Representatives in Washington. Maginnis took the matter to officials in the capitol and also expounded at length to a reporter from the *New York Bulletin*. The *Bulletin* outdid any of its Montana counterparts for invective, referring to the Weatherwax trial as a "drumhead court-martial" and editorializing that "it is a mockery to justice ... that a gang of ruffians should take all a man's property and divide it among themselves, after adjudging it to themselves."[54] It said that American traders "were at the mercy of the mounted police, and subject to the jealousy of the Hudson's Bay Company. It is to be hoped that there will not be any 'fifty-four-forty or fight' in the matter."[55]

Yet not all Montanans decried the arrest and conviction of Weatherwax. A Sun River citizen who seemed to be intimately familiar with the liquor traffic acknowledged that American traders had been flooding the British possessions with whisky and that this had pauperized and decimated the Blackfoot tribes. When the Mounted Police arrived, he said, they had been given extraordinary powers to cope with their situation. He added:

> The whisky traders, finding their occupation, formerly so profitable, gone, hated to give it up, but, thinking that they could evade this police force as they had formerly our authorities, have still been venturing in with more or less of this stuff they call whisky; but the British authorities, more vigilant than ours, and occasionally nabbing one of them, they naturally raise a hue and cry of unfairness.[56]

To all intents and purposes, the Weatherwax case ended the major whisky traffic in Whoop-Up country. There was only one more whimper before it died completely. When the Mounties arrived, "Dutch Fred" Wachter had a supply of whisky at his trading post at Standoff. He cached it over the winter, waiting for a chance to sell it, and when Berry's fort was burned down and Weatherwax's men were arrested, he thought the time was right for him to go north. He teamed up with "Spanish Joe" Aranna, John J. Sowers, and two other men; they then split into two groups. Wachter, with a supply of legitimate goods, passed through

Fort Macleod, while Aranna and the others took the whisky by another route. They reunited at Neil Campbell's post on Sheep Creek and decided to build a trading post nearby. However, on 25 February, during construction, a drunken argument broke out between the partners, and Wachter ended up crushing the Spaniard's skull with an iron bar.

Wachter voluntarily surrendered to the Mounties two months later, claiming that the killing was in self-defence. Initially, he was convicted of selling liquor to Indians and given a five-hundred-dollar fine and two months in jail. During this time, information was collected on the killing but there was not enough evidence to secure a conviction so he was acquitted.[57] By December, Wachter was back in Sheep Creek country but this time without any liquor.

By the end of 1875, the whisky trade on the Canadian side of the border was virtually finished. The Blackfoot, in their calendar system, recorded it as "*Itsixowatorpi/napiorki* – When it was finished/whiskey."[58] From time to time a few bootleggers tried to slip across the line, usually unsuccessfully, and established traders sometimes handled a little whisky on the side, but the amount was a mere trickle compared to the flood that had so decimated the Blackfoot tribes in the previous five years. But it was a different story south of the border.

15. *South of the Border*

The eradication of the whisky trade on the Canadian side of the border spelled chaos for the Peigans living on the Blackfeet Reservation in Montana. The few cautious traders who had given up the traffic in Whoop-Up country in 1873 in anticipation of the North-West Mounted Police (NWMP) were now reinforced by scores of others who fled the British side after the arrest of "Kamoose" Taylor and the incarceration of John Weatherwax. They moved onto the watercourses of the reservation where they put up temporary shacks and went back to wagon trading, invading Peigan villages along the Badger, Birch, Two Medicine, Marias, and other streams.

Not only did the Indians suffer because of this onslaught, but so did the licenced traders, most of whom were in the employ of either I. G. Baker or T. C. Power. They quickly found their business dwindling and their competition increasing because of illicit traders on the reservation. Their immediate response was to launch a writing campaign to get more police appointed to halt the trade. As a journalist commented, "Our government has but one or two men watching over the whole frontier, whereas the Canadian government has 300 men."[1] In fact, the Blackfeet Indian Agency had only one law enforcement officer, Detective Andrew Dusold, who simply could not cope with the influx.

Ironically, one of the first to participate in the writing campaign was Al Hamilton, former part-owner of Fort Whoop-Up. He wrote to the commissioner of Indian Affairs in Washington at the beginning of 1875, commenting:

> The Whisky traffic with Indians having been entirely suppressed by Her Majesty's Force of Mounted Police ... Men who have heretofore been carrying on that trade with Indians in that portion of the country ... are becoming bolder every day in introducing Whisky, Arms and Ammunition into the Blood and Piegan Camps on the Teton and Marias Rivers. Several of the leading Chiefs of the Piegan tribe of Indians have been killed during the past year in drunken rows, and there appears to be no successful attempt made by our Government to suppress this illicit traffic ... Being engaged in a legitimate trade with the Indians at the Post of I. G. Baker & Co. near the

Blackfoot Agency, I felt that it was my duty to inform you of this state of affairs.[2]

About the same time, Tom Power wrote to the commissioner from Fort Benton, calling his attention to the fact that "since the arrival of the British Mounted Police in the 'Whoop Up Country' where formerly whiskey was traded to the Indians without limit, those traders have now changed their base of operations and are carrying on a whiskey trade with impunity below here and between this point and Fort Clagett."[3] Like Hamilton, Power wanted more police and even offered to pay fifty dollars a month from his own pocket towards the salary of another detective.

Henry Kennerly, trader for T. C. Power at Fort Maginnis on Birch Creek, told the Indian agent that the Peigan chiefs were urging that the traffic be suppressed. The Peigans told Kennerly that on Medicine Lodge Creek, six men were building a number of houses "for the purpose of illegal traffic with Indians, their principal stock in trade being whiskey." He said these men were from Whoop-Up country who had been driven across the line.[4]

Yet this wasn't just a simple situation of interlopers trading illegally on the reservation, as claimed by the licenced traders. Some of the licenced traders themselves either sold whisky or sent the Indians a short distance from their forts to their cohorts who were waiting with whisky. Colonel John Gibbon, at Fort Shaw, explained the process:

The view of Front Street facing the Missouri River in Fort Benton, 1878. A steamboat can be seen on the right. (Montana Historical Society 947-051)

> The licensed trader establishes himself or his Agent on or near the
> line of the Reservation on the north bank of the Maria's [sic]
> River. Directly in the vicinity of this *licensed* Trader and on the
> *south* bank of the River (that is, off the Reservation), the illicit
> trafficer [sic] establishes himself and exposes his vile poison for
> sale or exchange for robes. The licensed Trader receives, entertains
> and harbors the illicit trader and his wares, and receives from the
> latter the robes, &c. which he gathers in from the Indians in trade
> for whiskey and ammunition. [italics in original][5]

Gibbon specifically identified the I. G. Baker company as one of the offending
parties while Detective Dusold said that Henry Kennerly and Charles Aubrey,
both trading for T. C. Power, were selling contraband, mostly in the form of
repeating rifles and ammunition, from their licenced posts.

According to Indian agent John S. Wood, it was almost impossible to ferret
out the whisky traders because white men camped on the reservation with their
Indian wives either tipped off the traders or were trafficking themselves.
Similarly, Peigans who had been caught with liquor refused to reveal their
sources. He said that recently there had been fifteen to twenty Indians and five
white men killed through whisky troubles. At the time of writing, the Indians
were "running about in small bands and say they don't care to go to the Agency
as their Father has no controll [sic] of the bad White Men, and we don't wish to
go there and get killed."[6] Like Hamilton and Power, Agent Wood complained
that the reservation was becoming infested with traders from the north. "The
British Government," he said, "has a Battalion of Mounted men on the border
and have run all the Whiskey traders out of what is called 'Whoopup' in the
British Possessions, the great rendezvous for men of that caractor [sic], down on
us and we have now what the British have had for a great many years."[7]

Probably the man fighting the whisky trade most effectively during this time
was Andrew Dusold, the Indian department detective. He had served five years
in the Union army, attaining the rank of captain and receiving a high commen-
dation from General Grenville Dodge. A staunch Republican, he had served as a
representative to the Montana Territorial convention in 1872 and was described
as "the untiring Republican war-horse."[8] He was appointed Indian department
detective in 1873 and, in the same year, was elected to the Territorial legislature.
As a detective, he soon gained the trust of the Peigans for his honesty and diligence; Indian Agent Wood commented: "His success in winning the friendship
and confidence of these Indians is remarkable."[9]

In 1875, Dusold set out to achieve three goals. One was the arrest or expul-
sion from the reservation of any of the Whoop-Up crowd who had moved south
of the border. The second was to put out of business the men who built shacks

just off the edge of the reservation and secretly sold whisky to the Peigans. And the third was to nab any of the licenced traders who were selling illegal arms or alcohol or working in collusion with illicit traders.

In an attempt to curtail the ex-Whoop-Up traffic, Detective Dusold and a detachment of one officer and nine soldiers from Fort Shaw made a foray into the heart of the whisky-trading area at the end of January 1875. When they reached the mouth of Badger Creek, Dusold learned that five men outfitted with whisky and fixed ammunition were now trading about 25 miles up the creek. He and his men followed their trail and caught them just as they were saddling up to leave. A search of their camp turned up four thousand rounds of Henry cartridges, but Dusold failed to find the whisky that he knew was cached some place nearby. The wagon, horses, and other gear were seized and the traders taken to the Indian agency to await trial. On their way back to the agency, Dusold learned of another party of seven men trading whisky at the head of Two Medicine River, but feared losing the prisoners they already had if they pursued them.

During this trip, one old chief came to him and said, "When I was young there was no Whisky and my people were happy; but now they get drunk and kill one another, and sometimes when they are drunk they will kill the whiskey traders."[10]

A second expedition took place in March, but because of blizzards, deep snow, and bitterly cold weather it met with little success. When Dusold and the soldiers arrived on Birch Creek, they were told by Peigans that white men were trading whisky on Badger Creek. Dusold led his men through deep snow and managed to get to Fort Maginnis just before their horses gave out. There they discovered that someone had gone ahead of them to warn the illicit traders, who had then decamped. Dusold reported, "I made inquiries among the Indians about Whisky Traders and was informed that there were 3 or 4 parties on the Reservation between Birch Creek and the St. Mary's River on the British line."[11]

As soon as the horses were rested, Dusold and the soldiers set out again and along Badger Creek found a known whisky trader named Fitzgerald, who claimed he had come down from the Whoop-Up country to buy provisions. A diligent search of the area failed to turn up his whisky cache, and he was reluctantly released but ordered to leave the reservation. From the whisky trader's camp, Dusold and his men went to visit White Calf Chief's village on Badger Creek, a Blood camp on Medicine Lodge Creek, and three others on Cut Bank River and at the forks of Milk River, but the whisky traders had left.

In April, the detective's diligence was finally rewarded when he was tipped off that John B. Smith (the notorious "Whiskey" Smith)[12] had recently come down from Whoop-Up and built a post just off the reservation, referring to it grandiloquently as Smith's Fort.[13] Through careful inquiry, Dusold found several Native witnesses willing to testify they had seen whisky sold by Smith and his associates. On the basis of this information, he arrested Smith, Leonard Leeman,

Charles Phemister, Charles Osborne, and James Arnoux. A sixth man, John E. McDonald, escaped.

It turned out that Dusold had rounded up some of the top men in Montana's whisky-trading clique, men with influence in both business and political arenas. In order to keep the cases out of court, these men launched a campaign of fear and intimidation against the Peigans. As the Indian agent reported, Henry Bostwick, a labourer at Fort Shaw, said openly that "if certain Indians appeared as witnesses against the parties accused of selling whisky to Indians that they would never come back alive."[14] Over the next several days, those who had agreed to testify were harassed, threatened, and even bribed to induce them to back off. But Detective Dusold's presence reassured them not to succumb to the pressures. As the Indian agent said, "No other person could have induced the Indian witnesses to go to Helena to appear against the whisky trafficers [sic] at the late trial. They were afraid and it was their great confidence in Mr. Dusold which alone emboldened them to do so."[15]

The witnesses were escorted to Helena for a hearing before a u.s. Grand Jury, with Dusold to follow as soon as he returned from gathering more evidence near the Canadian line. However, once the Peigans arrived in Helena, Smith and Leeman pressed charges against the leading witness, Big Brave, son of the great leader Mountain Chief, accusing him of trying to shoot and kill them. On the basis of these false charges, Big Brave was arrested and put in jail. Obviously, the whisky traders hoped this action would cause the other witnesses to withdraw and Big Brave's testimony to be discredited.

Dusold arrived in Helena a few days later and found Big Brave in jail on the false charges, but much to his pleasure and surprise, he learned that the other witnesses hadn't been intimidated and had stayed where they were. This was despite their belief that Smith really "had the power to have them imprisoned and punished, if they should appear in Court against them."[16] The detective immediately got Big Brave out on bail and had two lawyers successfully defend him—all paid for out of his own pocket.

In early May, the charges against Smith and the others "for disposing of spiritous liquors to Indians" came before Chief Justice Decius Wade and a jury. The defendants' lawyers claimed that the offences with which their clients were charged had actually occurred south of the Teton River and off the reservation. As such, they said, no crime had been committed. This time, Judge Wade sided with the government. He instructed the jury:

> If the evidence shows that the offence alleged to have been
> committed was committed on the Teton River in Choteau
> County in the Territory of Montana, at a place in the habitual
> and long continued occupation by the Indians, then the offence

was committed within Indian country as that term is used in the statute under which the indictment is drawn.[17]

On the basis of the evidence and Judge Wade's directive, Smith and his co-defendants were found guilty. But the whisky crowd was not ready to abandon Smith so easily. Less than a week later, one of the guards in the Helena jail conveniently had to go to church, leaving only one man on duty. When Smith asked to use the latrine, he was permitted to go unescorted into the yard where the outhouse was located. From there he quickly scaled the wooden fence, scrambled up a hillside on the west side of town, and made use of a fleet horse and a Henry rifle that were waiting for him.[18] Within minutes he was crossing the Great Cactus Plain and within days he was over the border into Whoop-Up country.

The implication of Justice Wade's instruction to the jury was far-reaching. It meant that the whisky shacks along the river that were off the reservation could be raided and closed down, as they were located in an area where the Peigans had a record of long occupation. This was a great victory for Detective Dusold, and he had no trouble getting the United States military to cooperate now that a court decision had gone its way. Accordingly, one company of cavalry and one of infantry were given the task of intercepting and searching all wagons and pack animals approaching the Teton River.

Dusold had accomplished one of his goals, for the Whiskey Smith decision had broken the back of the ex-Whoop-Up trade on the reservation. Now he was in a position to attack his second goal, that of putting the rest of the Teton traders out of business, including their kingpin, Sol Abbott. The detective was aware of five trading posts along the river, all run by men with Territorial or County licences and all selling whisky. The situation was so bad that he considered the Teton River to be "a second Whoop Up."[19] Most of these traders, he believed, were working in concert with the licenced traders on the reservation. As a result, in June, Detective Dusold raided T. C. Power's trading post near the agency, run by Charles Aubrey, seizing some 818 robes and closing the post down. Next he went to Birch Creek, where he seized all the goods of Henry Kennerly, valued at some five thousand dollars, and closed him down as well. His was another T. C. Power establishment.

This was too much for the whisky and arms moguls of Fort Benton to accept. The telegrams started flying, the political wheels turning, and then the axe fell. Dusold was still moving goods out of Kennerly's post when he received a telegram from Washington telling him that he had been transferred to the Crow Agency.[20]

There was a great hue and cry at this crude attempt to muzzle the Indian agency's most effective watchdog. The Indian agent exclaimed that Dusold was essential in the campaign to put down the whisky trade and implied that his departure would give the illicit traders a free reign. In the end, the government compromised by cancelling Dusold's transfer but instructing the u.s. attorney to discontinue any legal actions against T. C. Power & Bro. for their violations of the law.[21]

By summer, the worst of the excessive liquor trade had been suppressed on the Blackfeet Reservation and Indian Agent Wood could report:

> The detestable whisky traffic is destroyed, as the Indians have declared against its use, but a strict watch must be kept [on] the whisky trafficer [*sic*] during the coming winter, when the robes and peltries of the Indians will stimulate this class to extra exertion. The utmost vigilance will be necessary to prevent the misfortune of a relapse, even though temporary, to the degradation of the past.[22]

Trafficking in whisky would continue to be a major problem on the Blackfeet Reservation for the next five years, or as long as the Indians could still produce buffalo robes. But with the final destruction of the buffalo herds in 1880–81, the Blackfoot no longer had anything the traders wanted, and the trade simply withered away; what was left slipped into the hands of a few local bootleggers. In those same years, whisky remained just a memory to the Indians north of the line as the NWMP carried out their active program of complete suppression.

16. *What Became of Them?*

*W*hen the North-West Mounted Police (NWMP) came to Whoop-Up country in 1874, the Reverend John McDougall had some words of advice for them. In spite of the whisky traders' criticisms of him and the false stories they had circulated about him, the missionary was not prepared to condemn all of them now that the law had arrived. Wrote a reporter in the *Toronto Mail*:

> Mr. Macdougall says that a large number of the traders of that section of the country are as fine a class of men as can be found anywhere, and that they are not disposed to resist the authorities, but rather to co-operate with them. The class mostly to be dreaded are the roughs and blacklegs and outlaws who gamble and prospect in the summer, and in winter sell whiskey to the Indians. These men, as a rule, have little capital and are reckless. Many of those of the other class who have sold whiskey have not gone to excess in the business, and they all prefer to see it done away with, as they are men of means and want protection to life and property.[1]

The NWMP appeared to have followed McDougall's advice not to condemn a man for anything he may have done prior to their arrival. In fact, no sooner were the police in Whoop-Up country than they started to do business with the one-time whisky traders. Four days after the Mounties pitched their tents, they bought ten dollars' worth of goods from Kamoose Taylor and 5½ tons of hay from "Red" Buckland. The following week Fred Kanouse sold them 3 tons of hay, and Joe Carr began bringing them fresh buffalo meat on a regular basis.[2] Even when John Weatherwax offered to pay the fines of Kamoose Taylor and his men, the Mounties were willing to take goods instead of cash. In lieu of money they accepted 326 pounds of bacon, 5 gallons of syrup, a pitchfork, some axe handles, and 105 buffalo robes.[3]

Similarly, Charles Conrad and D. W. Davis became the two main agents for I. G. Baker & Co., even though both had been heavily involved in the whisky trade. Also, T. C. Power built a store at Fort Macleod and later at Fort Calgary, while a number of ex-whisky traders opened local businesses and became part of the southern Alberta community.

The whisky traders and suppliers who survived unruly Indians and their own alcoholic binges fell into three groups. One group remained in Canada and, by and large, became a positive part of the community. The second group returned to the United States, a few of its members settling on the Blackfeet Reservation with their Native wives, and the third group drifted farther afield. Of course, many of those involved in the trade simply dropped out of sight. These were the labourers, teamsters, and wolfers who had wandered in and out of the whisky-selling scene, often with no other identity than a last name or a nickname. The *Benton Record*, for example, listed some of them as Whistling Jack, Buckskin Joe, Four-Jack Bob, Toe-String Joe, Sweet-Oil Bob, Smooth Bill, and Whiskey Brown.[4] Others were remembered only by their surnames, such as O'Neill, Davidson, Stuart, and Annerson. They, and others like them, simply disappeared from the pages of history.

But many of those actively involved with the whisky trade, particularly those who had their own businesses or built their own trading posts, left a trail that can easily be followed, sometimes for only a year or two, but in other instances to the ends of their careers.

At the top of any such list must be John J. Healy and Alfred B. Hamilton, for they launched the northern whisky trade in the winter of 1869–70 and maintained the leadership of it with the largest and most impressive fort of any in Whoop-Up country. Of the two, Healy was the leader, the entrepreneur, and the most colourful.

After the NWMP arrived in 1874, Healy retained sole ownership of Fort Whoop-Up and continued with the Indian trade until he sold out in 1876 to his manager, Dave Akers. Healy then became a partner and reporter for the *Benton Record* in 1877, and during the flight of the Nez Perces, he provided a first-hand account of their battle with the U.S. army at Bear Paw Mountain. He also was present for Sitting Bull's meeting with General Alfred Terry at Fort Walsh and telegraphed his report to the *New York Herald*. But perhaps his most significant literary contribution was his series of reminiscences and articles on early Montana that were published in the *Record* between 1878 and 1880.

In addition to his editorial duties, Healy was named sheriff of Choteau county in 1877 and pursued a flamboyant and unorthodox style of law enforcement for the next eight years. During this time, he appointed his old partner, Al Hamilton, as one of his deputies. When Healy was voted out of office in 1885, he went to Alaska where he purchased a schooner, began trading with gold miners, and the following year opened a trading post at Dyea on the Lynn Canal. Gradually he expanded his business to other enterprises, at the same time serving as a deputy marshal. On his first trip "outside" in 1891, Montana greeted him as a returning hero, with a local newspaper commenting that "the reception of Mr. Healy by the old timers was in the nature of an ovation."[5]

On this trip, Healy was able to obtain financial backing to launch the North American Transportation & Trading Company to operate ships and handle supplies throughout Alaska and the Yukon Territory. After a short time in operation, Healy wrote to Hamilton, saying, "I think I have struck another Whoop-Up country, though much quieter and safer."[6]

Plying the Yukon River and keeping the miners outfitted with supplies, Healy was in a perfect position to capitalize on the Klondike gold rush in 1896–98. He opened a branch office in Dawson City and moved to the boom town in 1897. However, he was soon embroiled in trouble with the directors of the company when his order for a boatload of food for starving miners was countermanded and whisky was sent instead. An angry Healy physically attacked one of his investors on the deck of the boat, while hungry miners watched. He then created more trouble for himself when miners' orders were not properly filled as he tried to take advantage of inflated prices.

By 1898, Healy was being viciously attacked in the press, accused of price gouging and cheating. He weathered the storm but the complaints continued, the company's profits plunged, and in the summer of 1899 he was fired.

Undeterred, Healy organized the Yakutat Fishing Company in 1900 and, with outside backing, formed the Central Alaskan Exploration Company to prospect for gold. However, after a year, both companies expired. His next idea was to build a railroad from Valdez, on the Alaska coast, to the interior. He travelled to London to raise capital for the project, but like so many of his other dreams, it failed to materialize. The entrepreneur then embarked on a scheme to build a railroad across the Bering Sea and through Siberia, and although the plan created considerable interest in Washington, London, and Moscow, it too failed.

By this time, Healy was sixty-five years old with a string of failures behind him. With no other options open to him, he went back to his old occupations of prospecting and trading. When his health failed, he moved to his daughter's home in San Francisco and died there in 1908. Although he had been flamboyant and colourful throughout his life, he never got rich. The Whoop-Up years made him famous, but most of the money he earned went to Tom Power and the bankers, not into his own pocket. Similarly, if anyone profited in Alaska, it was the investors, not Healy.

By comparison, Al Hamilton's life was somewhat dull and pedestrian. In a deposition in 1910, he described his career as follows: "I have been a Justice of the Peace in the Territorial government; have been elected to the territorial legislature three times; have been Sheriff and Deputy Sheriff of Teton County; County Assessor of Choteau; six years Postmaster in Choteau; and doorkeeper of the Legislative Assembly of Montana."[7]

Hamilton had married Lucy, the daughter of Iron Breast, in the 1850s and they had two daughters, Grace and Ella. When Hamilton left Fort Whoop-Up in 1873, he opened a trading post on the Teton River. In the following year he became a licenced trader for I. G. Baker, and for most of his life he was never far from the Blackfeet Reservation. In 1875 he went into partnership with I. N. Hazlett in the mercantile firm of Hamilton & Hazlett. He founded the village of Choteau in 1879, became its first postmaster, and was appointed its deputy sheriff.[8]

Hamilton was considered to be a leading figure in the area and was highly respected by both Peigans and Indian agency staff. In 1885, when the Indian agent resigned, Hamilton's name was recommended by Martin Maginnis as his successor and supported by a petition from citizens of Choteau county.[9] However, he didn't get the job; it went instead to a faithful party member from Ohio. In 1886, Hamilton & Hazlett closed its doors, and Hamilton moved to the nearby village of Robare where he opened a general store. In 1895, when the Peigans were being pressed to surrender part of their reservation near the mountains, they demanded that Hamilton and Charles Conrad sit in on the meetings. Later, when negotiations were in danger of breaking down, Hamilton, together with Conrad, Joe Kipp, and George Steell, convinced the tribal council to settle for a lower price.[10] In 1897 Hamilton was permitted to build a trading post on the reservation but he had so many debts that, as soon as it opened, creditors rushed to attach his property.[11] After suffering these reverses, he welcomed an invitation from John Healy to join him in Alaska where his old partner had great plans for the future. Hamilton travelled there with his daughter Grace, but when Healy's schemes failed to materialize, they returned to Montana and he died in 1920 at his daughter's home on Cutbank Creek.

Of the two men, Hamilton was obviously the more reliable and stable. Also, evidence indicates that he was a somewhat reluctant participant in the whisky end of the business and gave it up when he had the chance to take over his uncle's trading post. There is no indication that he ever again was involved in liquor trafficking, even though there would have been plenty of opportunities while he lived on or near the Blackfeet Reservation.

Not so with Joe Kipp. He was, in many ways, a likeable scoundrel and an opportunist. His image, however, was given a shine and polish by author James Willard Schultz, who worked for Kipp and appears to have greatly admired him. Through Schultz's writings, Kipp comes through as a brave hero who overcame all the obstacles that confronted a mixed-blood trader on the frontier.

Kipp bailed out of the Whoop-Up country trade as soon as the NWMP appeared on the scene. Presumably he simply abandoned his post at the confluence of the Belly and Oldman Rivers or sold it to one of the other traders who had decided to stick around. According to Schultz, "From this time on, until the buffalo were finally exterminated, [Kipp] traded in different parts of Montana, one year in one place, the next season somewhere else, wherever the buffalo and Indians were."[12]

He spent the winter of 1874–75 at a post on the Marias River, where he traded with Gros Ventre, Assiniboine, and Blackfoot Indians and continued to deal in whisky. Al Wilkins told of an experience he had with Kipp in the spring of 1875 while hunting on the Teton River. He was about 4 miles from Benton when he saw a wagon racing along the trail and another wagon following some distance behind. "I headed for the river," recalled Wilkins, "where I thought the first team would strike it, to see what was up. When I reached the river, Joe Kipp had driven into it and thrown 10 kegs of whisky into the stream."[13] The kegs had just floated around a bend when Marshal X. Biedler arrived in the second wagon and told Kipp he was under arrest for trading whisky to the Indians. However, when the wagon was searched, no whisky was found and the trader was released. Later, Kipp followed the river downstream until he came to a riffle where all the kegs had been trapped. He recovered his stash and left that night for the Blackfoot camps, returning the following day with a load of buffalo robes.

Kipp had trading posts on Badger and Dupuyer Creeks in the succeeding years, then followed the Indians to the Bear Paw Mountains in 1878–79 as they pursued the declining buffalo herds. The next summer he was on Judith River and, for the first time in his checkered career, he traded no whisky.[14] For the winter of 1879–80, he had a post at Carroll on the Missouri, but the returns dropped so drastically that in the trading season of 1882–83 he acquired only a hundred robes. With buffalo hunting at an end and the Peigans returning to their reservation, Kipp and his partners bought Fort Conrad from I. G. Baker where they traded and ranched.

During the 1880s, Kipp had a number of trading posts in the vicinity of Robare, but in 1889 became a licenced trader and was permitted to move onto the reservation with his Peigan wife. There he took over a former trading post and ran it as a store and stopping place.

In the 1890s, a number of charges were made against Kipp for shady dealings on the reservation. He was accused of "borrowing" a government sawmill to fulfill commercial contracts;[15] of being part of an "Agency Ring," along with James Willard Schultz, that was illegally staking mineral claims on the reservation and agitating to have this area opened for settlement;[16] of helping to talk the Peigans into surrendering this "mineral belt" section of their reservation;[17] and of "shady practises" in operating his stores. He would have been ordered off the reservation had not Indian Agent George Steell interceded on his behalf.[18] Kipp remained on the reservation for the rest of his life and died in Browning in 1913. At the time of his death, ex-whisky-trader George Houk said: "Kipp had no trouble with the Alberta Indians. He got along well with them. He was well educated and had a lot of tact and diplomacy [but he] had troubles with the Montana tribes."[19]

Two other noteworthy figures in the whisky trade, particularly from the supply side, were John Weatherwax and Scott Wetzel. Weatherwax started out as an employee but eventually became a partner of Scott Wetzel to form the company Wetzel & Weatherwax. While he was serving his six-month sentence in the Fort Macleod guardhouse, he continued to maintain his company's trading post a short distance from the fort, placing L. C. Baker in charge. When he finished his jail term, Weatherwax returned to Fort Benton where a number of townsmen met him on the trail and escorted him in with a hero's welcome. For the winter of 1875–76, Weatherwax took charge of a trading post at Willow Rounds on the Blackfeet Reservation that was run jointly by Tom Power and Scott Wetzel. Under a complex deal, the post that had been owned by Wetzel & Weatherwax was sold to T. C. Power & Bro. at cost. It was operated jointly over the winter by Weatherwax, representing the Wetzel company, and Henry Kennerly, for T. C. Power, with each company having a half interest in the stock. In the spring, Wetzel & Weatherwax took the remaining stock and resumed ownership of the post.[20] Presumably, this deal enabled Power to have the post operate under his licence for the season.

Weatherwax continued in the mercantile business with Wetzel until 1880 when he sold out to his partner. Wetzel then carried on the business alone until 1884, when he went bankrupt; he died in 1891.

While Healy, Hamilton, Kipp, and Weatherwax did not stay in Canada for any length of time after the NWMP arrived, this was not true of other whisky traders. Fred Kanouse, Kamoose Taylor, "Dutch Fred" Wachter, Tony Lachappelle, and Dave Akers, for example, all decided to make Canada their home.

Fred Kanouse, the murderer of Jim Nabors, started doing business with the Mounties as soon as they arrived, as well as continuing to trade with the Indians. In 1877 he became one of Alberta's first ranchers when he imported twenty-one cows and a bull, successfully wintering them on the open range. For several years Kanouse lived in Fort Macleod, where he had a small drugstore and lived a hand-to-mouth existence. He was considered an unsavoury character and never became part of Macleod's social scene. Instead, he was regularly involved in gambling, horse racing, and drinking, continued to sell whisky, and was one of the town's main bootleggers. In 1881 he was twice arrested for illegal possession of liquor and once for selling whisky to Indians. In each instance he was let off with a fine. In 1885 he was fined for illegal possession, in 1889 he was convicted of gambling, and in 1893 he was arrested and "charged under the Indian Act with keeping a house and allowing an Indian squaw to prostitute herself therein."[21]

In 1901 Kanouse went to Blairmore, where he opened the Waldorf Hotel and pool hall; four years later he moved to the Frank sulphur springs where he had a small sanatorium. Then, in 1911, having determined that there were no longer any outstanding charges against him in the United States, he moved to Chehalis,

Washington, where he opened a hotel and pool hall. In 1912, he was invited back to Canada to be a guest at the first Calgary Stampede and to build a replica of Fort Whoop-Up. In his interviews at the time, he extolled the virtues of the whisky traders, claiming they were honest merchants who were given a bad name by the Hudson's Bay Company. He died a short time later in Tacoma, Washington.

Harry "Kamoose" Taylor also decided to make Canada his home. After suffering the humiliation of being the first whisky trader arrested by the NWMP, this former secretary of the Spitzee Cavalry soon came to see the red coats as his best potential customers. As soon as Fort Calgary was constructed, he travelled to Fort Benton where he purchased a pool table, had it hauled to the Bow River, and then he installed it in a restaurant-pool hall-stopping place not far from the NWMP fort. In 1881 he moved to Fort Macleod, where he constructed the Macleod Hotel, one of the most unique hostelries of its day. A sign at the entrance to the dining room showed a pistol with the words "settle up" issuing from its mouth. Another sign had a cartoon of a thin man "before dinner" and a fat man "after dinner."[22] But perhaps Taylor's most famous piece of frontier humour was his "Macleod Hotel Rules and Regulations." Among the thirty "rules" were:

> "Spiked boots and spurs must be removed at night before retiring." "Dogs are not allowed in the Bunks, but may sleep underneath." "To attract attention of waiters or bell boys, shoot a hole through the door panel. Two shots for ice water, three for a deck of cards, and so on." And "All guests are requested to rise at 6 a.m. This is imperative as the sheets are needed for tablecloths."[23]

When the town moved to a new site in 1884, Taylor built a large, two-storey hotel that became the main stopping place in Macleod. During these years, he was active in Conservative politics and was instrumental in having D. W. Davis, former trader at Fort Whoop-Up, elected to the House of Commons. Taylor himself was elected to the town council and served on the board of trade. In 1892 he sold his business and operated a ranch near the town until ill health forced him to move to Lethbridge in 1900, where he died a year later.

Another prominent whisky trader to stay in Canada was Dutch Fred Wachter, a former Confederate soldier. After being acquitted of killing "Spanish Joe" Aranna, he stayed around Fort Macleod for the winter of 1875–76, acting as an informer for the Mounties. He then moved to Standoff, where he carried on an active trade with the Blood Indians and sold a bit of whisky on the side. He expanded into ranching and dairying, receiving a patent for 500 acres of land on Standoff bottom and running a hundred head of range cattle, forty milk cows, and twenty horses.[24] In 1883 he sold his spread to the Oxley Ranch Company and moved to Baden, Germany; he remained there for only three years before returning to the West.

Another American who remained north of the border was Dave Akers, who had been a wood-cutter and prospector before becoming a whisky trader in 1871. He had worked for Tom Power during the 1870s but also traded on his own. By 1874 Akers was at Fort Whoop-Up, employed as manager by John Healy, and on 1 July 1876, he bought the fort from Healy for twenty-nine hundred dollars and paid another sixteen hundred dollars for the stock, furnishings, horses, etc.[25]

Akers continued to trade with the Blackfoot and regularly shipped large quantities of buffalo robes from Whoop-Up to Fort Benton. When a reporter visited him in 1882, the buffalo robe business was over and he had turned to market gardening, cultivating an area of 40 acres near the fort. "Mr. Akers showed me some of the finest specimens of vegetables, including potatoes, turnips, carrots, and cabbages that I have ever seen in any country," said the reporter. "His garden yields him a very substantial little income every year."[26] Akers also mined coal from the nearby hillside and earned extra money by renting part of the fort to the NWMP to use as an outpost. This ended in 1889 when a wing of the fort burned to the ground.

In 1894, Akers became embroiled in an argument with an old miner named Tom Purcell over a cattle deal. According to their agreement, Purcell was to transfer his share of a coal mine to Akers in exchange for cattle. When the deal fell through, Akers went to court but lost. Later, he went to Purcell's ranch and was forcibly trying to take a steer that he claimed was his when Purcell shot and killed him. At his trial, Purcell was given four years for manslaughter.

One man who never made the transition to a life of law and order was Tony Lachappelle, the Quebec-born whisky trader who was operating a post on the Oldman River when the NWMP arrived. He was one of the first to move to the village that sprang up around the police fort, and by the spring of 1875, he had installed two billiard tables and gambling tables, besides running a store that sold tobacco and candy. However, bootlegging was his real business. He took a contract with the Mounties to carry messages between Fort Macleod and Fort Benton, and at the same time he became an unofficial supplier of intoxicants to the police. Mountie Simon Clarke mentioned in 1879: "Tony Lachepelle [sic] arrived from Benton with quite a load of Jamica [sic] Ginger and Whiskey. The police Boys are on a drunk again."[27] In the spring of 1880 when he brought in another of his regular liquid supplies, a disgruntled policeman informed on him and he was arrested.[28] In the fall of the same year, Clarke noted, "Tony Lachapelle arrived from Benton and the boys are drinking again."[29] Two months later the trader was fined two hundred dollars for selling Jamaica ginger.[30]

This set the pace for Lachappelle's checkered existence. In 1882, he was fined for gambling and for selling intoxicants; in 1883, thirty dollars for assault; in 1885 and 1886, for illegal possession and illegal sale of intoxicants; in 1887, for illegal possession and for being drunk; in 1888, for being drunk; and in 1889, for selling liquor to Indians. The downward trend in his life continued as he became more and more erratic in his behaviour and finally culminated with his suicide in 1892.[31]

One of the most prominent men to remain after the arrival of the NWMP was D. W. Davis, who had been a trader for Healy & Hamilton; a tough, wild type of man, he seemed ideally suited to the whisky trade. While he was in the whisky trade, he was a relatively minor figure, seldom mentioned in the Montana newspapers of the day. With the arrival of the NWMP in 1874, Davis left Healy and became manager of the northern trade for I. G. Baker & Co., supervising the building of stores at Fort Macleod, Calgary, and other points. In 1878, when his mother asked him if he intended to stay in Canada, he said, "... while I can make money here easy and not have to work like they do in the states I shall stay."[32]

As southern Alberta grew, particularly after the arrival of the Canadian Pacific Railway in 1883, Davis became a social and business leader in the Fort Macleod area. He was a partner in the Strong horse ranch, president of the local board of trade, and helped finance the town's first newspaper. In 1887 he became a Conservative Party candidate for Parliament. His employer, Charles Conrad, said, "We would like rather our representative had not entered this political contest, but having done so ... we cannot afford to lose."[33] The I. G. Baker company donated two thousand dollars to the campaign fund and when Davis went north, he swung the vote in his favour when a sleigh loaded with hog carcasses was delivered to Métis villages in the area, each containing bladders full of whisky. Davis was elected.

As a Conservative MP, he served the ranching community until 1895 when he left office to become Collector of Customs in the Yukon Territory. There he met his old boss John Healy, and perhaps Al Hamilton as well. Davis died there in 1906. In later years, the whisky traders were proud of the fact that one of their own had reached such a high political office as Member of Parliament.

In addition to these men, there were a number of minor figures who also remained in Canada. Howell Harris became manager of the huge Circle Ranch; John B. "Whiskey" Smith had a small ranch on the upper waters of the Belly River; Lafayette French had a stopping house and ranch at High River; and William Gladstone moved into the foothills where he continued his trade as a carpenter. George Houk initially went back to Montana where he served a term as sheriff at Fort Benton. In 1885 he moved north to the Lethbridge area where he started a ranch and, over the years, became the "grand old man" of the district, leading the Lethbridge parade at the head of a contingent of local Indians. On the negative side, Neil Campbell drowned while driving a herd of Indian department cattle across the Battle River.[34]

In Montana, Moses Solomon went into farming and poultry raising; John Kerler became a bookkeeper for John Largent of Sun River,[35] John LaMott moved to Arrow Creek where he had a ranch and stopping house,[36] John Wren had a ranch on the Teton River,[37] Jim McDevitt established a livery and freighting business in Fort Benton and expanded into real estate,[38] Herman Brinkman had a butcher shop in Fort Benton,[39] and Red Buckland settled on a ranch at Highwood, Montana.[40] The Sample brothers continued to operate Spitzee Post in Whoop-Up country until 1878, importing horses from Idaho and Washington. Dan Sample then established his own ranch on the Teton River in Montana, while his brother Asa took charge of I. G. Baker's horse herd.

A number of other ex-whisky traders returned to Montana and settled on the Blackfeet Reservation with their Peigan wives. Some of them simply lived off their wives' families, while others had tiny ranches and a few head of cattle on their wives' allotments. Often they were referred to derisively as "squaw men" and were disliked and distrusted by the various Indian agents who saw them as interlopers and a disruptive faction on the reservation. Among those ex-traders living on the reservation were Sol Abbott, Charles Choquette, Henry Powell, Jack Miller, Charlie Thomas, Bill Fargo, Francois Vielle, Jim Grant, and Charles Phemister.

After the NWMP's arrival, Montana traders were quick to establish legitimate stores in Canada. This is a view of I. G. Baker's Fort Macleod store in 1879. Its manager, former whisky trader D. W. Davis, is leaning on the post at the left. (Glenbow Archives, NA-98-24)

The list of whisky traders who had children by Indian wives is fairly extensive. Those with Blood mates included Dave Akers, Frank Bostwick, James Brown, Charles Choquette, Charles Conrad, D. W. Davis, Ben Deroche, John Healy, Joe Healy, Barney Hughes, H. A. "Fred" Kanouse, Tony Lachappelle, Rock LaRoque, Ellis Miller, Henry Mills, John Riplinger, Daniel Sample, John Sample, John B. "Whiskey" Smith, Frank Spearson, Harry "Kamoose" Taylor, and A. A. Vice. Those with South Peigan mates included Sol Abbott, Thomas Bogy, Henry Bostwick, Herman Brinkman, Rowland "Red" Buckland, Joe Cobell, Louis Ell, Al Hamilton, Thomas Hardwick, Eugene "Paddy" Hasson, George Houk, Antoine Juneau, Joe Kipp, John LaMott, William Lee, Orrin S. "Hod" Main, Jack Miller, Charles Rose, Asa Sample, James Scott, William Teasdale, Charlie Thomas, Francois Vielle, John Weatherwax, Scott Wetzel, and John Wren.[41]

No comment about the whisky trade would be complete without mentioning the two principal suppliers, T. C. Power & Bro., represented by Tom Power, and I. G. Baker & Co., dominated by Charles Conrad. With the profits they accrued from the whisky trade, Power and Conrad branched into transportation, banking, real estate, and ranching, both ultimately becoming millionaires.

Their first major business ventures were joint ones in transportation and banking. Their companies acquired the steamer *Benton* in 1874, followed by the *Red Cloud* in 1875, and the *Colonel Macleod* a year later; these boats plied the Missouri as far south as St. Louis, bringing in supplies and taking out buffalo robes. The pair also formed a transportation company, equipped with bull and mule teams, to carry land freight throughout the Montana Territory. By controlling transportation, they were able to capitalize on the presence of the NWMP and the Indian department just north of the line. For almost ten years, both of these Canadian agencies received their supplies through Fort Benton, largely provided by the Baker company.

In the 1880s, the Bakers created the Benton & St. Louis Cattle Company,[42] later called the Circle Ranching Company, which became one of the largest outfits in Montana, with extensive holdings in Alberta. In the 1890s it was frequently in trouble with the United States Indian department for illegally running thousands of head of cattle on the Blackfeet Reservation.[43]

When the Northern Pacific Railway reached Great Falls in 1883, it soon spelled the end of Fort Benton as a business and transportation centre. Yet by 1885 I. G. Baker & Co. had amassed assets there of more than $1 million, over and above the Conrads' personal investments.[44] The bank in Benton was closed in 1891, and in the same year, Charles and William Conrad wound up the business of I. G. Baker and sold their Canadian stores to the Hudson's Bay Company. Charles then moved to Kalispell where he became an owner of the original townsite company. William, who had always been in the shadow of his brother, returned to Virginia.

In Kalispell, Charles started the Conrad National Bank, sold town lots, and built the finest house in the Flathead valley. He soon expanded his business to include extensive timber, real estate, ranch, and farm holdings. When he died in 1902, a newspaper stated, "He leaves an estate that is very conservatively valued at over one million dollars, his investments being in almost every branch of industry that exists in Montana, with great interest in the Canadian Northwest."[45]

In 1878, Tom Power moved from Fort Benton to Helena and, like Charles Conrad, expanded his financial and political empire. During the 1870s, he was accused of being a member of an Indian ring that conspired to get u.s. government contracts and to supply inferior or inadequate goods. In 1873, Power, along with clerk Charles Giddings, Indian agent William Ensign, and trader Hyram Upham, were indicted for conspiracy to defraud the u.s. government by stealing supplies intended for the Blackfoot Indians. In the end the indictment against Power was dropped when a witness and vital legal papers both disappeared and other evidence was ruled inadmissible. Ultimately, Upham was sentenced to a year in jail, Giddings got off on appeal, and Ensign skipped the Territory.

In 1881–82, T. C. Power & Bro. was said to have provided short-weighted bags of flour and to have failed to deliver goods to the Blackfoot on time, which led to the allegation that it was directly responsible for starvation on the reservation.[46] Also, in 1884 the firm tried to supply corn that was unfit to eat.[47]

In politics, Power was defeated when he ran in the 1889 gubernatorial election, but in 1890, he was selected as one of the first state senators from Montana. This was accomplished, said one of his detractors, "by the corrupt use of money."[48] This critic also claimed that Power influenced the awarding of government contracts, "which contracts relate to supplies and transportation in the Indian and Military service."[49] Power served in Washington until 1895.

In the business world, Power established a stagecoach line in 1879, the year after he moved to Helena. Over his career, he founded or invested in more than ninety-five companies in the fields of banking, merchandising, transportation, cattle and sheep ranching, real estate, lumbering, mining, electrical power generation, hotels, military and Indian contracting, agricultural implement sales, grain milling, oil, and irrigation. He died a millionaire in Helena in 1923.

And what became of the Blackfoot Indians? With the disappearance of the buffalo, they were obliged to settle on their various reserves—the South Peigans in Montana, the Bloods near Standoff, the North Peigans near Pincher Creek, and the Siksika east of Calgary. Those who were rescued from the deadly whisky trade now were obliged to cope with starvation, corruption, government lethargy, residential schools, and tuberculosis, but over the years they triumphed and survived. Indeed, today's tribal populations are larger than those at the beginning of the Whoop-Up era.

Conclusion

The whisky-trading era was relatively brief, about six years, but its effects were more devastating than any epidemic or massacre. Not only did the trade kill many people, but for the Blackfoot tribes, it devastated their cultural and social life, created internal dissension, and left them helpless in the face of the invasion of their hunting grounds by enemy tribes. Chiefs lost their power to control their bands, fathers could not control their young men, and the rush to sell their robes and everything they owned for whisky turned many families into virtual paupers.

Although a few Canadians were involved in the whisky trade, including some Métis from Manitoba, it was clearly dominated by Montanans working out of Fort Benton and Sun River. Traders, teamsters, hunters, wolfers, and artisans all used the Montana towns as their headquarters when they travelled south from trading and working in Whoop-Up country. In addition to being the headquarters of I. G. Baker and T. C. Power, Fort Benton also boasted at least a dozen saloons, a brewery, dance halls, and gambling joints.[1] It also was the embarkation point from the Missouri River and thus had all the facilities to handle the thousands of robes brought to the town each year.

The volume of trade through Fort Benton provides some indication of the scope of the Blackfoot trade and the devastation of the buffalo herds. In 1869, just prior to opening the Whoop-Up trade, some fifteen thousand robes were being shipped through Benton. This increased dramatically to twenty thousand robes in 1870, thirty thousand in 1871, and forty thousand in each year of 1872 and 1873.[2] The trade became so massive that in 1873 a trader commented, "I venture to say that there is not ten men in Benton who do not make a living directly from the whiskey trade."[3]

Yet there were a few Americans who honestly tried to halt the illicit traffic. In contrast to this indifference, Deputy Marshal Charles Hard and Detective Andrew Dusold travelled hundreds of miles, often under adverse conditions, in their attempts to nab traders on the Blackfeet Reservation, usually on their way to Whoop-Up country. Indian department superintendent Alfred Sully and his successor, Jasper Viall, with a few of their agents, made heroic efforts to stamp out the trade, and if the cases got to court they were aggressively prosecuted by United States attorney Merritt Page. Officials made appeals to Washington to enforce the Intercourse Law of 1834 and even tried to declare Fort Benton to be part of the Blackfeet Reservation and thus ban the sale of alcohol from that point. These actions may have made a minor difference, but the whisky trade was too organized, too profitable, and too influential to be suppressed.

By the early 1870s, opportunists had learned that the Americans did not have the resources on the frontier to stop the trade, and the British were doing nothing at all. Once a trader took his whisky supply across the border, there was effectively no law to stop him from selling wares, taking in buffalo robes, killing with impunity, and making his own laws. As a journalist stated, "No u.s. detective or spy dare invade their quiet rendezvous; nor is whisky ever confiscated when it gets to that 'happy hunting ground.'"[4]

These traders were outfitted, and probably financed, by Fort Benton's two leading suppliers—T. C. Power & Bro., which was essentially run by Tom Power, and I. G. Baker & Co., ultimately dominated by Charles Conrad. These firms in turn received credit from Helena bankers like Sam Hauser and from fur dealers and wholesalers such as P. B. Weare, Field Lister, and Burnham and Son, of Chicago: from Roche and McCabe; from Erford and Whitney, of St. Louis; and from Main and Winbeck, of San Francisco. These companies extended credit to be paid after robe deliveries were made in the spring.

The end of the whisky trade in Canada came very quickly after the arrival of the NWMP in 1874. This photograph shows (L–R) Constable Malcolm J. Millar, Inspector E. D. Clark, Colonel James F. Macleod, and Dr. John Kittson. (Glenbow Archives, NA-52-1)

Both Tom Power and Charles Conrad became millionaires from investing the profits they made from the whisky traffic. But the traders themselves garnered no such fortunes, and at times seemed to be working more for the Baker and Power firms than for themselves. John Healy, for example, seemed to be constantly in debt to Power and his friends and sometimes had trouble meeting his notes. Not infrequently, he had to ask for extensions in order to accumulate enough robes to cover his debts. Neither he, Al Hamilton, Joe Kipp, Fred Kanouse, nor any other trader ever became rich.

Meanwhile, the Canadian government took no action to halt the trade in spite of protests and pleas from missionaries and others. In fact, the government only became officially aware of the noxious trade more than a year and a half after it had started. Even when the horror stories began to circulate and Lieutenant-Governor Alexander Morris began making repeated appeals for help, he was ignored in Ottawa. As late as 1873, Morris's request for 150 men was met with a response from the Privy Council "that the Government after a full consideration of all the facts, has come to the conclusion that the state of affairs in the North West is not so grave a character as to warrant them in incurring so heavy an expense as the measure you suggest would involve."[5] Only after the Cypress Hills Massacre was the government forced to act and later in 1873 the North-West Mounted Police (NWMP) were dispatched to the West.

Their arrival was unique in the frontier history of North America. Usually, agricultural settlers arrived first and had their own idea of justice, often including conflicts with Indians. In this instance, law preceded settlement and when the first permanent settlers arrived, they were quite willing to abide by the rules of the country. This resulted in the peaceful settlement of the southern prairies. It also formed a bond of trust and friendship between the Blackfoot and the NWMP after the red coats drove the whisky traders from their lands. But this friendship proved to be a double-edged sword. The whisky, combined with the smallpox epidemic of 1869–70, and the Baker Massacre of 1870, had virtually destroyed the ability of the Blackfoot to put up any type of organized resistance to any invaders—Métis, Cree, or white. The deaths of great war chiefs like Seen From Afar and the loss of control by other chiefs made it virtually impossible for the tribes to staunch the flow of government agents, railway surveyors, settlers, and others who followed the Mounties into their lands.

The damage done, physically and psychologically, by the whisky trade is hard to measure. In 1871, Jean L'Heureux indicated that some eighty-nine members of the Blackfoot nation had been killed that year either in drunken brawls or from the effect of the liquor.[6] Donald Graham estimated that seventy Indians from the Blood tribe alone were killed in drunken quarrels during the winter of 1872–73. And missionary John McDougall was told that liquor caused the death of forty-two Siksika over the winter of 1873–74.[7] Multiply these figures by four tribes and spread it over six years and one can appreciate the calamity that befell the Blackfoot tribes. Chiefs lost control over their followers, inter-tribal disputes arose as drunken killings resulted in acts of revenge, and people were afraid to meet each other on the trail.

It can be argued that the Blackfoot did not need to drink, that no one was forcing them. Yet the wholesale availability of liquor was something new to them and fitted tragically into their way of life. The entire culture of the Blackfoot had been built around a nomadic life, excessive behaviour, and little concern for the future. As nomads, the Blackfoot could not store and save. Everything they had was carried with them, so if they killed a buffalo, they might eat it right away. If they bought objects at a trading post, they had to be portable and in a form that could be of immediate use. If the item was whisky, the men carried it away in skin bags or 1-gallon kegs and consumed it at once. While visiting the forts, some men carried their own tin cups, tied to their waist,[8] so they could drink the whisky on the spot. Everything was practical and immediate.

Intoxicants of any kind had been unknown to the Blackfoot prior to European contact. Although rum or whisky had been around since the 1770s, the tribes had had only limited access to it when they visited the trading posts twice a year. Then, they had a big debauch, going into it wholeheartedly, just as they did when celebrating a victory over an enemy or performing a ritual or ceremony. After, they returned to their camps and remained sober for several months, until their next trip to the fort. This pattern was well established over the years, but when the whisky traders came into their midst, they were encouraged to extend their drinking year-round.

Some Blackfoot responded by having their wives turn out tanned robes as quickly as possible and then drinking up the proceeds. Others were more temperate in their use of alcohol, but could never keep a supply on hand because of the pressures from friends and relatives to share their whisky. Some became exceedingly depressed while drunk and would cry for hours, mourning those who had died during these difficult years. They created "drinking songs" that often had no words, but were simply sad melodic sounds. One had the words, "Bear Chief give me a drink, Bear Chief give me a drink, Ah hai a hai yo, a hai yo a ho."[9] This was sung by women, apparently to cadge a drink.

Given the terrible chaos created by the liquor traffic, are there any mitigating circumstances that could justify the role of the whisky traders? In later years they described themselves as pioneers, pathfinders, and men who opened the way for settlement. In fact, they were glorified bootleggers, breaking American law each time they crossed the Blackfeet Reservation, and Canadian law each time they sold liquor. They were opportunists who found a loophole in the law—or rather a lack of enforcement of the law—and exploited it to the extreme. Their only goal was to make money, and if their actions created misery, hardship, and death for the Indians, it was no concern of theirs. There was no law north of the line so they lived lawless lives, killing friend and foe at random, doling out potent and sometimes deadly brews with impunity, and caring for nothing except their profits.

When engineer Frank Wilkeson visited Fort Whoop-Up in 1871, he noted:

> The whiskey traders ... told me they came here to make money ... Far from being an injury to the United States, they said they were a great benefit as they keep the Indians poor, and kill directly or indirectly more Indians of the most warlike tribe on the continent every year, at no cost to the United States government, than the more regular army did in ten years! The Indians ... were British subjects and had a right to exercise all the freedom of British subjects; and if the British subjects saw fit to pay big prices for poor whiskey and get immensely drunk on the Saskatchewan plains, it is the subjects' affair, and not that of the United States.[10]

There were no innocent parties in the trade. The whisky suppliers such as Tom Power, Isaac Baker, Charles Conrad, and Scott Wetzel were just as guilty of destroying the lives of Indians as were John Healy, Al Hamilton, Joe Kipp, Fred Kanouse, and the host of others who actually dispensed the liquid death. The guilt extended to a lesser degree to the freighters, artisans, interpreters, guides, labourers, and anyone else whose activities helped to keep the trade alive. And at a distance, bankers, politicians, and liquor manufacturers were guilty of greasing the wheels of industry, government, and finance to keep the liquor flowing unimpeded into Blackfoot country.

If there were any who were guiltless, it was the Blackfoot themselves. Although they were one of the most warlike nations on the continent, they did not deserve to be decimated, victimized, and pauperized by the illicit trade in a deadly commodity that was foreign to their culture. For generations they had succeeded in repelling the forces of Cree, Assiniboine, and other tribes that tried to invade their hunting grounds but they were powerless against the relentless onslaught of the traders and their whisky.

For that reason, the North-West Mounted Police can truly be described as saviours of a people. The Blackfoot recognized this and established a bond of friendship with the red coats that lasted for more than a century. The relationship was aptly described by Medicine Calf at the Blackfoot treaty with the Canadian government in 1877. "I can sleep safely now," he said. "Before the arrival of the Police, when I laid my head down at night, every sound frightened me; my sleep was broken; now I can sleep sound and am not afraid."[11]

Yet the help from the police had its price. It put down the whisky traffic and enabled the Blackfoot to rebuild their shattered lives, but the police also made it easy for the government to negotiate a treaty with them and for settlers to come streaming into Blackfoot lands unimpeded. The influx of settlers created a completely new set of problems for the Blackfoot by confining them to reserves, where starvation and disease replaced whisky as their new enemies.

Notes

Introduction

1. Letter, Lorenzo B. Lyman to Indian Agent R. F. May, 28 January 1874. Montana Superintendency of Indian Affairs, Record Group 75, M234, roll 499, pp. 532–37, National Archives & Records Administration, Washington, DC (hereinafter cited as RG 75, M234, NARA).
2. Hugh A. Dempsey, *Crowfoot, Chief of the Blackfeet* (Norman, OK: University of Oklahoma Press, 1972), 78.
3. *Helena Daily Herald*, 12 February 1872.
4. The term "British possessions" was the common one used by Montanans when referring to the area north of the forty-ninth parallel. This was the case even after 1869–70 when the area became part of the Dominion of Canada. For simplicity, this term will be used throughout the book.

Chapter 1: Beginnings of the Liquor Trade

1. Robert E. Pinkerton, *Hudson's Bay Company* (London: Thornton Butterworth Ltd., 1932), 204.
2. Journal of Manchester House, entry for 10 April 1787. Hudson's Bay Company Records, Provincial Archives of Manitoba, Winnipeg.
3. Ibid.
4. Edward Umfreville, *The Present State of Hudson's Bay* (Toronto: Ryerson Press, 1954), 104.
5. Arthur S. Morton, ed., *The Journal of Duncan M'Gillivray of the North West Company at Fort George on the Saskatchewan, 1794–95* (Toronto: Macmillans, 1929), 47.
6. Ibid., 30.
7. William F. Butler, *The Great Lone Land* (London: Sampson Low, Marston, Low & Searle, 1874), 286.
8. Elliott Coues, ed., *New Light on the Early History of the Greater Northwest* (New York: Francis P. Harper, 1897), 723.
9. Ibid., 729.
10. Ibid., 730.
11. Butler, *Great Lone Land*, 287.
12. Pinkerton, *Hudon's Bay Company*, 206.
13. Cited in Arthur S. Ray, *Indians in the Fur Trade* (Toronto: University of Toronto Press, 1974), 198.
14. E. H. Oliver, *The Canadian North-West: Its Early Development and Legislative Records* (Ottawa, ON: Government Printing Office, 1915), 754.
15. *The Nor'Wester*, 5 March 1862.
16. Interview with White Fat, Blackfoot Indian, 19 June 1941. Lucien & Jane Hanks, Papers, Glenbow Archives, Calgary, AB.
17. Interview with One Gun, Blackfoot Indian, 24 July 1939. Lucien & Jane Hanks, Papers.
18. Interviews with One Gun, 24 July 1939, and Dog Chief, Blackfoot Indian, 1 August 1939. Lucien & Jane Hanks, Papers.
19. Interview with Sleigh, Blackfoot Indian, 25 August 1938. Lucien & Jane Hanks, Papers.
20. Oliver, *Canadian North-West*, 438.
21. Ibid., 444–45.
22. Earl of Southesk, *Saskatchewan and the Rocky Mountains* (Edinburgh: Edmonston & Douglas, 1875), 327.
23. Hiram M. Chittenden, *The American Fur Trade of the Far West* (Stanford, CA: Academic Reprints, 1954), 26.
24. Ibid.
25. Ibid., 28.
26. Ibid., 29.
27. Ibid., 30.
28. Ibid., 358.
29. Charles Larpenteur, *Forty Years a Fur Trader on the Upper Missouri* (Chicago: Lakeside Press, 1933), 46.
30. Ibid., 77–78.
31. J. N. B. Hewitt, ed., *Journal of Rudolph Friederich Kurz*. Bulletin 115, Smithsonian Institution (Washington, DC: United States Government Printing Office, 1937), 176–77.
32. Ibid., 177.
33. John E. Sunder, *The Fur Trade on the Upper Missouri, 1840–1865* (Norman, OK: University of Oklahoma Press, 1965), 91.
34. Interview with Many Tail Feathers, South Peigan Indian, 11 August 1929. James Willard Schultz, Papers, Montana State University, Special Collections, Bozeman.

Chapter 2: The Turbulent Sixties

1. Charles J. Kappler, ed., *Indian Affairs. Laws and Treaties*, vol.1 (New York: AMS Press, 1971), 736.
2. Durfee & Peck were said to have smuggled repeating rifles, stolen Indian supplies, and defrauded the government. The son of Columbus Delano, Secretary of the Interior, was said to be a partner in the firm. See *Rocky Mountain Gazette*, 7 May & 10 September 1873.
3. *Helena Daily Herald*, 24 September 1875.
4. James H. Bradley, "Blackfoot War with the Whites," *Contributions to the Historical Society of Montana* 9 (1923) 253–54.
5. *Montana Radiator*, 27 January 1866.
6. Petition, 10 January 1866. Montana Superintendency of Indian Affairs, RG 75, M234, roll 488, p. 237, NARA.
7. *Montana Post*, 28 April 1866.
8. George B. Wright to secretary of the interior, 5 July 1867. SC 895, Montana Historical Society (MHS).
9. Letter, Culbertson to Gen. Alfred Sully, 2 September 1869. U.S. Congress, House, *Piegan Indians: Letter from the Secretary of War*. Ex. Doc. 269, (1870), 51.
10. *Helena Weekly Herald*, 25 April 1867.
11. Ibid., 20 February 1868.
12. *Montana Post*, 23 May 1868.
13. Ibid., 4 June 1866.
14. Interview with Mrs. Split Ears by James Willard Schultz. Manuscript No. 9, James Willard Schultz, Papers, Montana State University, Special Collections, Bozeman.
15. *Montana Post*, 29 April 1866.
16. Letter, Pope to commissioner, 20 September 1867. Montana Superintendency of Indian Affairs, RG 75, M234, roll 488, p. 814, NARA.
17. Ibid., 813–14.
18. Interview with Mrs. Split Ears by James Willard Schultz (see n. 14).
19. Letter, Hubbell to commissioner, 14 March 1868. Montana Superintendency of Indian Affairs, RG 75, M234, roll 488, p. 1133, NARA.
20. Letter, Wright to commissioner, 31 March 1868. Montana Superintendency of Indian Affairs, RG 75, M234, roll 488, pp. 1415–16, NARA.

21. *Helena Herald*, 29 November 1866.
22. *Helena Daily Herald*, 1 April 1869.
23. Letter, Nathaniel Pope to commissioner Cullen, 21 January 1869. Montana Superintendency of Indian Affairs, RG 75, M234, roll 489, p. 211, NARA.
24. Letter, Secretary O. H. Browning to commissioner N. G. Taylor, 24 March 1868. Montana Superintendency of Indian Affairs, RG 75, M234, roll 488, p. 1147, NARA.
25. Letter, Nathaniel Pope to Commissioner Cullen, 9 October 1868. Montana Superintendency of Indian Affairs, RG 75, M234, roll 488, p. 1333, NARA.
26. Declaration by Governor Clay Smith, 25 March 1868. Montana Superintendency of Indian Affairs, RG 75, M234, roll 488, p. 1248, NARA.
27. Ibid., 1249.
28. Ibid., 1250–52.
29. Ibid., 1253.

Chapter 3: The Merchants

1. Joel Overholser, *Fort Benton: World's Innermost Port* (Helena, MT: Falcon Press, 1987), 230.
2. James H. Bradley, "Notes on the Business of I. G. Baker & Company at Fort Benton," *Contributions to the Historical Society of Montana* 9 (1923), 346.
3. Ibid.
4. Undated article in the *Jordan Gazette*, c.1918. Charles B. Benton Power, Papers, SC 55a, Montana Historical Society (MHS).
5. James E. Murphy, *Half Interest in a Silver Dollar: The Saga of Charles E. Conrad* (Missoula, MT: Mountain Press, 1983), 19.
6. Undated article in the *Jordan Gazette*, c.1918. Charles B. Benton Power, Papers, SC 55a, MHS.
7. The legal partnership between the two brothers was signed on 1 May 1870, with Tom providing $58,053.58 of the capitalization and John $10,732.23. (T. C. Power, Papers, MC55, vol. 137, p. 232, MHS.)
8. Deposition of Roswell Tibbetts, 15 October 1867. Montana Superintendency of Indian Affairs, RG 75, M234, roll 488, p. 989, NARA.
9. Deposition of Jacob Korn, 9 October 1867. Montana Superintendency of Indian Affairs, RG 75, M234, roll 488, p. 986, NARA.
10. Letter, Nathaniel Pope to Indian commissioner, 20 September 1867. Montana Superintendency of Indian Affairs, RG 75, M234, roll 488, pp. 817–18, NARA.
11. Letter, J. B. Hubbell to Indian commissioner, 14 March 1868. Montana Superintendency of Indian Affairs, RG 75, M234, roll 488, p. 1135, NARA.
12. Murphy, *Half Interest in a Silver Dollar*, 6.
13. Ibid., 1.
14. Reminiscences of John LaMott. James Willard Schultz, Papers, Montana State University, Special Collections, Bozeman.
15. Ibid.
16. *Montana Post*, 5 September 1868.
17. Helen B. Clarke, "Sketch of Malcolm Clarke," *Contributions to the Historical Society of Montana* 2 (1896), 260.
18. S. C. Ashby, "An Opportunity Presented Itself," in *We Seized Our Rifles: Recollections of the Montana Frontier*, ed. Eugene Lee Silliman (Missoula, MT: Mountain Press, 1982), 87.

19. I. G. Baker and the North West Fur Company both had licences issued in 1866 that permitted them to trade with the Blackfoot but not to encroach on their reservation.
20. Ashby, "An Opportunity," 89.
21. Ibid., 90.
22. Ibid.
23. *Helena Weekly Herald*, 10 December 1868.
24. Letter, I. G. Baker to Indian commissioner, 2 February 1869. Montana Superintendency of Indian Affairs, RG 75, M234, roll 489, p. 86, NARA.
25. Letter, Secretary of the Interior O. H. Browning to commissioner of Indian affairs, 10 February 1869. Letters sent by the Indian division of the office of the secretary of the interior, Record Group 75, roll 9, p. 6, NARA.
26. Letter, Abel Farwell to Durfee & Peck, 15 October 1869. Montana Superintendency of Indian Affairs, RG 75, M234, roll 490, p. 909, NARA.
27. Letter, Nathaniel Pope to W. J. Cullen, 21 January 1869. Montana Superintendency of Indian Affairs, RG 75, M234, roll 489, p. 209, NARA.
28. Ibid.
29. Letter, W. J. Cullen to Indian commissioner, 2 February 1869. Montana Superintendency of Indian Affairs, RG 75, M234, roll 489, pp. 173–74, NARA.
30. Letter, Inspector General James A. Hardie to Major General George L. Hartsuff, 28 December 1869. U.S. Congress, House, *Piegan Indians: Letter from the Secretary of War*, Ex. Doc. 269 (1870), 22.
31. *Helena Weekly Herald*, 15 April 1869.
32. Ibid., 23 September 1869.
33. *Great Falls Tribune*, 29 August 1937.
34. Letter, Col. P. R. de Trobriand to Gen. O. D. Greene, 13 August 1869. Montana Superintendency of Indian Affairs, RG 75, M234, roll 489, p. 23, NARA.
35. Jack Holterman, *Kings of the High Missouri: The Saga of the Culbertsons* (Helena, MT: Falcon Press, 1987), 172. See also John C. Ewers, *The Blackfeet: Raiders on the Northwestern Plains* (Norman, OK: University of Oklahoma Press, 1958), 246.
36. Charles Rowe, "Pioneer Tales by Charlie Rowe," in *Rowe Family History* (Great Falls, MT: Edithann Rowe Janetski, n.d.), 72.
37. Ben Bennett, *Death, Too, For The-Heavy-Runner* (Missoula, MT: Mountain Press, 1981), 21; Overholser, *Fort Benton*, 310.
38. *Helena Weekly Herald*, 28 August 1869.
39. Also listed as Sam Pecks.
40. *Helena Weekly Herald*, 19 August 1869.
41. Letter, Gen. James A. Hardie to Gen. George L. Hartsuff, 29 January 1870. U.S. Congress, House, *Piegan Indians: Letter from the Secretary of War*, Ex. Doc. 269 (1870), 30.
42. Letter, Gen. Henry A. Morrow to Gen. O. D. Greene, 15 August 1869. Montana Superintendency of Indian Affairs, RG 75, M234, roll 489, p. 27, NARA.
43. Letter, Alfred Sully to W. B. Pease, 14 November 1869. Records of the Montana Superintendency of Indian Affairs, RG 75, M833, roll 3, p. 100, NARA.
44. Col. P. R. de Trobriand to chairman, 6 October 1869. U.S. Congress, House, *Piegan Indians: Letter from the Secretary of War*, Ex. Doc. 269 (1870), 61.
45. *Helena Weekly Herald*, 23 September 1869.
46. *Great Falls Tribune*, 29 August 1937.
47. *Helena Weekly Herald*, 30 September 1869.

48. "Report of the U.S. Grand Jury 3rd Judicial Dist. M.T. on Indian outrages in said district," 13 October 1869. Montana Superintendency of Indian Affairs, RG 75, M234, roll 489, p. 812, NARA.

49. Letter, John Riplinger to S. H. Eastman, 14 December 1869. Montana Superintendency of Indian Affairs, RG 75, M234, roll 489, pp. 912–16, NARA.

50. Ibid.

51. Letter, John Riplinger to S. H. Eastman, 8 January 1870. Montana Superintendency of Indian Affairs, RG 75, M234, roll 490, p. 918, NARA.

52. As his son Joe Culbertson recalled, "After my father had done everything in the world for my mother and took her east and marrie [sic] her as a white laddy [sic] and raised a big family, she left him and went off with a man by the name of John Ripgner [Riplinger]." Letter, Culbertson to C. N. Kessler, 12 July 1919. C. N. Kessler, Papers, William Andrews Clark Memorial Library, University of California Library, Los Angeles.

Chapter 4: Off to the British Possessions

1. Letter, John Riplinger to S. H. Eastman, 14 December 1869. Montana Superintendency of Indian Affairs, RG 75, M234, roll 489, p. 915, NARA.

2. Edmonton House Journals, entry for 5 December 1869. Hudson's Bay Company Records, Provincial Archives of Manitoba, Winnipeg.

3. *Montana Post*, 16 May 1868.

4. Ibid., 10 August 1868.

5. Letter, Marshal W. F. Wheeler to S. H. Eastman, 16 December 1869. Montana Superintendency of Indian Affairs, RG 75, M234, roll 489, p. 917, NARA.

6. Clark C. Spence, *Territorial Politics and Government in Montana, 1864–89.* (Urbana, IL: University of Chicago Press, 1975), 46.

7. Ibid., 160.

8. Letter, Charles Aubrey to Tom Power, 14 May 1890. T. C. Power, Papers, box 1, folder 1, MC 55, Montana Historical Society (MHS).

9. Spence, *Territorial Politics*, 79.

10. Telegram, Tom Power to Alfred Sully, 9 November 1869. Montana Superintendency of Indian Affairs, RG 75, M833, roll 2, p. 603, NARA.

11. Letter, Tom Power to Alfred Sully, 11 November 1869. Montana Superintendency of Indian Affairs, RG 75, M833, roll 2, p. 607, NARA.

12. Letter, S. H Eastman to W. F. Wheeler, 27 November 1869. Montana Superintendency of Indian Affairs, RG 75, M833, roll 2, p. 631, NARA.

13. Ibid.

14. Letter, Alfred Sully to district attorney, 6 December 1869. Montana Superintendency of Indian Affairs, RG 75, M833, roll 3, p. 109, NARA.

15. Telegram, E. S. Parker to Alfred Sully, 1 December 1869. Letters Sent by the Office of Indian Affairs, Washington, D.C., RG 75, M21, roll 93, p.180, NARA; also Montana Superintendency of Indian Affairs, RG 75, M234, roll 489, p. 731, NARA.

16. Letter, Secretary of the Interior Columbus Delano to Hon. J. M. Cavanaugh, 14 December 1870. Letters Sent by the Indian Division of the Office of the Secretary of the Interior, RG 75, M606, roll 10, p. 116, NARA.

17. Telegram, Alfred Sully to commissioner, 8 December 1869. Montana Superintendency of Indian Affairs, RG 75, M234, roll 489, p. 729, NARA.

18. "Permit to Messrs. Hamilton & Healy to travel through the Blackfoot Country," 6 December 1869. Copy in Glenbow Archives, Calgary, AB, file 184.

19. Letter, W. F. Wheeler to S. H. Eastman, 16 December 1869. Montana Superintendency of Indian Affairs, RG 75, M234, roll 489, p. 917, NARA.

20. Letter, J. B. Hubbell to Hon. M. D. Wilkinson, 9 January 1870. Montana Superintendency of Indian Affairs, RG 75, M234, roll 490, p. 922, NARA.

21. For a sample promissory note for 1873, see T. C. Power, Papers, file 372–21, MC 55, MHS.

22. "Healy & Hamilton In a/c with Tom C. Power & Bro.," 17 May 1870. Power, Papers, MC 55, vol. 178–1, p. 305, MHS.

23. Letter, Tom Power to John D. Brown, 9 September 1873. T. C. Power, Papers, MC 55, vol.178–4, p. 346, MHS.

24. Alex Staveley Hill, *From Home to Home: Autumn Wanderings in the North-West* (New York: O. Judd Co., 1885), 263.

25. Haney's name is shown as Pat Heany in *The Browning Review*, 3 June 1922 article but as Pat Haney in T. C. Power's account book, Power, Papers, MC 55, vol. 63, p. 339, MHS.

26. The name has been variously spelled as Way, Wye, and Wey, but Power in his correspondence and accounts consistently spells it Wei.

27. Letter, Alfred Sully to Commissioner, 27 December 1869. Montana Superintendency of Indian Affairs, RG 75, M234, roll 489, p. 773, NARA.

28. Ibid. See also *The Browning Review*, 3 June 1922.

29. Letter, John Riplinger to S. H. Eastman, 8 January 1870. Montana Superintendency of Indian Affairs, RG 75, M234, roll 489, p. 918, NARA.

30. *Rocky Mountain Gazette*, 9 February 1870.

31. Ibid.

32. "Hugh Kirkendall vs. The United States and the Blackfeet and Piegan Indians," 1910. SC 83, p. 15, MHS.

33. Apparently I. G. Baker & Co. had not followed this procedure in 1868 when they built their post on the Marias River and were threatened by angry Peigans. See S. C. Ashby, "An Opportunity Presented Itself," in *We Seized Our Rifles: Recollections of the Montana Frontier*, ed. Eugene Lee Silliman (Missoula, MT: Mountain Press, 1982), 90.

34. Interview with Laurie Plume, Blood Indian, 24 October 1955, by the author.

35. Cecil Denny, *The Riders of the Plains* (Calgary, AB: The Herald Company, 1905), 4.

36. U.S. Congress, House, *Piegan Indians: Letter from the Secretary of War*, Ex. Doc. 269 (1870), 23.

37. Ibid.

38. *Helena Daily Herald*, 18 January 1870.

39. U.S. Congress, House, *Piegan Indians*, 24.

40. Ibid., 32.

41. Letter, Alfred Sully to the commissioner of Indian affairs, Washington, 10 July 1870. Montana Superintendency of Indian Affairs, SC 895, MHS.

42. *Helena Daily Gazette*, 20 March 1870.

43. *Rocky Mountain Gazette*, 1 February 1870.

44. *The Browning Review*, 3 June 1922.

45. Ibid.
46. Ibid.
47. Ibid.
48. "Statement of Mr. A. B. Hamilton," 16 January 1915. The United States v. Blackfeet Tribe, 1855–1950, Docket 279-D, MHS. I wish to thank Stan Gibson for this reference.
49. Ben Bennett, *Death, Too, For The-Heavy-Runner* (Missoula, MT: Mountain Press, 1981), 163.
50. *Helena Weekly Herald*, 23 September 1874.
51. Letter, Father Camillus Imoda to Alfred Sully, 11 April 1870. Montana Superintendency of Indian Affairs, SC 895, MHS.
52. E. Tappen Adney, "Incidents of Indian-fighting and Fur Trader days in Montana, the Canadian Northwest, and Alaska, related by the late Captain John J. Healy," 1937. MF 95, p. 61, MHS.
53. Ibid., 62.
54. *Lethbridge Herald*, 15 November 1924.
55. Ibid., 26 July 1913. See also Cecil Denny, "Traders of the Early West," *Alberta Historical Review* 6, no. 3 (summer 1958), 20. Trader Fred Kanouse claimed that the name was given by Charlie Choquette but there is no evidence that he was at Fort Hamilton during the first winter.
56. "Healy & Hamilton In a/c with Tom C. Power & Bro.," 17 May 1870. T. C. Power, Papers, MC 55, vol. 178–1, p. 305, MHS.
57. "Hugh Kirkendall vs. The United States and the Blackfeet and Piegan Indians", 1910, SC 83, p. 21, MHS.
58. *Benton Weekly Record*, 12 March 1880. The author and witness to the event was probably John Healy.
59. Ibid.
60. "Hugh Kirkendall vs. The United States and the Blackfeet and Piegan Indians," 1910. SC 83, p. 14, MHS.

Chapter 5: Rush to the North

1. Letter, Alfred Sully to Indian commissioner, 2 March 1870. Montana Superintendency of Indian Affairs, RG 75, M234, roll 490, p. 364, NARA.
2. Letter, Alfred Sully to Indian commissioner, 27 April 1870. Montana Superintendency of Indian Affairs, RG 75, M234, roll 490, p. 43, NARA.
3. *Helena Daily Herald*, 15 June 1870. The use of "Lo" to describe an Indian is based upon Alexander Pope's eighteenth-century poem that begins, "Lo, the poor Indian! whose untutor'd mind/Sees God in the clouds/or hears him in the wind."
4. Letter, I. G. Baker to Alfred Sully, 31 May 1870. Selected Documents Relating to the Montana Superintendency of Indian Affairs, RG 75, NARA. Copy in Montana Historical Society (MHS); also letter, Acting Commissioner H. F. Cady to Alfred Sully, 15 June 1870. Letters sent by the Office of Indian Affairs, Washington, D.C., RG 75, M21, roll 88, p. 276, NARA.
5. Letter, Alfred Sully to commissioner, 30 June 1870. Selected Documents Relating to the Montana Superintendency of Indian Affairs, RG 75 , NARA. Copy in MHS.
6. Letter, Acting Commissioner H. F. Cady to Alfred Sully, 15 June 1870. Letters Sent by the Indian Division of the Office of the Secretary of the Interior, Washington, D.C., RG 75, M21, roll 26, p. 276, NARA.

7. Letter, N. W. Osborne to Merchants of Benton, 23 April 1870. U.S. War Department, Correspondence, Fort Benton Post, 1867–74. SC 933, MHS.
8. Letter, T. C. Power to Pool Nagro & Co., 21 June 1870. T. C. Power, Papers, MC 55, vol. 178–1, p. 355, MHS.
9. Letter, T. C. Power to Durfee & Peck, 3 July 1870. Power, Papers, MC 55, vol. 178–1, p. 395, MHS.
10. Peter Koch, "Life at Muscleshell in 1869 and 1870," *Contributions to the Historical Society of Montana* 2 (1896), 297.
11. Letter, T. C. Power to Roche & McCabe, 17 July 1870. Power, Papers, MC 55, vol. 178–1, p. 430, MHS.
12. Letter, Columbus Delano to J. M. Cavanaugh, 14 December 1870. Letters Sent by the Indian Division of the Office of the Secretary of the Interior, RG 75, M606, roll 10, p. 116, NARA.
13. Letter, Columbus Delano to secretary of the treasury, 15 December 1870. Letters Sent by the Indian Division of the Office of the Secretary of the Interior, RG 75, M606, roll 10, pp. 117–18, NARA.
14. Ibid.
15. Ibid.
16. Letter, Columbus Delano to J. M. Cavanaugh, 14 December 1870. Letter sent by the Indian Division of the Office of the Secretary of the Interior, RG 75, M606, roll 10, p. 116, NARA.
17. E. Tappen Adney, "Incidents of Indian-fighting and Fur Trader days in Montana, the Canadian Northwest, and Alaska, related by the late Captain John J. Healy," 1937. MF 95, p. 62, MHS.
18. *Toronto Daily Mail*, 5 April 1875.
19. *Benton Weekly Record*, 15 November 1878.
20. Letter, Charles Hard to Jasper Viall, 22 November 1870. Montana Superintendency of Indian Affairs, RG 75, M234, roll 490, p. 800, NARA.
21. *Rocky Mountain Gazette*, 13 March 1871.
22. *Helena Daily Herald*, 16 March 1871.
23. Letter, J. V. D. Reeves to I. G. Baker and others, 13 November 1867. Montana Superintendency of Indian Affairs, RG 75, M833, roll 1, p. 583, NARA.
24. Letter, Charles Hard to Jasper Viall, 24 November 1870. Montana Superintendency of Indian Affairs, RG 75, M234, roll 490, p. 802, NARA.
25. Letter, Jasper Viall to Indian commissioner, 5 December 1870. Montana Superintendency of Indian Affairs, RG 75, M234, roll 490, p. 798, NARA.
26. T. C. Power to Collector of Customs, W. W. Johnson, Helena, 10 December 1870. Power, Papers, letter-book 178–2, SC 83, p. 182, MHS.
27. Letter, Charles Hard to Jasper Viall, 22 November 1870. Montana Superintendency of Indian Affairs, RG 75, M234, roll 490, p. 800, NARA.
28. *Rocky Mountain Gazette*, 26 December 1870.
29. Jean L'Heureux, "Description of a Portion of the Nor'West and the Indians," Rocky Mountain House, November 1871. Glenbow Archives, Calgary, AB.
30. *Rocky Mountain Gazette*, 24 April 1871.
31. L'Heureux, "Description."
32. John McDougall, *George Millward McDougall, The Pioneer, Patriot and Missionary* (Toronto: William Briggs, 1902), quoting a letter of 1 April 1871 by George McDougall, 175.
33. Ibid., 174.

34. Mike Mountain Horse, *My People the Bloods* (Calgary, AB: Glenbow Museum, 1979), 50.

35. Frank Wilkeson, "The Last of the Indian Treaties," *New York Times*, 17 April 1887. In his flamboyant account, Wilkeson identifies the attackers as Pend d'Oreilles and Flatheads. I wish to thank Patricia McAndrew of Bethlehem, PA, for sending me this reference.

36. Joseph K. Dixon, *The Vanishing Race* (New York: Doubleday & Co., 1913), 112–15.

37. *Lethbridge News*, 30 April 1890.

38. Interview with John Cotton, Blood Indian, 29 December 1955, by the author.

39. Bad Head, in Hugh A. Dempsey, *A Blackfoot Winter Count* (Calgary, AB: Glenbow Museum, 1965), 15.

40. *Helena Daily Herald*, 2 December 1870.

41. Letter, A. J. Simmons to Viall, 30 November 1870. Montana Superintendency of Indian Affairs, SC 895, MHS.

42. Ibid.

43. *Rocky Mountain Gazette*, 28 December 1870.

44. *Helena Daily Herald*, 10 January 1871.

45. Letter, Jasper Viall to Indian commissioner, 7 March 1871. Montana Superintendency of Indian Affairs, RG 75, M234, roll 491, p. 520, NARA.

46. *Helena Daily Herald*, 18 March 1871.

47. Letter, Cornelius Hedges to Jasper Viall, 11 April 1871. Montana Superintendency of Indian Affairs, RG 75, M234, roll 491, p. 552, NARA. Interestingly, Warren was described as a "bitter uncompromising democrat, of the most malignant type" [Clark C. Spence, *Territorial Politics and Government in Montana, 1864–89* (Urbana, IL: University of Chicago Press, 1975), 226], who had been appointed when the Democrats were in power in Washington and as such he was prone to espouse the pro-trader cause. However, he resigned later in the year during a Republican drive to depose him.

48. Letter, Jasper Viall to Indian commissioner, 14 April 1871. Montana Superintendency of Indian Affairs, RG 75, M234, roll 491, pp. 562–64, NARA.

49. Letter, Columbus Delano to Indian commissioner, 12 May 1871. Montana Superintendency of Indian Affairs, RG 75, M234, roll 491, p. 210, NARA.

50. Interview with Many Tail Feathers, South Peigan, by James Willard Schultz, 7 August year unknown. James Willard Schultz, Papers, Montana State University, Special Collections, Bozeman.

51. Ibid.

52. Wilkeson, "Last of the Indian Treaties."

53. Ibid.

54. Ibid.

55. Ibid.

56. Note by H. J. Moberly, March 1872. Adams G. Archibald, Papers, MG 12, A1, item 783, Provincial Archives of Manitoba, Winnipeg. Wren was identified in the note as John Rann.

57. *Rocky Mountain Gazette*, 10 April 1871; John Maclean, *The Indians of Canada: Their Manners and Customs* (London: Charles H. Kelly, 1892), 228–29; Hugh A. Dempsey, ed., "Howell Harris and the Whiskey Trade," *Montana Magazine of History* 3, no. 2 (spring 1953), 2.

58. Maclean, *The Indians of Canada*, 229. For variations of the story, see also Alex Staveley Hill, *From Home to Home: Autumn Wanderings in the North-West* (New York: O. Judd Co., 1885), 145; Dempsey, ed., "Howell Harris," 3.

59. *Rocky Mountain Gazette*, 24 April 1871.

Chapter 6: The Standoff

1. James Willard Schultz, "Raven Quiver, the Trader," *Forest and Stream* (18 July 1903), 42–43.

2. According to George Houk (*Lethbridge Herald*, 22 December 1913) "Joe was the medium between the I. G. Baker Co. and the Indians and remained in Alberta until the Baker Co. quit the business."

3. Letter, B. F. Potts to Columbus Delano, 26 May 1871. Montana Superintendency of Indian Affairs, RG 75, M234, roll 491, p. 343, NARA.

4. *Helena Daily Herald*, 18 May 1871.

5. Letter, Jasper Viall to Indian commissioner, 20 June 1871. Montana Superintendency of Indian Affairs RG 75, M234, roll 491, p. 767, NARA.

6. "Interview of Mr. Forest Chrissy of the Chicago Evening Post with Captain John J. Healy on Friday evening at 9 P.M., May 5, 1899." Microfilm in Montana Historical Society (MHS). See also, Raymond W. Thorp and Robert Bunker, *Crow Killer: The Saga of Liver-Eating Johnson* (Bloomington, IN: University of Indiana Press, 1983). Interestingly, these latter authors completely omitted any reference to Johnson's whisky-trading career.

7. Schultz, "Raven Quiver," 42.

8. *Helena Weekly Herald*, 18 April 1872. See also *Helena Weekly Gazette*, 12 November 1873. William Gladstone, who was in the area at the time, makes no mention of him being with the traders (*Pincher Creek Echo*, 24 February 1910), while Alfred Burrows claims John Wren was leading the party (*Manitoba Free Press*, 15 June 1872). This might explain why no legal action was taken against Kipp.

9. Telegram, William Goodyear to Jasper Viall, 11 April 1872. Montana Superintendency of Indian Affairs, RG 75, M234, roll 493, p. 4, NARA.

10. Letter, W. F. Wheeler to Indian commissioner, 7 July 1871. Montana Superintendency of Indian Affairs, RG 75, M234, roll 491, pp. 1122–23, NARA.

11. Schultz, "Raven Quiver," 42.

12. *Pincher Creek Echo*, 24 February 1910.

13. *The Manitoban* (Winnipeg), 14 March 1874.

14. *Great Falls Tribune*, 5 July 1914.

15. Permits issued 16 August 1871 to Frank W. Eastman and on 17 August 1871 to Durfee & Peck. Montana Superintendency of Indian Affairs, RG 75, M833, roll 3, pp. 168–75, NARA.

16. Permit issued 30 September 1871 to Isaac and George Baker. Montana Superintendency of Indian Affairs, RG 75, M833, roll 3, pp. 176, NARA.

17. The various statements by John LaMott and Howell Harris, while not at variance with each other, are sometimes confusing. Harris changed his dates when revising his reminiscences, while LaMott implies that I. G. Baker had two separate posts. The one documented fact is a newspaper report in the spring of 1872 regarding the death of Dan Hardin over the winter of 1871–72. As LaMott says this took place at Conrad's Standoff post, and Harris says he built the Captain Jack's post in 1872, it is consistent to state that the I. G. Baker post was built at Standoff in 1871

and abandoned in favour of the second post a year later. Such problems of dating are not unusual in reminiscences, although the whisky traders have shown a high degree of accuracy, especially when the statements can be compared to contemporary newspaper reports.

18. Theresa Berglund, "The Reminiscences of John LaMott," SC 365, p. 18, MHS.
19. Charley Rowe, *Pioneer Tales*. Private printing, 1959; T. C. Power, Papers, MC 55, vol. 140, inside front cover. Rowe identified Jerry Potts as Jim Potts.
20. Ibid. He may have meant Slide Out, although according to Gladstone, this post was not built until 1873.
21. Ibid.
22. There is some confusion as to whether there was one trading post or two. In a map drawn by LaMott, he shows a single post identified as "Bond, Girard, Moses Solomon." However, in his narrative he states that Dick Berry and Bond had a trading post below Standoff. On the basis of existing information, it seems likely that there was only one post at that time. LaMott sometimes spells Bond as "Bahn."
23. Permit issued 20 October 1871 to Fred F. Girard. Montana Superintendency of Indian Affairs, RG 75, M833, roll 3, p. 186, NARA.
24. *Kendall Miner*, 31 August 1906.
25. Dan Hardin had been a member of the infamous Slade's gang in Montana in the 1860s when its members were being hunted and executed by the Vigilantes. Hardin had fled one step ahead of the rope, and had been on the fringe of society ever since.
26. Interview with John LaMott by James Willard Schultz, n.d. James Willard Schultz, Papers, Montana State University, Special Collections, Bozeman. All conversations in this story were told to Schultz by LaMott.
27. *Helena Daily Herald*, 13 March 1872.
28. John McDougall, *On Western Trails in the Early Seventies* (Toronto: William Briggs, 1911), 66.
29. Letter, T. C. Power & Bro. to J. D. Weatherwax, 25 September 1871. Power, Papers, MC 55, file 178–2, MHS.
30. *The Manitoban* (Winnipeg), 14 March 1874.
31. Ibid.
32. Letter, John J. Healy to T. C. Power, 29 September 1871. Power, Papers, MC 55, file 113–7, MHS.
33. Letter, John J. Healy to T. C. Power, 2 October 1871. Power, Papers, MC 55, file 13A–1, MHS.
34. Accounts ledger, Power, Papers, MC 55, vol. 228, MHS.
35. Letter, T. C. Power & Bro. to Whom it may Concern, 29 November 1871. Power, Papers, MC 55, file 178–2, MHS.
36. Letter, T. C. Power & Bro. to J. D. Weatherwax, 6 December 1871. Power, Papers, MC 55, file 178–2, MHS.
37. *Helena Weekly Herald*, 15 February 1872.
38. Letter, Jasper Viall to Indian commissioner, 15 December 1871. Montana Superintendency of Indian Affairs, RG 75, M234, roll 492, pp. 678–84, NARA.
39. Ibid., 680.
40. Schultz, "Raven Quiver," 42–43.
41. Berglund, "John MaMott," 20.
42. Interview with John LaMott by James Willard Schultz, n.d.
43. Ibid.
44. Berglund, "John LaMott," 32.
45. Ibid., 33.
46. Interview with John LaMott by James Willard Schultz, n.d.
47. George H. Ham, "Whoop Up," *The Globe* (Toronto), 30 December 1882.
48. Winter counts of Many Guns, Bull Plume, Houghton Running Rabbit, Teddy Yellowfly, Percy Creighton, and Jim White Bull. Copies in author's collection.
49. Interview with Crooked Meat Strings, Siksika Indian, 17 August 1938. Lucien & Jane Hanks, Papers, Glenbow Archives, Calgary, AB.
50. Interview with Pretty Young Man, Siksika Indian, 1939. Lucien & Jane Hanks, Papers.
51. Hugh A. Dempsey, *Crowfoot, Chief of the Blackfeet* (Norman, OK: University of Oklahoma Press, 1972), 78.
52. Joel Overholser, *Fort Benton: World's Innermost Port* (Helena, MT: Falcon Press, 1987), 31.
53. Ibid., 178.
54. Interview with George Houk by James Willard Schultz, n.d. Schultz, Papers, Montana State University, Special Collections, Bozeman.
55. *Helena Weekly Herald*, 18 April 1872.
56. *Rocky Mountain Gazette*, 27 August 1873.

Chapter 7: A Devastating Traffic

1. Letter, T. C. Power to Sam T. Hauser, 26 May 1872. T. C. Power, Papers, MC 55, file 178–3, p. 113, Montana Historical Society (MHS).
2. Letter, John Healy to T. C. Power, 2 June 1872. Power, Papers, MC 55, file 134–2, MHS.
3. Letter, Healy Hamilton & Co to T. C. Power, 17 June 1872. Power, Papers, MC 55, file 134–2, MHS.
4. Letterbook of Statements and Copy Book, Power, Papers, MC 55, file 252–23, p. 687, MHS.
5. Letter, Healy Hamilton & Co. to T. C. Power, 10 July 1872. Power, Papers, MC 55, file 134–2, MHS.
6. Petty ledger C, 1871–72, vol. 64, and petty ledger D, 1872–73, vol. 65, Power, Papers, MC 55, MHS.
7. Various entries, Bill Book, vol. 214, Power, Papers, MC 55, MHS.
8. George M. Dawson, diary, microfilm in Glenbow Archives, Calgary, AB, M 339.
9. Charles Schafft, "A Visit to 'Whoop Up' in the Days Gone By," *Benton Weekly Record*, 16 January 1880. Unless otherwise stated, any direct references in this story are from this source.
10. *Pincher Creek Echo*, 24 February 1910. By this time, the North West Fur Company had been bought out by Durfee & Peck.
11. Letter, C. E. Giddings to Indian commissioner, 23 August 1872. Montana Superintendency of Indian Affairs, RG 75, M234, roll 492, pp. 483–84, NARA.
12. James Willard Schultz, "Raven Quiver, the Trader," *Forest and Stream* (18 July 1903), 43.
13. Margaret A. Kennedy, *The Whiskey Trade of the Northwestern Plains: A Multidisciplinary Study* (New York: Peter Lang, 1997), 78.
14. James E. Murphy, *Half Interest in a Silver Dollar: The Saga of Charles E. Conrad* (Missoula, MT: Mountain Press. 1983), 27.
15. Hugh A. Dempsey, ed., "Howell Harris and the Whiskey Trade," *Montana Magazine of History*, 3, no. 2 (spring 1953), 4.

16. "Statement of Mr. I. G. Baker of Fort Benton, Montana," Royal Canadian Mounted Police, Papers, RG 18, vol. 4, file 98, National Archives of Canada (NAC).
17. Letter, N. C. Thum to C. Peck, 17 January 1873. Montana Superintendency of Indian Affairs, RG 75, M234, roll 495, p. 551, NARA.
18. Theresa Berglund, "The Reminiscences of John LaMott," SC 365, p. 43, MHS.
19. Ibid., 55.
20. Ibid., 40–41.
21. Joel Overholser, Fort Benton: World's Innermost Port (Helena, MT: Falcon Press, 1987), 254.
22. Dempsey, "Howell Harris," 5. Harris is not reliable regarding dates and admitted such when he made changes to his recollections. He states he was at High River during the winter of 1871–72 and that the troubles with the Spitzee Cavalry occurred in May 1872; however, documents show that the latter event happened in April 1874. John LaMott has proven to be much more accurate, his dates generally agreeing with documented sources.
23. High River Pioneers & Old Timers Association, Leaves from the Medicine Tree (Lethbridge, AB: Lethbridge Herald, 1960), 168.
24. Ibid.
25. Ibid., 169–70.
26. Leroy Victor Kelly, The Range Men (Toronto: Coles, 1980), 93–94.
27. In the spring of 1873, Berry estimated that he had made some $3,000. He kept up the post, but some time later he sold out to the Sample brothers and they operated it long after the arrival of the Mounted Police.
28. Helena Daily Herald, 8 April 1873.
29. Interview with John Cotton, Blood Indian, 4 January 1957 by the author.
30. Ibid.
31. Interview with John LaMott by James Willard Schultz, n.d. James Willard Schultz, Papers, Montana State University, Special Collections, Bozeman.
32. Kelly, Range Men, 94. Like so many people giving their reminiscences, Kanouse tended to make himself the hero of the story when he was interviewed by Leroy Kelly. He also claimed to have been the one who shot the chief, White Eagle. Kanouse told Kelly that one white man and one Blood were killed in the initial onslaught, and that several Indians were killed during the siege. The Helena Herald said three traders were wounded and three Indians killed. LaMott, who seems to be the most reliable source, states that one trader and one Indian were killed and Kanouse wounded.
33. Helena Daily Herald, 8 April 1873.
34. Interview with John LaMott by James Willard Schultz, n.d.
35. Helena Daily Herald, 27 August 1873.
36. Ibid.
37. Interview with John Cotton, Blood Indian, 4 January 1957 by the author.
38. Letter, John Healy to Tappen Adney, 25 August 1905. E. Tappen Adney, Papers, MHS.
39. Letter, T. C. Power to D. W. Davis, 18 September 1873. Power, Papers, MC 55, file 1783, MHS.
40. John McDougall, On Western Trails in the Early Seventies (Toronto: William Briggs, 1911), 69, 191.
41. Letter, D. W. Davis to Daniel Davis, 28 June 1873. Reprinted in Lewis O. Saum, "From Vermont to Whoop-Up Country: Some Letters of D. W. Davis, 1867–1878," Montana the Magazine of Western History (summer 1958), 67.
42. Visitor Donald Graham said the post was occupied by Berry, rather than Kanouse. See Hugh A. Dempsey, "Donald Graham's Narrative of 1872–73," Alberta Historical Review 4, no. 5 (winter 1956), 16.
43. Ibid.
44. Ibid., 17.
45. Hugh A. Dempsey, Red Crow, Warrior Chief (Saskatoon, SK: Western Producer Prairie Books, 1980), 75.
46. Ibid., 76.
47. Ibid., 77.
48. Ibid.
49. Letter, William Ensign to Indian commissioner, 14 October 1872. Montana Superintendency of Indian Affairs, RG 75, M234, roll 493, p. 467, NARA.
50. Viall also was under investigation at this time, accused of failing to take appropriate action when Blackfoot agent Jesse Armitage was charged with diverting Indian department flour and other goods to John Riplinger, of the North West Fur Company. Viall was also accused of arranging for Deputy Marshal Hard to bribe one of the witnesses to leave the Territory. (See letter, Secretary Delano to Indian commissioner, 7 December 1872, Montana Superintendency of Indian Affairs, RG 75, M234, roll 492, NARA.)
51. Letter, A. J. Simmons to Indian commissioner, 11 January 1873. Montana Superintendency of Indian Affairs, RG 75, M234, roll 495, p. 775, NARA.
52. Letter, James Wright to Indian commissioner, 11 March 1873. Montana Superintendency of Indian Affairs, RG 75, M234, roll 496, pp. 335–36, NARA.
53. Licence, 10 November 1871. Montana Superintendency of Indian Affairs, RG 75, M234, roll 491, p. 1050, NARA.
54. E. Tappen Adney, "Incidents of Indian-fighting and Fur Trader days in Montana, the Canadian Northwest, and Alaska, related by the late Captain John J. Healy," 1937, MF95, pp. 17–18, MHS. In his recollections, Healy said this incident occurred in 1869 during a presidential election year, but as he was in possession of a permit that year, which included the transportation of whisky, there was no need for subterfuge. Tappen Adney says of the 1869 date, "Healy is probably a little off on the date, giving it 1869; but it was no great while before the presidential election in the States, and that was to be in 1872." (pp. 56–57). In an interview [Alex Stavely Hill, From Home to Home (New York: O. Judd Co., 1885), 159], Healy also implies the date was 1872.
55. The Helena Weekly Herald, 29 August 1872, indicated that Hamilton was in Helena at the time.
56. Adney, "Incidents," 18–19.
57. Peter Koch, "Life at Muscleshell in 1869 and 1870," Contributions to the Historical Society of Montana 2 (1896), 298.
58. Schultz, "Raven Quiver," 43.
59. Letter, T. C. Power to Mike, 31 August 1873. Power, Papers, MC 55, file 178–4, pp. 327–28, MHS.
60. Letter, John Bunn to Richard Hardisty, 22 March 1875. Richard Hardisty, Papers, Glenbow Archives.
61. Kennedy, Whiskey Trade, 162–64.

62. Ibid., 161–65.
63. *Helena Daily Herald*, 17 May 1873.
64. Letter, James Wright to commissioner, 16 June 1873. Montana Superintendency of Indian Affairs, RG 75, M234, roll 497, p. 169, NARA.

Chapter 8: The Wolfers & the Cypress Hills Massacre

1. *Helena Herald*, 10 September 1868.
2. *The River Press* (Fort Benton), 20 January 1886.
3. Enoch Gilbert, "From Fort Benton," *The Weekly Montanian* (Missoula), 23 May 1872.
4. William Rodney, *Kootenai Brown: His Life and Times* (Sidney, BC: Gray's Publishing Co., 1969), 114.
5. Hugh A. Dempsey, "Donald Graham's Narrative of 1872–73," *Alberta Historical Review* (winter 1956), 18.
6. Ibid.
7. Ibid.
8. *Great Falls Tribune*, 22 July 1934.
9. Report, F. D. Pease to secretary of the interior, 19 February 1874. Montana Superintendency of Indian Affairs, RG 75, M234, roll 458, pp. 11–12, NARA.
10. Ibid.
11. "Interview of Mr. Forest Chrissy of the Chicago Evening Post with Captain John J. Healy on Friday evening at 9 P.M., May 5, 1899." Microfilm in Montana Historical Society (MHS).
12. Ibid.
13. Ibid.
14. Ibid.
15. Peter Koch, "Life at Muscleshell in 1869 and 1870s," *Contributions to the Historical Society of Montana* 2 (1896), 301.
16. *Lethbridge Herald*, 17 September 1927.
17. *Helena Weekly Herald*, 23 May 1872.
18. Ibid., 9 May 1872.
19. *History of Montana, 1739–1885* (Chicago: Warner, Beers & Co., 1885), 1136.
20. Statement of John Evans in *Bozeman Avant Courier*, 4 July 1873.
21. *Helena Daily Herald*, 11 June 1873.
22. Ibid., 13 November 1871.
23. Philip Goldring, "Whisky, Horses and Death: The Cypress Hills Massacre and its Sequel," in *Canadian Historic Sites: Occasion Papers in Archaeology and History* (Ottawa: National Historic Parks & Sites Branch, 1979), 51.
24. "Court of Queen's Bench," *Manitoba Free Press*, 21 June 1876.
25. It is possible that Farwell's post in the Cypress Hills was being operated for Durfee & Peck of Fort Peck. A year later, 4 January 1874, Tom Power was still referring to the trader as "your man Farwell" when writing to Durfee & Peck, implying that his employment with the firm had been continuous.
26. Letter, M. C. Thum to Hon. N. J. Turney, 16 January 1873. Montana Superintendency of Indian Affairs, RG 75, M234, roll 456, p. 167, NARA.
27. Statement of John Evans in *Bozeman Avant Courier*, 4 July 1873.
28. See Dan Kennedy, *Recollections of an Assiniboine Chief* (Toronto: McClelland & Stewart, 1972), 42–47. The depositions of survivors of the massacre indicate that

they were from Wood Mountain, in what later became Man Who Took the Coat's band. For depositions, see Alexander Morris, Papers, MG12, #1177, Provincial Archives of Manitoba (PAM), Winnipeg.
29. "Court of Queen's Bench," *Manitoba Free Press*, 20 June 1876.
30. Ibid.
31. "Court of Queen's Bench," *Manitoba Free Press*, 20 June 1876. Alexis Lebombard said in his testimony that Farwell could not understand the Assiniboine language. This seems unlikely, as he had been trading with that tribe for at least three years. But if his knowledge of the language was limited, he should have had a working knowledge of the Plains Indian sign language, which was just as effective.
32. Ibid.
33. Ibid.
34. Statement of John Evans in *Bozeman Avant Courier*, 4 July 1873.
35. Ibid.
36. Statement of Woman Who Eats Grizzly Bear, 21 December 1875. Morris, Papers, MG12, #1177, PAM. Punctuation has been added to the statements where necessary.
37. Statement of Apasteeninchaco, 20 December 1875. Morris, Papers, MG12, #1177, PAM.
38. Statement of The Man Who Took the Coat, 20 December 1875. Morris, Papers, MG12, #1177, PAM.
39. Statement of John Evans in *Bozeman Avant Courier*, 4 July 1873.
40. Statement of Woman Who Eats Grizzly Bear, 21 December 1875. Morris, Papers, MG12, #1177, PAM.
41. Ibid.
42. Statement of Cutter, 20 December 1875. Morris Papers, MG12, #1177, PAM.
43. Statement of John Evans in *Bozeman Avant Courier*, 4 July 1873.
44. In relating this account of the Cypress Hills Massacre, the author gives greatest credibility to the accounts of Abel Farwell and the Assiniboine survivors of the attack. Also, the statement by John Evans is probably the most honest account by any of the wolfers. Evidence of others involved in the massacre is simply not credible.
45. *Helena Daily Herald*, 11 June 1873.
46. Letter, A. J. Simmons to Indian commissioner, 12 July 1873. Montana Superintendency of Indian Affairs, RG 75, M234, roll 495, p. 863, NARA.
47. Ibid.
48. *History of Montana, 1739–1885*, 1136.
49. *Helena Gazette*, 22 October 1873.
50. Ibid.
51. *The River Press* (Fort Benton), 13 January 1886.
52. Ibid.
53. *Helena Gazette*, 22 October 1873.
54. Letter, T. C. Power & Bro. to P. B. Weare Co., 18 December 1873. T. C. Power, Papers, MC 55, file 178–4, p. 516. MHS.
55. Letter, L. F. Williams to T. C. Power, 31 March 1874. Power, Papers, MC 55, file 178–4. MHS.
56. "A Plea for the Old-Timer," *The River Press* (Fort Benton), 20 January 1886.

Chapter 9: The Canadian Response

1. *The Manitoban*, 5 November 1870.
2. William F. Butler, *The Great Lone Land* (London: Sampson Low, Marston, Low & Searle, 1874), 366.
3. Ibid., 375.
4. Ibid., 378–79.
5. Letter, W. J. Christie to Government House, 26 April 1871. Adams G. Archibald, Papers, MG 12, A1, #272, Provincial Archives of Manitoba (PAM).
6. John McDougall, *George Millward McDougall: The Pioneer, Patriot and Missionary* (Toronto: William Briggs, 1902), 174.
7. Letter, Jean L'Heureux to W. J. Christie, 1871 [no other date]. Richard Hardisty, Papers, Glenbow Archives, Calgary, AB.
8. Jean L'Heureux, "Description of a Portion of the Nor-West and the Indians," Rocky Mountain House, November 1871, Glenbow Archives.
9. Letter, A. G. Archibald to John A. Macdonald, 18 January 1872. Sir John A. Macdonald, Papers, #78134, National Archives of Canada (NAC).
10. Ibid.
11. Undated notes from Moberly in Archibald, Papers, MG 12, A1, item 783, PAM.
12. Ibid.
13. Hugh A. Dempsey, ed., "Robertson-Ross' Diary: Fort Edmonton to Wildhorse, B.C., 1872," *Alberta Historical Review* 9, no. 3 (summer 1961), 5–22.
14. Ibid., 12–13.
15. Ibid., 7.
16. John Peter Turner, *The North-West Mounted Police* (Ottawa, ON: King's Printer, 1950), 81.
17. S. W. Horrall, "The March West," in *Men in Scarlet*, Hugh A. Dempsey, ed. (Calgary, AB: McClelland & Stewart West, 1974), 17.
18. Letter, Archibald McDonald to Lieutenant-Governor, 16 April 1873. Alexander Morris, Papers, MG 12, R.1, item 189, PAM.
19. Letter, Edward McKay to Lieut.-Governor, 18 May 1873. Morris, Papers, MG 12, R.1, item 164, PAM.
20. Letter, William Traill to Lieut.-Governor, 7 July 1873. Morris, Papers, MG 12, R.1, item 317, PAM.
21. Letter, Minister of the Interior to Lieut.-Governor, 13 August 1873. Morris, Papers, MG 12, R.1, item 1944, PAM.
22. Letter, Edward McKay to Lieut.-Governor, 24 August 1873. Morris, Papers, MG 12, R.1, item 1945, PAM.
23. Letter, Alexander Morris to Minister of the Interior, 26 August 1873. Morris, Papers, MG 12, R.1, item 45, PAM.
24. Deposition of Narcisse Lacerte, 8 September 1873. Morris, Papers, MG 12, R.1, item 1946, PAM.
25. Letter, David Laird to Lieut.-Governor, 8 May 1875. Morris, Papers, MG 12, R.1, item 997, PAM.
26. E. Tappen Adney, "Incidents of Indian-fighting and Fur Trader days in Montana, the Canadian Northwest, and Alaska, related by the late Captain John. J. Healy," 1937, MF 95, p. 63, Montana Historical Society (MHS).
27. "Interview of Mr. Forest Chrissy of the Chicago Evening Post with Captain John J. Healy on Friday evening at 9 P.M., May 5, 1899." Microfilm in MHS.
28. *Benton Weekly Record*, 16 January 1880.
29. James Willard Schultz, *Friends of My Life as an Indian* (Boston: Houghton Mifflin Co., 1923), 101.
30. James Willard Schultz, "Raven Quiver, the Trader," *Forest and Stream* (18 July 1903), 43.
31. Letter, Angus Fraser to Richard Hardisty, 27 August 1872. Hardisty, Papers, Glenbow Archives.
32. Letter, Angus Fraser to Richard Hardisty, 25 April 1873. Hardisty, Papers, Glenbow Archives.
33. Letter, Donald A. Smith to Richard Hardisty, 21 March 1873. Hardisty, Papers, Glenbow Archives.
34. *Benton Weekly Record*, 16 January 1880.
35. John McDougall, *On Western Trails in the Early Seventies* (Toronto: William Briggs, 1911), 64.
36. Ibid., 66.
37. Letter, Robert Hamilton to Government House, 10 December 1873. Morris, Papers, MG 12, B1, item 575, PAM.
38. Letter, George Young to Morris, 3 December 1873. Morris, Papers, MG 12, B1, item 566, PAM.
39. Letter, George McDougall to Donald A. Smith, 8 January 1874. Morris, Papers, MG 12, B1, item 606, PAM.

Chapter 10: Chaos and Misery

1. Margaret A. Kennedy, *The Whiskey Trade of the Northwestern Plains: A Multidisciplinary Study* (New York: Peter Lang, 1997), 95.
2. Alexander Morris, *The Treaties of Canada, with the Indians of Manitoba and the North-West Territories* (Toronto: Willing & Williamson, 1880), 248.
3. Ibid.
4. Red Tail Feathers, a.k.a. Joe Beebe, "Bygone Days of the Blackfeet Nation," December 1937. Copy in author's possession.
5. Interview with Wolf Leg, Siksika Indian, 8 July 1939. Lucien & Jane Hanks, Papers, Glenbow Archives, Calgary, AB.
6. Interview with Heavy Shield, Siksika Indian, 22 June 1939. Lucien & Jane Hanks, Papers.
7. Interview with Mrs. One Gun, Siksika Indian, 16 July 1939. Lucien & Jane Hanks, Papers.
8. Interviews with George Calling Last, Blood Indian, 24 July 1954, and Bobtail Chief, 8 October 1954, by the author.
9. Thomas Kehoe and Alice B. Kehoe, "A Historical marker, Indian Style," *Alberta Historical Review* 5, no. 4 (autumn 1957), 8.
10. Ibid., 9.
11. Ibid.
12. Interview with Buck Running Rabbit, Siksika Indian, 1939. Lucien & Jane Hanks, Papers.
13. Kehoe, "Historical Marker," 9–10.
14. Interview with Buck Running Rabbit, 1939.
15. Ibid.
16. Interview with Wolf Leg, 8 July 1939.
17. Interview with White Headed Chief, Siksika Indian, 3 September 1938. Lucien & Jane Hanks, Papers.
18. Ibid.
19. Interview with Many Guns, Siksika Indian, 16 September 1938. Lucien & Jane Hanks, Papers.
20. Ibid.
21. Interview with Crooked Meat Strings, Siksika Indian, 19 July 1939. Lucien & Jane Hanks, Papers.
22. Hugh A. Dempsey, "Donald Graham's Narrative of 1872–73," *Alberta Historical Review* 4, no. 5 (winter 1956), 17.
23. Interview with Jim White Bull, 1 January 1955, by the

author. Author's collection. All quotations in this story are from this source.

24. Interview with Jack Low Horn, Blood Indian, 29 December 1954, by the author. Author's collection.

25. Unidentified newspaper article, 28 November 1924, in the Charles Rowe clipping file, Montana Historical Society.

26. Ibid.

27. *Lethbridge Herald*, 11 July 1935.

28. Henry Standing Alone, "The Death of Calf Shirt," *Kainai News*, 1 September 1972.

29. Cecil Denny, *The Riders of the Plains: A Reminiscence of the Early and Exciting Days in the North West* (Calgary, AB: Herald Print, 1905), 4.

30. Alex Staveley Hill, *From Home to Home: Autumn Wanderings in the North-West* (New York: O. Judd Co., 1885), 161.

31. Denny, *Riders of the Plains*, 2.

32. *Benton Weekly Record*, 13 February 1880.

33. Ibid.

34. Interview with John LaMott by James Willard Schultz, n.d. James Willard Schultz, Papers, Montana State University, Special Collections, Bozeman.

35. Ibid.

36. Interview with Kate Shade, Blood Indian, 27 October 1994, by Pauline Dempsey. Interview provided courtesy of Margaret Kennedy.

37. Interview with Katie Wells, Blood Indian, 15 September 1994, by Pauline Dempsey. Interview provided courtesy of Margaret Kennedy.

Chapter 11: Unsettled Times

1. According to Flanagan, in 1873 "I. G. Baker had an office in Montreal on St. Joseph Street for the sale of furs bought in Canada." Mae Flanagan, "A Perspective View of the Life and Times of I. G. Baker." SC 1236, 16, Montana Historical Society (MHS).

2. Letter, William Wright to commissioner, 2 June 1873. Montana Superintendency of Indian Affairs, RG 75, M234, roll 497, p. 69, NARA.

3. Ibid.

4. Letter, Isaac Baker to Hon. James Harlan, 7 July 1873. Montana Superintendency of Indian Affairs, RG 75, M234, roll 495, pp. 72–73, NARA.

5. Letter, Charles Hard to William Wright, 9 June 1873. Montana Superintendency of Indian Affairs, RG 75, M234, roll 497, p. 165, NARA.

6. Letter, William Wright to commissioner, 16 June 1873. Montana Superintendency of Indian Affairs, RG 75, M234, roll 497, pp. 166–67, NARA.

7. *History of Montana, 1739–1885* (Chicago: Warner, Beers & Co., 1885), 1029.

8. Letter, M. A. Flanagan to T. C. Power, 27 November 1873. T. C. Power, Papers, MC 55, letter-book, file 178–4, p. 506, MHS.

9. Letter, T. C. Power to John Kerler, 25 July 1874. Power, Papers, MC 55, file 179–1, MHS.

10. Letter, T. C. Power to Mike, 31 August 1873. Power, Papers, MC 55, file 178–4, pp. 337–38, MHS.

11. Letter, T. C. Power to Ben Stickney Jr., 8 September 1873. Power, Papers, MC 55, file 178–4, p. 345, MHS.

12. Discharge book, 1873. Power, Papers, MC 55, file 287–6, p. 42, MHS.

13. Ibid.

14. Letter, Charles D. Hard to commissioner, 13 August 1873. Montana Superintendency of Indian Affairs, RG 75, M234, roll 495, p. 77, NARA.

15. *Rocky Mountain Gazette*, 10 September 1873.

16. Ibid.

17. Ibid.

18. Ibid.

19. John McDougall, *On Western Trails in the Early Seventies* (Toronto: William Briggs, 1911), 191.

20. *Helena Weekly Herald*, 8 April 1873.

21. *Helena Independent*, 22 March 1874.

22. *Lethbridge Herald*, 6 January 1891.

23. A variation of this letter has been published in a number of books and pamphlets. One of the first was by Edmonton historian Ernest Brown, who wrote: "Dear Friend. Bill Geary got to putting on airs and I shot him, and he is dead, my potatoes are looking fine. Yours truly, Skookum Jim." (Ernest Brown, *Old Trading Forts in Southern Alberta* [pamphlet] [Edmonton, AB: Private printing, 1930]. It was also cited by Longstreth, Sharp, McInnis, and others.

24. *Lethbridge Herald*, 26 July 1913.

25. Ibid.

26. Power, Papers, MC 55, vols. 63 & 139, MHS.

27. *Lethbridge Herald*, 11 July 1936, 51.

28. "Memorandum of information given by Johnston, April 20th, 1874." Alexander Morris, Papers, MG 12, B1, item 710, Provincial Archives of Manitoba (PAM).

29. *Helena Weekly Herald*, 19 June 1873.

30. Letter, Charles D. Hard to commissioner, 17 June 1873. Montana Superintendency of Indian Affairs, RG 75, M234, roll 497, p. 175, NARA.

31. Letters, Charles Hard to commissioner, 7 July 1873. Montana Superintendency of Indian Affairs, RG 75, M234, roll 495, p. 75, NARA; Attorney General George J. Williams to Secretary of the Interior Columbus Delano, 17 July 1873, ibid., p. 36, NARA; William Wheeler to attorney general, 24 July 1873, ibid., p. 228, NARA; M. C. Page to attorney general, 25 July 1873, ibid., p. 229, NARA.

32. Letter, William Ensign to commissioner, 10 September 1873. Montana Superintendency of Indian Affairs, RG 75, M234, roll 404, p. 655, NARA.

33. *Rocky Mountain Gazette*, 22 October 1873.

34. Letter, T. C. Power to P. B. Weare & Co., 3 February 1874. Power, Papers, MC 55, file 178–4, pp. 632–33, MHS.

35. Letter, T. C. Power to S. F. Williams, 3 February 1874. Power, Papers, MC 55, file 178–4, pp. 635–36, MHS.

36. Ibid.

37. Ibid., 637.

38. *Rocky Mountain Gazette*, 22 October 1873.

39. Leroy Victor Kelly, *The Range Men* (Toronto: Coles, 1913), 95; Robert J. Vaughn, *Then and Now, or 36 Years in the Rockies, 1864–1900* (Minneapolis, MN: Tribune Printing Co., 1900), 89. In his account ledger for 1 January 1874 [mistakenly entered as 1873], Power lists William Berry as being deceased (Power, Papers, MC 55, petty ledger D, vol. 64, p. 490, MHS). Kelly identifies the dead man as Dick Berry, but this person was still alive several years later. Vaughn identifies him as William. Also, Kelly attributes the date of the event as 1872, but Vaughn's 1874 date appears to be the accurate one.

40. Cecil Denny, *The Riders of the Plains; A Reminiscence of the Early and Exciting Days in the North West* (Calgary, AB: The Herald Company, 1905), 81.
41. Letter, Constantine Scollen to Samuel Livingston, 24 February 1874. Alexander Morris, Papers, MG 12, B1, item 646, PAM. Also, John McDougall commented in March 1874 that his brother David had "gone south to the Conrad establishment, on Sheep Creek. This was the only post that did not traffic in whiskey; but alongside of this, were several of the other sort." (McDougall, *On Western Trails*, 131)
42. James Willard Schultz, Papers, Montana State University, Special Collections, Bozeman.
43. McDougall, *On Western Trails*, 148–49.
44. Schultz, Papers.
45. Ibid.
46. Ibid.
47. *Pincher Creek Echo*, 31 March 1910.
48. Ibid.
49. *Helena Independent*, 22 March 1874. In another version of this story, Calf Shirt was trying to reclaim a shield he had left with the trader, resulting in a fatal argument. (Hugh A. Dempsey, *The Amazing Death of Calf Shirt and Other Blackfoot Stories* [Norman, OK: University of Oklahoma Press, 1994], 55.)
50. James Willard Schultz, "Raven Quiver, the Trader," *Forest and Stream* (18 July 1903), 43.
51. James Willard Schultz, *Blackfeet and Buffalo* (Norman, OK: University of Oklahoma Press, 1962), 66.
52. Ibid.
53. Hugh A. Dempsey, "The Amazing Death of Calf Shirt," *Montana Magazine of History* 3, no. 1 (January 1953), 71.
54. Interview with James Willard Schultz by George Houk. Schultz, Papers.
55. Ibid.
56. Julius F. Morley, "Account of a Prospecting Trip North to Canada by way of Sun River, St. Mary's in 1873." Manuscript in MHS archives.
57. George M. Dawson, diary, M-339, Glenbow Archives, Calgary, AB.
58. Ibid.

Chapter 12: Vagaries of the Law

1. Letter, Andrew Dusold to D. W. Buck, 1 January 1874. Montana Superintendency of Indian Affairs, RG 75, M234, roll 498, p. 339, NARA.
2. *Helena Weekly Herald*, 27 November 1873.
3. *Rocky Mountain Gazette* cited on p. 2.
4. Letter, Martin Maginnis to Indian commissioner, 29 December 1873. Montana Superintendency of Indian Affairs, RG 75, M234, roll 499, pp. 458–61, NARA.
5. Ibid.
6. Letter, I. G. Baker Bro. & Co. to Martin Maginnis, 7 February 1874. Martin Maginnis, Papers, MC 50, file 1–3. Montana Historical Society (MHS).
7. Letter, T. C. Power to Martin Maginnis, 8 January 1874. T. C. Power, Papers, MC 55, file 178–4, pp. 563–64, MHS.
8. Petition signed by chiefs of the Blackfeet, Bloods, and Peigans, 1 August 1874. Montana Superintendency of Indian Affairs, RG 75, M234, roll 499, pp. 904–08, NARA.
9. *Helena Daily Herald*, 8 November 1873.
10. Letter, Merritt Page to attorney general, 7 May 1874. Montana Superintendency of Indian Affairs, RG 75, M234, roll 499, pp. 72–73, NARA.
11. "United States v. Carr," *Report of Cases Argued and Determined in the Supreme Court of Montana Territory* (Virginia City: George F. Cope, 1875), 235.
12. Letter, Merritt Page to Columbus Delano, 7 August 1874. Montana Superintendency of Indian Affairs, RG 75, M234, roll 500, pp. 173–75, NARA. See also "United States v. Carr," Report of Cases, 235–36.
13. Letter, Hiram Knowles to R. F. May, 5 May 1874. Montana Superintendency of Indian Affairs, RG 75, M234, roll 499, p. 117, NARA.
14. Letter, M. C. Page to Indian commissioner, 13 January 1874. Montana Superintendency of Indian Affairs, RG 75, M234, roll 500, pp. 116–22, NARA.
15. Letter, Merritt Page to Columbus Delano, 7 August 1874 (see n. 12).
16. Ibid.
17. Ibid.
18. Letter, Charles D. Hard to Indian superintendent, 17 June 1873. Montana Superintendency of Indian Affairs, RG 75, M234, roll 497, pp. 175–76, NARA.
19. *Helena Daily Herald*, 25 May 1874; *New North West* (Deer Lodge), 19 September 1874.
20. Letter, R. F. May to commissioner, 19 January 1874. Montana Superintendency of Indian Affairs, RG 75, M234, roll 499, pp. 504–6, NARA.
21. Thomas J. Dimsdale, *The Vigilantes of Montana, or Popular Justice in the Rocky Mountains* (Helena, MT: State Publishing Co., c.1934), 9.
22. *The Globe* (Toronto), 30 December 1882.
23. E. Tappen Adney, "Incidents of Indian-fighting and Fur Trader days in Montana, the Canadian Northwest, and Alaska, related by the late Captain John J. Healy," 1937. MF 95, p. 65, MHS.
24. Taylor's name, which in Blackfoot meant "woman thief," was given when he stole a Blackfoot woman after her father had refused to let him marry her.
25. Adney, "Incidents."
26. *The Globe* (Toronto), 30 December 1882.
27. James Willard Schultz, "Raven Quiver, the Trader," *Forest and Stream* (18 July 1903), 43.
28. *The Globe* (Toronto), 30 December 1882.
29. Ibid.
30. Letter, S. F. Williams to T. C. Power, 31 March 1874. Power, Papers, MC 55, file 178–4, pp. 728–30, MHS.
31. *Helena Daily Independent*, 11 April 1874.
32. *Helena Daily Herald*, 17 April 1874.
33. Adney, "Incidents."
34. Later in 1874, for example, Power wrote to his agent at Fort Kipp, "We have hired & will send Mr. Dave Acres out to aid you." (Letter, T. C. Power to John Kerler, 9 December 1874. Power, Papers, MC 55, file 178–4, MHS.)
35. Adney, "Incidents."
36. Ibid.
37. Ibid.
38. Ibid.
39. Ibid.
40. Ibid.
41. Ibid.
42. Ibid.
43. Ibid.

44. Ibid.
45. Ibid.
46. Ibid.
47. Ibid.
48. Ibid.
49. Ibid.
50. Ibid. Dave Akers' version of the story is similar to that told by Healy, except that Healy was said to have placed kegs of dynamite around the fort, rather than using a cannon (*The Globe* [Toronto], 30 December 1882). Ex-Mountie G. E. Grogan incorrectly attributed the incident to Joe Kipp, rather than Healy, also using the dynamite version (*Calgary Herald*, 26 January 1907), and Norman T. Macleod said that Joe Kipp had surrendered to the wolfers at Fort Kipp but that Healy had stood them off with dynamite at Whoop-Up (*Lethbridge Herald*, 24 January 1944).

Chapter 13: Beginning of the End

1. John McDougall, *On Western Trails in the Early Seventies* (Toronto: William Briggs, 1911), 128.
2. *Helena Daily Independent*, 22 March 1874.
3. Jack Blunt in *Benton Record*, 15 May 1875.
4. *The Globe* (Toronto), 6 March 1875.
5. Letter, John Bunn to Richard Hardisty, 25 October 1874. Richard Hardisty, Papers, Glenbow Archives, Calgary, AB.
6. Letter, R. F. May to commissioner, 24 January 1874. Montana Superintendency of Indian Affairs, RG 75, M234, roll 499, p. 530, NARA.
7. *Helena Daily Herald*, 17 April 1874.
8. Ibid., 15 November 1871.
9. Letter, T. C. Power to John Kerler, 25 July 1874. T. C. Power, Papers, MC 55, file 179–1, pp. 128–30, Montana Historical Society (MHS).
10 Ibid.
11. Ibid.
12. "I. G. Baker - Information re Ft. Macleod District 1875." Royal Canadian Mounted Police, Papers, RG 18, vol. 4, file 98, National Archives of Canada (NAC).
13. Leroy Victor Kelly, *The Range Men* (Toronto: Coles, 1980), 95.
14. Interview with Mrs. Axe, Siksika Indian, 25 July 1939. Lucien & Jane Hanks, Papers, Glenbow Archives.
15. *The New North-West* (Deer Lodge), 24 October 1874.
16. Letter, William Winder to James F. Macleod, 6 August 1875. RCMP, Papers, RG 18, vol. 7, file 362, NAC.
17. *Helena Daily Herald*, 15 September 1874, publishing a letter from Fort Benton, 10 September 1874.
18. Report of Inspector J. W. Daniel, 6 November 1873. Montana Superintendency of Indian Affairs, RG 75, M234, roll 494, p. 543, NARA.
19. Letter, Charles D. Hard to D. W. Buck, 31 December 1873. Montana Superintendency of Indian Affairs, RG 75, M234, roll 498, p. 408, NARA.
20. *Helena Daily Herald*, 15 September 1874.
21. *Helena Weekly Herald*, 23 September 1874.
22. *Helena Daily Herald*, 5 October 1874.
23. *Report of Cases Argued and Determined in the Supreme Court of Montana Territory* (Virginia City, MT: George F. Cope, 1875), 239–40.
24. Letter, Andrew Dusold to R. F. May, 31 October 1874. Montana Superintendency of Indian Affairs, RG 75, M234, roll 499, pp. 1036–45, NARA.
25. Ibid.
26. Ibid.
27. E. Tappen Adney, "Incidents of Indian-fighting and Fur Trader days in Montana, the Canadian Northwest, and Alaska, related by the late Captain John J. Healy," 1937, MF 95, MHS.
28. Ibid.
29. Letter, R. F. May to commissioner, 2 November 1874. Montana Superintendency of Indian Affairs, RG 75, M234, roll 499, pp. 1036–37, NARA.

Chapter 14: The Queen's Mounted Police

1. Reprinted in *Toronto Mail*, 24 October 1874.
2. Report of George A. French, in *Opening Up the West, 1874–1881* (Toronto: Coles, 1973), 22.
3. Ibid., 25.
4. Simon John Clarke, diary, entry for 9 October 1876. Glenbow Archives, Calgary, AB.
5. Diary of George A. French, in *Opening Up the West*, 47.
6. Ibid.
7. Letter, R. B. Nevitt to Lizzie, 24 September 1874. Richard Barrington Nevitt, Papers, Glenbow Archives.
8. Diary of George A. French, in *Opening Up the West*, 50.
9. Joel Overholser, *Fort Benton: World's Innermost Port* (Helena, MT: Falcon Press, 1987), 360.
10. Letter, R. B. Nevitt to Lizzie, 9 October 1874. Nevitt, Papers, Glenbow Archives.
11. *Helena Daily Herald*, 28 September 1874.
12. Ibid., 4 October 1874.
13. *Benton Weekly Record*, 16 January 1880.
14. *The New North-West* (Deer Lodge), 24 October 1874.
15. *Toronto Daily Mail*, 5 April 1875.
16. *Helena Daily Herald*, 15 March 1875. These were probably Fred Kanouse (murderer), Neil Campbell (horse thief), and Kamoose Taylor (preacher).
17. *Toronto Mail*, 8 March 1875.
18. Unaware of the Canadian system of justice planned for the West, the United States government considered recommending the implementation of a unique two-country law to suppress the whisky trade. According to Secretary of the Interior Delano, the proposed law would read: "Any person selling, bartering or giving or attempting to sell, barter or give intoxicating liquors to any Indian on the continent of North America or any of the Islands adjacent thereto, shall be liable on conviction for such offence, to a fine not exceeding five hundred dollars." He does not explain how the law would be enforced. The matter was forwarded to Hamilton Fish, Secretary of State, with the recommendation that it be forwarded to the British government. (Letter, Interior Secretary Columbus Delano to Hamilton Fish, Secretary of State, 29 November 1873. Letters Sent by the Indian Division of the Office of the Secretary of the Interior, RG 75, M606, roll 14, pp. 59–60, NARA.)
19. Letter, James Macleod to George French, 30 October 1874, in *Opening Up the West*, 58.
20. Ibid., 60.
21. Letter, R. B. Nevitt to Lizzie, 26 October 1874. Nevitt, Papers, Glenbow Archives.
22. Ibid.
23. Cecil Denny later claimed in a work of semi-fiction that Bond had discovered a rich source of gold near the Porcupine Hills, and after his escape, he met some

cohorts and they were taking the horde south when he was shot in the back and killed.

24. Norman T. Macleod in *Lethbridge Herald*, 14 January 1944.
25. *The Daily Citizen* (Ottawa), 7 April 1875.
26. Letter, T. C. Power to John Kerler, 9 December 1874. T. C. Power, Papers, MC 55, file 179–1, Montana Historical Society (MHS).
27. Ibid.
28. Letter, T. C. Power to P. R. Pease, 5 December 1874. Power, Papers, MC 55, letter-book in file 179–1, p. 400, MHS.
29. Letter, T. C. Power to John Kerler, 9 December 1874. Power, Papers, MC 55, file 179–1, MHS.
30. *Helena Daily Herald*, 5 January 1875.
31. Ibid., 5 April 1875.
32. *Havre Plaindealer*, 27 September 1919.
33. Letter, James Macleod to George French, 4 December 1874, in *Opening Up the West*, 62.
34. Letter, James Macleod to Arthur French, 2 February 1875. RCMP Papers, RG 18, vol. 4, file 115, National Archives of Canada (NAC).
35. Ibid.
36. Ibid.
37. Ibid.
38. W. D. Antrobus, "A Mid-Winter North West Mounted Patrol in 1875," *Scarlet & Gold* 9 (1938), 44.
39. Ibid.
40. Ibid.
41. Ibid.
42. Ibid.
43. Ibid.
44. Ibid.
45. Ibid.
46. Richard Barrington Nevitt, *A Winter at Fort Macleod* (Calgary, AB: Glenbow-Alberta Institute, 1974), 57.
47. *Toronto Mail*, 5 April 1875.
48. *Helena Daily Herald*, 18 March 1875.
49. *The Daily Citizen* (Ottawa), 7 April 1875.
50. *Benton Record*, 15 March 1875.
51. *Helena Daily Herald*, 20 March 1875.
52. Ibid.
53. Ibid.
54. *New York Bulletin*, 11 April 1875.
55. Ibid.
56. *Helena Daily Herald*, 9 April 1875.
57. M. H. Williams, *Manitoba and the North-West: Journal of a Trip from Toronto to the Rocky Mountains* (Toronto: Hunter, Rose & Co., 1882), 143.
58. Hugh A. Dempsey, *A Blackfoot Winter Count* (Calgary, AB: Glenbow Museum, 1965), 16.

Chapter 15: South of the Border

1. *Helena Daily Herald* 5 January 1875.
2. Letter, A. B. Hamilton to commissioner, 4 January 1875. Montana Superintendency of Indian Affairs, RG 75, M234, roll 502, pp. 14–15, NARA.
3. Letter, T. C. Power to commissioner, 6 January 1875. Montana Superintendency of Indian Affairs, RG 75, M234, roll 502, pp. 721–22, NARA.
4. Letter Henry A. Kennerly to J. S. Wood, 29 January 1875. Blackfeet Reservation files, Browning, MT. Note: these files were examined in the 1950s while in possession of the tribe, but are now in the National Archives.

5. Letter, John Gibbon to O. D. Greene, 6 March 1875. Montana Superintendency of Indian Affairs, RG 75, M234, roll 503, pp. 305–7, NARA.
6. Letter, John S. Wood to commissioner, 2 February 1875. Montana Superintendency of Indian Affairs, RG 75, M234, roll 503, pp. 199–203, NARA.
7. Ibid.
8. *Helena Weekly Herald*, 26 June 1872.
9. Letter, John Wood to commissioner, 17 June 1875. Montana Superintendency of Indian Affairs, RG 75, M234, roll 503, pp. 418–21, NARA.
10. Ibid. Paraphrased from Dusold's report.
11. Letter, Andrew Dusold to John Wood, 31 March 1875. Blackfeet Reservation files, Browning, MT (see n. 4).
12. Ibid.
13. *Helena Daily Herald*, 6 April 1875.
14. Letter, John Wood to M. C. Page, 29 April 1875. Blackfeet Reservation files, Browning, MT (see n. 4).
15. Letter, John Wood to commissioner, 17 June 1875. Montana Superintendency of Indian Affairs, RG 75, M234, roll 503, pp. 418–21, NARA.
16. Letter, John Wood to commissioner, 15 June 1875. Montana Superintendency of Indian Affairs, RG 75, M234, roll 503, pp. 423–25, NARA.
17. *Benton Record*, 19 June 1875.
18. *Helena Daily Herald*, 17 May 1875.
19. Letter, Andrew Dusold to John Wood, 11 February 1875. Montana Superintendency of Indian Affairs, RG 75, M234, roll 503, pp. 238–42, NARA.
20. Letter, Andrew Dusold to John Wood, 30 June 1875. Blackfeet Reservation files, Browning, MT (see n. 4).
21. Letter, attorney general to secretary of the interior, 19 November 1875. Montana Superintendency of Indian Affairs, RG 75, M234, roll 502, pp. 254–55, NARA.
22. Report, John Wood to commissioner, 28 September 1875. Montana Superintendency of Indian Affairs, RG 75, M234, roll 503, pp. 705–14, NARA.

Chapter 16: What Became of Them?

1. *Toronto Mail*, 27 September 1874.
2. Canada, *Sessional Papers of Canada*. Public Accounts #188, vol. 12, no. 1 (1879), 23–27.
3. Ibid., 25.
4. *Benton Record*, 1 May 1875.
5. Cited in William R. Hunt, *Whiskey Peddler: Johnny Healy, North Frontier Trader* (Missoula, MT: Mountain Press, 1993), 135. Much of the biographical material dealing with Healy's Alaskan adventures are from this source.
6. Ibid., 143.
7. "Hugh Kirkendall vs. The United States and the Blackfeet and Piegan Indians," 1910. SC 83, p. 16, Montana Historical Society (MHS).
8. Teton County History Committee, comp. *Teton County, A History* (Choteau, MT: Teton County History Committee, 1988), 81, 84, 195.
9. Michael F. Foley, "An Historical Analysis of the Administration of the Blackfeet Indian Reservation by the United States, 1855–1950s" (Washington, DC: Indian Claims Commission), Docket #279-D, p. 77.
10. Idem, 193.
11. Idem, 214.
12. James Willard Schultz, "Raven Quiver, the Trader," *Forest and Stream* (18 July 1903), 43.
13. *Great Falls Tribune*, 1 July 1934.

14. Schultz, "Raven Quiver," 43.
15. Foley, "Historical Analysis," 119–20.
16. Ibid., 181–83.
17. Ibid., 185–94.
18. Ibid., 214.
19. *Lethbridge Herald*, 22 December 1913.
20. T. C. Power, Papers, MC 55, letter-book of Statements and Copy Book, file 252–53, p. 613, MHS.
21. *Macleod Gazette*, 10 March 1893.
22. M. H. Williams, *Manitoba and the North-West: Journal of a Trip from Toronto to the Rocky Mountains* (Toronto: Hunter, Rose & Co., 1882), 130.
23. John D. Higinbotham, *When the West was Young* (Toronto: Ryerson Press, 1933), 79–81.
24. Williams, *Manitoba and the North-West*, 142.
25. Report by William Pearce, 2 September 1888. Department of the Interior papers, RG 10, vol. 7765, file 27103-1, p. 24661, National Archive of Canada.
26. *The Globe* (Toronto), 30 December 1882.
27. Simon John Clarke, diary, entry for 13 April 1879. Glenbow Archives, Calgary, AB.
28. Ibid., entry for 16 March 1880.
29. Ibid., entry for 17 September 1880.
30. Ibid., entry for 1 November 1880.
31. *Macleod Gazette*, 12 May 1892.
32. Beverley A. Stacey, "D. W. Davis: Whiskey Trader to Politician," *Alberta History* 38, no. 3 (summer 1990), 1–11.
33. Ibid., 7.
34. *Manitoba Free Press*, 26 September 1876.
35. *Sun River Sun*, 22 January 1885.
36. *History of Montana 1739–1885* (Chicago: Warner, Bears & Co., 1885), 1016.
37. Ibid., 1030.
38. Ibid., 1021.
39. Ibid., 1007.
40. Ibid., 1008.
41. These names were gleaned from various sources, but primarily Roxanne DeMarce, *Blackfeet Heritage, 1906–07* (Browning, MT: Blackfeet Heritage Program, 1980); "Indians of the Blood Reserve," Oblate Collection, 71.220, Provincial Archives of Alberta; and annuity paysheets of the Blood tribe.
42. *History of Montana*, 1009.
43. Foley, "Historical Analysis," 59 (see n. 9).
44. "Condition Fort Benton House of Messrs. I. G. Baker & Co., at close of business, February 28th, 1885." SC 293, MHS.
45. James E. Murphy, *Half Interest in a Silver Dollar: The Saga of Charles E. Conrad* (Missoula, MT: Mountain Press, 1983), 228.
46. Foley, "Historical Analysis," 50, 65, 67 (see n. 9).
47. Ibid., 72.
48. Undated draft of a resolution attributed to T. H. Carter. Power, Papers, MC 55b, file 1–17, MHS.
49. Ibid.

4. *Helena Herald*, 12 February 1872.
5. Letter, minister of the interior to lieutenant-governor, 13 August 1873. Alexander Morris, Papers, MG 12, R.1, item 1944, Provincial Archives of Manitoba.
6. Hugh A. Dempsey, ed., "Robertson-Ross' Diary: Fort Edmonton to Wildhorse, B.C., 1872," *Alberta Historical Review* 9, no. 3 (summer 1961), 11.
7. John McDougall, *On Western Trails in the Early Seventies* (Toronto: William Briggs, 1911), 128.
8. Interview with Harry Undermouse, Blood Indian, 3 November 1950. Claude Schaeffer, Papers, Glenbow Archives, Calgary, AB.
9. Ibid.
10. Ibid.
11. Alexander Morris, *The Treaties of Canada, with the Indians of Manitoba and the North-West Territories* (Toronto: Willing & Williamson, 1880), 270.

Conclusion

1. Jack Holterman, *King of the High Missouri: The Saga of the Culbertsons* (Helena, MT: Falcon Press, 1987), 248–49.
2. Ibid., 31–32.
3. Letter, M. C. Thum to Colonel C. K. Peck, 17 January 1973. Montana Superintendency of Indian Affairs, RG 75, M234, roll 495, p. 551, NARA.

Bibliography

Bennett, Ben. *Death, Too, For The Heavy-Runner*. Missoula, MT: Mountain Press, 1981.

Berry, Gerald L. *The Whoop-Up Trail*. Edmonton, AB: Applied Art Products, 1953.

Brown, Ernest. *Old Trading Forts in Southern Alberta* [pamphlet]. Edmonton, AB: Private printing, 1930.

Butler, William F. *The Great Lone Land*. London: Sampson Low, Marston, Low & Searle, 1874.

Canada. *Sessional Papers of Canada*, Public Accounts #188, vol. 12, no. 1, 1879. Ottawa, ON: King's Printer, 1879.

Chittenden, Hiram M. *The American Fur Trade of the Far West*. Stanford, CA: Academic Reprints, 1954.

Coues, Elliott, ed. *New Light on the Early History of the Greater Northwest*. New York: Francis P. Harper, 1897.

DeMarce, Roxanne. *Blackfeet Heritage, 1906–07*. Browning, MT: Blackfeet Heritage Program, 1980.

Dempsey, Hugh A. *A Blackfoot Winter Count*. Calgary, AB: Glenbow Museum, 1965.

———. *Crowfoot, Chief of the Blackfeet*. Norman, OK: University of Oklahoma Press, 1972.

———. *Red Crow, Warrior Chief*. Saskatoon, SK: Western Producer Prairie Books, 1980.

———. *The Amazing Death of Calf Shirt and Other Blackfoot Stories*. Calgary, AB: Fifth House, 1994.

Denny, Cecil. *The Riders of the Plains: A Reminiscence of the Early and Exciting Days in the North West*. Calgary, AB: The Herald Company, 1905.

Dimsdale, Thomas J. *The Vigilantes of Montana, or Popular Justice in the Rocky Mountains*. Helena, MT: State Publishing Co., c.1934.

Dixon, Joseph K. *The Vanishing Race*. New York: Doubleday & Co., 1913.

Ewers, John C. *The Blackfeet: Raiders on the Northwestern Plains*. Norman, OK: University of Oklahoma Press, 1958.

Hewitt, J. N. B., ed. *Journal of Rudolph Friederich Kurz*, Bulletin 115, Smithsonian Institution. Washington, DC: United States Government Printing Office, 1937.

High River Pioneers & Old Timers Association. *Leaves from the Medicine Tree*. Lethbridge, AB: Lethbridge Herald, 1960.

Higinbotham, John D. *When the West was Young*. Toronto: Ryerson Press, 1933.

Hill, Alex Staveley. *From Home to Home: Autumn Wanderings in the North-West*. New York: O. Judd Co., 1885.

History of Montana, 1739–1885. Chicago: Warner, Beers & Co., 1885.

Holterman, Jack. *King of the High Missouri: The Saga of the Culbertsons*. Helena, MT: Falcon Press, 1987.

Hunt, William R. *Whiskey Peddler: Johnny Healy, North Frontier Trader*. Missoula, MT: Mountain Press, 1993.

Kappler, Charles J., ed. *Indian Affairs. Laws and Treaties*. New York: AMS Press, 1971.

Kelly, Leroy Victor. *The Range Men*. Toronto: Coles, 1980.

Kennedy, Dan. *Recollections of an Assiniboine Chief*. Toronto: McClelland & Stewart, 1972.

Kennedy, Margaret A. *The Whiskey Trade of the Northwestern Plains: A Multidisciplinary Study*. New York: Peter Lang, 1997.

Larpenteur, Charles. *Forty Years a Fur Trader on the Upper Missouri*. Chicago: Lakeside Press, 1933.

McDougall, John. *George Millward McDougall, The Pioneer, Patriot and Missionary*. Toronto: William Briggs, 1902.

———. *On Western Trails in the Early Seventies*. Toronto: William Briggs, 1911.

Maclean, John. *The Indians of Canada: Their Manners and Customs*. London: Charles H. Kelly, 1892.

Morris, Alexander. *The Treaties of Canada, with the Indians of Manitoba and the North-West Territories*. Toronto: Willing & Williamson, 1880.

Morton, Arthur S., ed. *The Journal of Duncan M'Gillivray of the North West Company at Fort George on the Saskatchewan, 1794–95*. Toronto: Macmillans, 1929.

Mountain Horse, Mike. *My People the Bloods*. Calgary, AB: Glenbow Museum, 1979.

Murphy, James E. *Half Interest in a Silver Dollar: The Saga of Charles E. Conrad*. Missoula, MT: Mountain Press, 1983.

Nevitt, Richard Barrington. *A Winter at Fort Macleod*. Calgary, AB: Glenbow-Alberta Institute, 1974.

Oliver, E. H. *The Canadian North-West: Its Early Development and Legislative Records*. Ottawa, ON: Government Printing Office, 1915.

Overholser, Joel. *Fort Benton: World's Innermost Port*. Helena, MT: Falcon Press, 1987.

Pinkerton, Robert E. *Hudson's Bay Company*. London: Thornton Butterworth Ltd., 1932.

Ray, Arthur S. *Indians in the Fur Trade*. Toronto: University of Toronto Press, 1974.

Report of Cases Argued and Determined in the Supreme Court of Montana Territory. Virginia City, MT: George F. Cope, 1875.

Rodney, William. *Kootenai Brown: His Life and Times*. Sidney, BC: Gray's Publishing Co., 1969.

Rowe, Charles. *Pioneer Tales*. Private printing, 1959.

Royal Canadian Mounted Police, comp. *Opening Up the West, 1874–1881*. Toronto: Coles, 1973.

Schultz, James Willard. *Friends of My Life as an Indian*. Boston: Houghton Mifflin Co., 1923.

———. *Blackfeet and Buffalo*. Norman, OK: University of Oklahoma Press, 1962.

Sharp, Paul F. *Whoop-Up Country: The Canadian-Amerian West, 1865–1885*. Minneapolis, MN: University of Minnesota Press, 1955.

Southesk, Earl of. *Saskatchewan and the Rocky Mountains*. Edinburgh: Edmonston & Douglas, 1875.

Spence, Clark C. *Territorial Politics and Government in Montana, 1864–89*. Urbana, IL: University of Chicago Press, 1975.

Sunder, John E. *The Fur Trade on the Upper Missouri, 1840–1865*. Norman, OK: University of Oklahoma Press, 1965.

Teton County History Committee, comp. *Teton County, A History*. Choteau, MT: Teton County History Committee, 1988.

Thorp, Raymond W., and Robert Bunker. *Crow Killer: The Saga of Liver-Eating Johnson*. Bloomington, IN: University of Indiana Press, 1983.

Turner, John Peter. *The North-West Mounted Police*. Ottawa, ON: King's Printer, 1950.

Umfreville, Edward. *The Present State of Hudson's Bay*. Toronto: Ryerson Press, 1954.

U.S. Congress. House. *Piegan Indians. Letter from the Secretary of War*. Ex. Doc. 269, 1870.

Vaughn, Robert J. *Then and Now, or 36 Years in the Rockies, 1864–1900*. Minneapolis, MN: Tribune Printing Co., 1900.

Williams, M. H. *Manitoba and the North-West: Journal of a Trip from Toronto to the Rocky Mountains*. Toronto: Hunter, Rose & Co., 1882.

Articles
Antrobus, W. D. "A Mid-Winter North West Mounted Patrol in 1875," *Scarlet & Gold* 9 (1938), 44–47.

Ashby, S. C. "An Opportunity Presented Itself." In *We Seized Our Rifles: Recollections of the Montana Frontier*. Edited by Eugene Lee Silliman. Missoula, MT: Mountain Press, 1982, 86–95.

Bradley, James H. "Blackfoot War with the Whites." *Contributions to the Historical Society of Montana* 9 (1923): 252–56.

———. "Notes on the Business of I. G. Baker & Company at Fort Benton." *Contributions to the Historical Society of Montana* 9 (1923), 345–47.

Clarke, Helen B. "Sketch of Malcolm Clarke." *Contributions to the Historical Society of Montana* 2 (1896), 254–68.

Dempsey, Hugh A. "The Amazing Death of Calf Shirt." *Montana Magazine of History* 3, no. 1 (January 1953): 65–72.

Dempsey, Hugh A., ed. "Howell Harris and the Whiskey Trade." *Montana Magazine of History* 3, no. 2 (spring 1953): 1–8.

Dempsey, Hugh A. "Donald Graham's Narrative of 1872–73." *Alberta Historical Review* 4, no. 5 (winter 1956): 10–19.

Dempsey, Hugh A., ed. "Robertson-Ross' Diary: Fort Edmonton to Wildhorse, B.C., 1872." *Alberta Historical Review* 9, no. 3, (summer 1961): 5–22.

Denny, Cecil. "Traders of the Early West." *Alberta Historical Review* 6, no. 3 (summer 1958): 20–24.

Goldring, Philip. "Whisky, Horses and Death: The Cypress Hills Massacre and its Sequel." In *Canadian Historic Sites: Occasional Papers in Archaeology and History*. Ottawa, ON: National Historic Parks & Sites Branch, 1979, 41–70.

Horrall, S. W. "The March West," In *Men in Scarlet*. Edited by Hugh A. Dempsey. Calgary, AB: McClelland & Stewart West, 1974, 13–26.

Kehoe, Thomas, and Alice B. Kehoe. "A Historical Marker, Indian Style." *Alberta Historical Review* 5, no. 4, (autumn 1957): 6–10.

Koch, Peter. "Life at Muscleshell in 1869 and 1870." *Contributions to the Historical Society of Montana* 2 (1896): 292–303.

Rowe, Charles. "Pioneer Tales by Charlie Rowe." In *Rowe Family History*. Great Falls, MT: Edithann Rowe Janetski, n.d, 1–79.

Saum, Lewis O. "From Vermont to Whoop-Up Country: Some Letters of D. W. Davis, 1867–1878." *Montana the Magazine of Western History* (summer 1958): 57–71.

Schultz, James Willard. "Raven Quiver, the Trader." *Forest and Stream* (18 July 1903): 42–43.

Stacey, Beverley A. "D. W. Davis: Whiskey Trader to Politician." *Alberta History* 38, no. 3 (summer 1990): 1–11.

Standing Alone, Henry. "The Death of Calf Shirt." *Kainai News*, 1 September 1972, 8.

Manuscripts & Documents

Adney, E. Tappen. "Incidents of Indian-fighting and Fur Trader days in Montana, the Canadian Northwest, and Alaska, related by the late Captain John J. Healy," 1937. MF 95, Montana Historical Society, Helena.

Adney, E. Tappen. Papers. Letter, John Healy to Tappen Adney, 25 August 1905. Montana Historical Society, Helena.

Archibald, Adams G. Papers. MG 12, A1, Provincial Archives of Manitoba, Winnipeg.

Beebe, Joe, a.k.a. Red Tail Feathers. "Bygone Days of the Blackfeet Nation." December 1937. Copy in author's possession.

Berglund, Theresa. "The Reminiscences of John LaMott." SC 365, Montana Historical Society, Helena.

Canada. Department of the Interior Papers. RG 10, National Archives of Canada, Ottawa.

Canada. Royal Canadian Mounted Police Papers. RG 18, National Archives of Canada, Ottawa.

Clarke, Simon John. Diary, 1876. Glenbow Archives, Calgary, AB.

Dawson, George M. Diaries. M 339, Glenbow Archives, Calgary, AB.

Flanagan, Mae. "A Perspective View of the Life and Times of I. G. Baker." SC 1236, 16, Montana Historical Society, Helena.

Foley, Michael F. "An Historical Analysis of the Administration of the Blackfeet Indian Reservation by the United States, 1855–1950s." Washington: Indian Claims Commission, Docket #279-D.

Hanks, Lucien & Jane. Papers. Glenbow Archives, Calgary, AB.

Hardisty, Richard. Papers. Glenbow Archives, Calgary, AB.

Hudson's Bay Company Records, Provincial Archives of Manitoba, Winnipeg.

"Hugh Kirkendall vs. The United States and the Blackfeet and Piegan Indians," 1910. SC 83, Montana Historical Society, Helena.

"Indians of the Blood Reserve." Oblate Collection, 71.220, Provincial Archives of Alberta, Edmonton.

"Interview of Mr. Forest Chrissy of the Chicago Evening Post with Captain John J. Healy on Friday evening at 9 P.M., May 5, 1899." Microfilm in Montana Historical Society, Helena.

Kessler, C. N. Papers. William Andrews Clark Memorial Library, University of California Library, Los Angeles.

L'Heureux, Jean. "Description of a Portion of the Nor'West and the Indians," Rocky Mountain House, November 1871. Glenbow Archives, Calgary, AB.

Macdonald, Sir John A. Papers. National Archives of Canada, Ottawa.

Maginnis, Martin. Papers. MC 50, Montana Historical Society, Helena.

Morley, Julius F., "Account of a Prospecting Trip North to Canada by way of Sun River, St. Mary's in 1873." Montana Historical Society, Helena.

Morris, Alexander. Papers. MG 12, Provincial Archives of Manitoba, Winnipeg.

Nevitt, Richard Barrington. Papers. Glenbow Archives, Calgary, AB.

Power, T. C. Papers. MC 55, Montana Historical Society, Helena.

Schaeffer, Claude. Papers. Glenbow Archives, Calgary, AB.

Schultz, James Willard. Papers. Montana State University, Special Collections, Bozeman.

Selected Documents Relating to the Montana Superintendency of Indian Affairs. Record Group 75, National Archives & Records Administration (NARA). Copy in Montana Historical Society, Helena.

"Statement of Mr. I. G. Baker of Fort Benton, Montana." RG 18, vol. 4, file 98, National Archives of Canada, Ottawa.

United States. Montana Superintendency of Indian Affairs, 1864 to 1876. Microfilm rolls #488 to 503, M234, Record Group 75, NARA.

United States. Records of the Montana Superintendency of Indian Affairs, 1867 to 1873. Microfilm rolls #1 to 3, M833, Record Group 75, NARA.

United States. Letters Sent by the Office of Indian Affairs, Washington, D.C., September 1868 to December 1870. Record Group 75, microfilm rolls #88 to 98, M21, NARA.

United States. Letters Sent by the Indian Division of the Office of the Secretary of the Interior, 1849 to 1876. Microfilm rolls #1 to 16, M606, Record Group 75, NARA.

United States. Report Books of the Office of Indian Affairs, Washington, D.C., 1869 to 1876. Microfilm rolls #19 to 27, M348, Record Group 75, NARA.

United States. Montana Executive Proceedings & Official Correspondence, 1867–89. Interior Department Territorial Papers. Microfilm rolls #1 & 2, M192, Record Group 48, NARA.

United States. Monthly Returns from Fort Shaw, 1867 to 1891. Microfilm rolls #1156 to 1158, M617; Returns from United States Military Posts, Record Group 94, NARA.

Index